How to save
a post-truth era

Manchester University Press

How to save politics in a post-truth era

Thinking through difficult times

Ilan Zvi Baron

Manchester University Press

Published by Manchester University Press
Altrincham Street, Manchester M1 7JA

www.manchesteruniversitypress.co.uk

British Library Cataloguing-in-Publication Data
A catalogue record for this book is available from the British Library

ISBN   978 1 5261 2684 9   paperback
ISBN   978 1 5261 2682 5   hardback

First published 2018

Typeset
by Toppan Best-set Premedia Limited
Printed in Great Britain
by CPI Group (UK) Ltd, Croydon CR0 4YY

For Sony and Yael

Contents

Foreword

Where do we find ourselves?

My title is drawn from the first line of Ralph Waldo Emerson's great essay "Experience." It is a question perhaps even more salient in our times than it was in his. It is in the context of that question that Ilan Zvi Baron has written a book that confronts this question directly, both as diagnosis and as prescription. This is a book, I may say, that we have been, or should have been, waiting for. It is written not only for those who are distressed with the election of Donald Trump and the Brexit decision in the United Kingdom, but even more importantly, for those who are *not* distressed by the two events. Drawing upon a very wide range of material – from philosophy, from political science, from economics, from literature, from international relations – he faces head on the problem of our relation to politics in a "post-truth" age. For ours is an age in which it appears, as a Trump spokesperson once said, that "anything is true if enough people believe it."

The novel move in Baron's book is not to discount such claims as "scientifically" silly, but to accept the reality that any claim of fact is potentially defeasible. Hannah Arendt – one of the major voices here – had said as much. Hence our world is increasingly characterized as "post-truth." The consequence of this – and this is Baron's starting point – is that many of us increasingly have the sense that the world is falling apart and that all responses to that experience seem pointless. This is not just an issue for "left-leaning" folk: neither we nor those who voted for Trump or Brexit have much faith in the state any more. As I write, positive support for the US Congress is at 11%.

Baron identifies several failures consequent to this situation. The legitimacy of "normal" modern politics seems at best tenuous; our politics is manifestly unable to address seriously and democratically the world of global capitalism; the dominant economic and neoliberal powers seem to be beyond control. An important contribution of this book is also to show that much contemporary political theory, especially liberal political theory, does not and cannot deal with these failures convincingly.

Baron's formation places him well to address the complexity of these issues. He is not only well versed in political theory, both the canon and contemporary material, but also in a wide range of philosophical thought, particularly phenomenology, as well as in Jewish thought and experience ("saving politics" is not irrelevant to contemporary Israeli experience). He has worked with several NGOs in Geneva and Zurich. A central theme throughout his work in these areas has been the question of responsibility, not only in terms of *who* is responsible, but, more importantly, of *how* ones assumes responsibility for oneself.

How does his formation shape the claims of this book? The problems we face, he writes, are not primarily economic (though they are not not economic), but they are political and social-cultural. Let us look at his argument about "post-truth."

Whether or not there is "the" truth, *knowing* the truth is in any case not the primary problem. It is rather "acknowledging it" – I borrow the term from Stanley Cavell, one of the thinkers who appear in Baron's book. What does this mean? Picture: you are late. You know you are late. I know you are late. I know you know you are late. You know I know you know you are late – an ethical version, perhaps, of the third man problem in philosophy. Such *knowledge is not enough*. You have to *do something appropriate to the particular situation* – in this case likely say something like: "I am sorry I was late, I ..." and file an *appropriate* excuse ("my child was sick"; "the car broke down"; "there was an accident on the highway"; but probably *not* "I was having too much fun in bed" or "I was abducted by aliens"). "Appropriate" means that you recognize the situation as another would. When Trump says something false, it is not that he does not *know* that it is false that matters, but that he does not, perhaps cannot, acknowledge it – that is, actually mean what he says. One cannot successfully call him on the "facts of the matter," that is, on it *being* "false." To mean actually what one says is the ground of responsibility. And to not mean what one says is to be missing something about oneself much more than it is an attempt to deceive.

Thus, what do those in power increasingly miss? This understanding has, for me and Baron, the consequence of making our political situation even more perilous than one might have thought. The problem is not that the administration lies; the problem is not that people do not or cannot deliberate. The problem is rather that the administration lacks any sense of responsibility to that human capacity that makes discourse public. Here "public" does not at first mean "true," but rather more something like what Kant meant: to speak as a human being and not as a socially defined role. To lack that responsibility is to be a tyrant.

Baron does not use the word "tyrant," but he might have. In what does our present tyranny consist? In the *Persian Letters*, Montesquieu argued that it consists in requiring that others have no existence for oneself except that which one allows them. This seems to me exactly right. What is missing in Trump *et al.* is an acknowledgement that there are those who, still to some shrinking degree, think that he (and much of the administration) is of the same community as others.

The emphasis on responsibility in Baron's book has a radical consequence. It means that, contrary to our still standard way of appraising judgments, the validity of a judgment or claim depends on the particular character of the person making that claim. In our age, we are required first to judge not the judgement but the judger. Baron unpacks this in a clear-headed way. Our life, he writes, may be said to be in some sense coordinated with the narrative of who we are and the positions we hold. Should we at some point not behave in a manner compatible with that narrative – say that out of deference to power we overlook an incidence of misogyny (one of Baron's examples) – we will to that degree be acting non-responsibly. This in turn leads Baron to develop a very interesting twist on the general question of identity as it relates to politics. Identity is important not so much as a fallback ground but in that what we know depends on who we are – and given the encomium about responsibility, there may be times that we do not act as who we are – and what we claim then to know cannot be authentically our own. Finally, there are, Baron argues, different facets of responsibility in relation to the question of identity: we can be liable for a choice; we can be complicit in going along with a choice that should not be ours, and we can be ontologically irresponsible, in that we have simple forgone being what or who we are.

Note that his argument is not a judgment about what policies might be preferable to follow. Baron is less concerned with that than he is concerned with the relation of human beings to the policies that they pursue and endure. His intention is to save politics, not to push for a particular policy. And the case he makes is convincing: without a redemption of politics, it will not matter what policy is pursued.

Tracy B. Strong
Professor of Political Thought and Philosophy, University of Southampton
Distinguished Professor Emeritus of Political Science, University of California, San Diego

Acknowledgements

Thank you to Jonathan Havercroft, Caroline Wintersgill, Alun Richards, and the anonymous reviewers.

Introduction

In 1989, in the American journal *The National Interest*, Francis Fukuyama wrote how, "In watching the flow of events over the past decade or so, it is hard to avoid the feeling that something very fundamental has happened in world history."[1] His conclusion was about the triumph of Western democratic liberal capitalism over communism. This triumph, if indeed it ever was one, by now ought to look to many like a pyrrhic victory.

The forces of liberal capitalism that he saw as representing the end of history—the end of any real choice of alternative models of political economy—have unleashed a powerful wave of anger directed at the winning elites. David Remnick, editor of *The New Yorker*, could not have expressed it better when he wrote on the morning of Donald Trump's victory as President-elect of the United States: "The election of Donald Trump to the Presidency is nothing less than a tragedy for the American republic, a tragedy for the Constitution, and a triumph for the forces, at home and abroad, of nativism, authoritarianism, misogyny, and racism."[2] Except, this was a tragedy that many should have anticipated. The documentary filmmaker Michael Moore did so by highlighting just how many people were being left behind by a liberal capitalist system that was destroying the social fabric they grew up in, and diminishing their career prospects and life dreams.[3] The American Dream had become precisely that, a dream that could never become reality. Horatio Alger's rags-to-riches fiction remains fictional.

In 2007 Naomi Klein highlighted how modern capitalism, what is often described as neoliberalism, grows out of various social and political crises, and out of the harm subsequently caused to our social and political fabrics.[4] In 2015 Wendy Brown argued against neoliberalism's attack on democracy,[5] adding yet another voice to a long list of scholars and journalists who have warned us against the political consequences of economic neoliberalism, of the displacement of politics by economics.[6]

Trump's election has certainly sent shockwaves among progressives, but I am not an American. I have never lived in the US. I am from Canada, although I currently live in the UK. For me, living in the UK as an immigrant, it was the EU referendum that sent the first shock. It was not that this event revealed previously ignored injustices; it was more like a blow to the system. Just like the election of Trump, the Leave side's campaign was based on lies, fears, nativism, anti-immigrant racism, and anti-intellectual populism—fears that immigrants were stealing local jobs, taking away access to health care, that "experts" were good-for-nothing and out-of-touch, and that the EU was somehow some large authoritarian entity that defied the sovereignty of Parliament. The Remain campaign was not much better, and it is worth reflecting that the entire referendum was not about the national interest, but was about playing politics within the Conservative Party. David Cameron, who should go down as one of the worst Prime Ministers in the UK's history, held the referendum as a way to cement his position against the Eurosceptic wing in the Conservative Party. He lost. He resigned as PM. He left Parliament. He got the entire UK into a massive mess with no plan about what to do if he lost, and so he quit.

As a Canadian, I was eligible to vote in the referendum— which seems rather unfair since citizens from EU countries living in the UK could not. In addition to exercising my right to vote, I did what little I could. I donated money, wrote an op-ed for an international newspaper arguing the Remain case,[7] and volunteered to help get out the vote. It was the first time I was out on the street as a political activist since I marched in London against the Iraq War. Before that, I protested tuition fee rises in Canada, logging in Clayoquot Sound, and engaged in lengthy debates with activist friends about capitalism, globalization, and democracy.

In those days of the anti-globalization movement and the Battle in Seattle (which I was unable to attend, even though I was frustratingly only hours away), there was a sense of anger and injustice against the forces of capitalism that were taking away our democratic rights, protecting the interests of capital at the expense of society. We debated the works of Naomi Klein and Noam Chomsky, visited Spartakus Books in Vancouver, and sought out copies of *Z Magazine*. I still remember seeing anti-NAFTA placards on lawns, including in front of one restaurant that had really good apple pie. Depressingly, none of the anti-globalization concerns have gone away, but in meeting Leave voters in the streets of a north-eastern town in England, I found that there was a visceral anger that was qualitatively different from that which I recall from the 1990s, even though many of the issues remain the same.

Arlie Russell Hochschild notes a similar anger in the US. In her book, *Strangers in Their Own Land: Anger and Mourning on the American Right*,[8] she argues that this anger is directed toward a political system that is seen as helping others, usually immigrants and minorities, and not the white working class, who feel that while they work hard, others are cutting in line, and the government appears to be on the side of these queue jumpers. Betrayal—the American Dream is being given to others—and anger at a political system that does not care about them are the driving forces of the Tea Party and alt-right movements in American politics (although religion also often plays a role). That many of these same people benefit from state welfare programmes or witness the destruction wrought on their communities by nefarious corporations is irrelevant: they distrust government a whole lot more and some are prepared to suffer in this life knowing that eternal salvation awaits them as good Christians.

For Hochschild, part of the reason for her book and her journey into Louisiana (where the book's fieldwork was carried out) was to try to understand these right-wing voters on their own terms. Part of what animated her book is the elitist left-wing dismissal of these right-wing rural voters. From this vantage point, the upper and lower classes are expected to vote for their own economic interests, whereas the middle class (the centre and centre-left) vote according to normative concerns of universal significance. Hence, when low-income rural voters support a right-wing party whose policies clearly benefit the upper classes the most, they are being duped.[9] Supposedly, the left-wing middle class, however, sees things as they are and makes the educated choice that benefits the greatest number of people.

This kind of progressive political elitism has a long history that can be easily traced back to Karl Marx and the important role of the intellectual who could point out the systems of oppression that those being oppressed could not see. Yet, in the case of neoliberal economic globalization, it is clear to people across a spectrum of demographics that something is seriously amiss. A large part of the left-wing anti-globalization movement was its open antipathy toward the neoliberal forces of an economic system whereby market forces, laissez-faire capitalism, and de-regulation are treated with reverence. The International Monetary Fund's structural adjustment policies and so-called aid in Pacific Asia caused lots of hurt in those countries that were forced to give up local accountability and instead acquiesce to the demands of an international neoliberal economic agenda. And a host of left-wing authors, from Naomi Klein to Noam Chomsky, highlighted a variety of injustices that seemed to follow from the misleadingly described post-1989 new world order, one that Chomsky pointed out looks very much like the old one.[10]

It was obvious to anyone who looked that, with the fall of the Berlin Wall and the end of history, the march of capitalism was going to be very hard to rein in. Even the mainstream left got in on the act with Bill Clinton and Tony Blair, two brilliant politicians (at least at the time) who clearly understood that the political economy of the world was changing with globalization, but who got the answers wrong by succumbing to the vested interests of global capital.

When Gordon Brown was doing his UK tour during the EU referendum he spoke about how, because of the economic forces of globalization and the increasing interconnectedness of our economies, the only way to push back and retain the ability to legislate effectively against a race to the bottom of deregulation and resist the narrow self-interests of large multinationals was to work collectively within the EU as a member-state. With this argument, Brown highlighted an important shift from the anti-globalization arguments of many on both the left and the populist right, whose views seemed to synthesize into variations of a strengthen-the-state mantra. Now the argument was not to strengthen the state, or to idealize small-scale direct democracy, but to strengthen our international institutions. The problem, however, is that politics happens locally and people need to see the positive effects of political decisions and feel invested and connected with both the political process and the outcomes. Local direct democracy is not really a viable solution—Gordon Brown was right in emphasizing the importance of our international institutions—and considering the usually abysmal local voting turnout in municipal and county elections,[11] we are deluding ourselves if we think people will suddenly change their voting turnout habits.

We have become disconnected from politics for a whole range of reasons.[12] Our connection with politics is grounded in our understanding of ourselves and of where we find ourselves in the world; but these groundings are always unstable, open to fluctuations of how we feel, who we want to be, who we think we are expected to be, what we believe we ought to get out of life, and how our communities never remain the same. Our groundings are, in effect, stories, authored by ourselves and others. We cannot control the stories, however much we may try, as each of our stories is always co-authored by others and through our moments of contact with the forces or structures of society. Our political and public sense of connection and investment follows from the narratives we construct and engage with in our negotiations with the world we find ourselves in. Our choices reflect our interpretation of these narratives. When the world starts to appear as if it is spinning outside of our narratives and thus undermining them, we are faced with difficult choices.

One choice that many appear to have made is anger—anger at the elites who have gained at the expense of the rest. It is very hard to understand the results of both the EU referendum and the Trump election without acknowledging that many voted as they did precisely as a means of attacking the system, to throw a spanner into the works and mix things up, to "drain the swamp" as Trump would say. The few Leave voters that I met were angry. Very angry. And even though their logic often made little sense (voting to leave the EU as a protest against Margaret Thatcher) and they harboured a self-righteousness that is ugly whatever economic or social class you belong to, it was not hard to understand—although our politicians do not seem to, at least not fully. The populists use it to their advantage, and the rest are struggling to find legitimacy and a voice in a post-truth world.

One of the arguments that politicians are having to address is a fairly simple economic one—that the working class is struggling, the middle class is shrinking, and the political elites are getting richer. The post-political careers of Tony Blair and Rudy Giuliani are no longer extreme examples of where the revolving door out of public service now leads, and of the riches available in a post public-service career. Blair reportedly can earn £200,000 for a single speaking engagement,[13] and not long after leaving office Giuliani was already making himself a very rich man with his consulting firm earning over $100 million within five years.[14]

In June 2016, YouGov UK noted how 31% of lower-middle-class to upper-middle-class members of society would be unable to pay an unexpected bill of £500.[15] This statistic helped cement the idea of the "squeezed middle," a term used to describe how the middle class is finding it harder to get by on existing salaries. For the traditional working classes, 41% would be unable to cover such a bill. Most alarmingly, the survey revealed that 14% of all respondents could not afford an unexpected bill of £100.

The story is similarly bleak in the US. In May 2016, the Pew Research Centre released a report pointing out how the American middle class in metropolitan areas is shrinking:

"From 2000 to 2014 the share of adults living in middle-income households fell in 203 of the 229 U.S. metropolitan areas examined in a new Pew Research Center analysis of government data."[16] In December 2015 they published the results of a survey identifying how the American middle class is "losing ground." As they put it: "After more than four decades of serving as the nation's economic majority, the American middle class is now matched in number by those in the economic tiers above and below it."[17] There is, in short, increasing income inequality.

We have, by now, all heard about the decline in local manufacturing, the outsourcing of industries, and the dwindling professional opportunities for the working classes. But one of the more concerning pieces of data is about mortality rates among non-Hispanic white Americans—they are rising. How, in one of the wealthiest countries on the planet, is that possible? To place this in context, one of the underlying narratives of the present age is how peaceful liberal democracies are. We live in a world where democracies don't go to war with one another, and consequently, where violence is decreasing. This is the argument we find in Michael Doyle's work on democratic peace theory,[18] which suggests a solution to international war that nicely corresponds with the end of history thesis: the spread of liberal democratic capitalist states will yield a more peaceful world. More recently, Steven Pinker, in his book *The Better Angels of Our Nature*, goes further and argues that, "The decline of violence may be the most significant and least appreciated development in the history of our species."[19] His very lengthy book paints a picture of the human race as progressing from being somehow very violent ("What is it about the ancients that they couldn't leave us an interesting corpse without resorting to foul play?"[20]) to more peaceful. That he never defines what exactly he has in mind by the term violence, or that parts of his argument are based more on rhetorical flourish than the evidence he ostensibly provides (the Bible contains violent episodes, but that does not mean people were more violent back then), are only two problems in this narrative. The more significant problem in regard to

Brexit and the 2016 presidential election is that if we are
living in such a peaceful world, why are the citizens in these
countries so angry at the political establishment? If the world
has become such a great and peaceful place that history has
been "won," what exactly is the problem? How do we square
this hopeful vision of decreasing violence and peace with the
rather ugly reality of the disproportionate deaths of African
Americans by police, and the mortality rate of the American
working class? As *The Washington Post* reported in regard to
the former of these, African Americans are "2.5 times as likely
as white Americans to be shot and killed by police officers."[21]

In regard to the latter, Anne Case and Angus Deaton note
in an often-cited article that the death rates of non-Hispanic
white Americans between the ages of 45 and 54 have increased
significantly. Or, to be more precise, they are not declining as
they are among other demographic groups in the US and in
other comparable countries, and since 1998 the mortality rate
among this constituency has increased by "half a percent per
year."[22] The group for whom this decline applies appears to
be the white working class and those with at most an education level of a high school diploma. The correlation between
education and mortality is by itself interesting, although clearly
not causal. Rather, the article goes on to suggest that one
reason for this increase in mortality could be due to increased
economic insecurity:

> Although the epidemic of pain, suicide, and drug overdoses
> preceded the financial crisis, ties to economic insecurity are
> possible. After the productivity slowdown in the early 1970s,
> and with widening income inequality, many of the baby-boom
> generation are the first to find, in midlife, that they will not be
> better off than were their parents.[23]

Combined with increasingly weakened pensions, the American
working class is suffering an epidemic. If there is a moment
when the social contract is failing, this could be it, as the
state is letting an entire segment of its population down. The
contract, however, does not exist, as there is very little that
people for whom the contract is not working can do, except

try to wreck the institutions of governance when given the chance, which Trump appeared to offer them. Importantly, this increase in mortality rates is counter to the idea, to the story, that we tell ourselves about Western liberal society. If our countries are so great, why the squeezed middle and the demise of the working class?

The tendency is to view these problems ideologically.[24] We read the numbers to suit our ideological predisposition, so we ignore proportionality and concentrate on the sum totals, or instead advance fictional notions of individual responsibility that ignore the structures of injustice and mitigate any possibility of collective responsibility. The solutions are thus fabricated according to our preconceived views of how to understand the problems, which means that we turn either to demanding more of individuals or searching for policy changes that government can enact to address whichever structures of inequality we hold responsible. In either case, the political system is not at fault, it is rather a question of implementation, of choice, and perhaps of political will.

However, politics has always been about the protection of some interests over others, and those with greater resources at their disposal tend to have the deck stacked in their favour. Living in a democracy does not necessarily mean that our political leaders really represent the people they are elected to serve. Rather, politics is a profession in which the goal is not service but the holding of public office. This is why people have so little faith in our politicians and why outliers like Trump can succeed. It also explains why Politics, Philosophy, and Economic graduates in the UK who make it into the high tiers of government appear inclined to regularly undermine the very education that got them there, emphasize the STEM subjects (Science, Technology, Engineering, and Maths) as more economically important, and devalue the Liberal Arts in the process. By doing so they are protecting their status and damaging the chances of others to climb the same ladder. The same forces are also behind the anti-intellectual populism of the conservative right who have managed to tap into working-class anger. These forces also contribute to the reaction toward antiquated socialist ideologies that have taken hold of the Labour Party in the UK. In each of these cases, it is people's anger at our political elites, plus the system that got them there and the culture which rewarded them, that provides the foundation for the convergence of right-wing ideology with working-class populism. The last time we saw such a convergence was with the rise of fascism in the 1930s (if we emphasize science and technology instead of politics and history in our education system, who would be able to notice?).[25]

People are grasping at straws for leaders who appear either authentic in their beliefs and not as opportunistic politicians, or for people who appear to be outsiders and thus stand a shot of breaking up a system that has harmed, disenfranchised, impoverished, and disillusioned way too many people. Many who voted to leave the EU, and those who voted for Trump, were—I think it is fair to assume—not voting *for* something so much as they were voting *against* something and looking for an opportunity to make their voices heard. That doing so put the populist right and the traditional left together is one of the consequences of where our political culture and political economy have taken us.

It is in this vein that politicians who appear as obstructionist can be rewarded with re-election, because they are not taking the system for granted. This is the story of the Republican Party in the US, who have, time and time again, demonstrated that they are more interested in halting government than in actually governing.[26] Just as the EU referendum was not about the national interest, the election of Donald Trump is almost certainly part of the trajectory created by the Republican Party who have demonstrated themselves to be less interested in governing and working for the national interest and more interested in getting into political power; once in power, they do all they can to act like muckrakers. By thwarting the possibility of governance in a system that to many appears bankrupt, they can lay false claim to acting against the established interests, thus promoting their (patently false) anti-establishment populist credentials for the next election cycle.

Politics is failing us—that much seems clear. But who is this "us?" Claims to membership and collective identity are inevitably complicated claims to make. The polls regularly use all sorts of classifications—economic, age, religion, gender, education, geographical location, ethnicity (or "race")—to help identify who votes for whom and what policies which people care the most about. But both the EU referendum and the US election revealed significant problems with these usual classification schemes. In the UK, the referendum brought together Conservative and traditional Labour voters. Rich and poor. In the US, while the politics of polarization clearly played its part in ensuring party (tribal?) loyalty, most of the polls got it wrong—almost all the major ones predicted a Clinton victory, or at least the likelihood of one. Was the problem here one of interpretation and of how polls are read and used publicly, of data, or that our traditional ways of identifying voting groups is out of sync with the way people vote? Or perhaps something even more fundamental, that the polls got it wrong because the way in which polls work or how data is collected no longer seem to function, that we are living in a different world; that it is no longer clear who "we" are, nor where to find "us." Are our traditional categories fraying at the seams? How else to understand why people who hold so dearly to religious faith could vote for someone who clearly does not live up to any standard of good conduct according to any major religion (I am not aware of any religion that condones sexual assault, and rewards bullying or abusive behaviour). Yet, according to exit polls, 53% of women who voted[27] chose a misogynist who advocated sexual assault—this is just confusing.

As Gérard Araud, the French ambassador to the US, wrote on Twitter after the election of Trump, "A world is collapsing before our eyes."[28] Indeed. A world is collapsing. It is not hyperbole to say that we could be witnessing the end of the post-war liberal order (although we can share at least some relief in the result of the Austrian presidential election). While this order came with a lot of negative baggage in its political economy, it also came with a lot of good intentions about

internationalism, pluralism, peace, and justice. This post-war
order was built on the idea of hope for a better future. The
GI Bill, the civil rights movement, feminism, and yes, even
the anti-globalization and occupy movements, Black Lives
matter, the creation of the NHS, all of these were products
of this post-war order, even though they are also about trying
to repair a broken world that emerged out of two World Wars
and the Holocaust. But now, this world seems to be falling
apart. As a political activist who marched with anarchists,
socialists, and democrats, I always knew that the fight for a
better world would not follow a straight line. There would
be hiccups along the way. But that idea is now shattered.
We are not living in any dialectic where crisis will eventually lead to gradual improvements toward a better world.
We are, instead, rejecting this very idea, and are burrowing
down into a false comfort zone of populist insularity and
zero-sums.

The world that I felt I belonged to is falling apart, and
I've got no home. I know I'm not alone here. Many of us
feel homeless in a Brexit-Trump world. Yes, I've done well
for myself, and I work in a top university. But that does not
mitigate the fact that I too belong to a community, indeed to
multiple communities, and from what I can tell by speaking
with friends here and abroad, many of us are deeply shocked
by where we see the world heading. Moreover, the standards
of how we understand politics do not appear to be working
to help make sense out of this ongoing crisis that so many
of us feel. It seems as though we are on the wrong side
of history—even if by slim margins, or in the US, a slim
majority.

We are now living in a state of permanent crisis—crisis of
faith, economy, violence, and of politics—where the extreme
has become normalized. But how are we to understand this
new world, one in which those who believe in the values of
inclusivity, respect for diversity, openness, and compassion
appear to have no place? Instead, our political leaders are
taking us down a road of fear, racism, nativism, misogyny, and

closed-mindedness. Whatever happened to the world where we cared for others who are not like us?

> Give me your tired, your poor,
> Your huddled masses yearning to breathe free,
> The wretched refuse of your teeming shore.
> Send these, the homeless, tempest-tost to me, I lift my lamp
> beside the golden door![29]

This book is written with two purposes in mind. The first is to try to make some sense of what appears to be a world that is falling apart around us. The second is to try to advance an argument about where we go from here. While it may be the pragmatic second purpose that is more appealing, we cannot begin to have that conversation in any meaningful sense if we do not address the first. Without understanding where we are and how we got here, we cannot explore where we go from here.

The challenge, however, is that it is not at all clear where "here" is. The liberal order that was seemingly rejected in both the US election and the UK referendum was not a peaceful world order. It was (and still is) a dangerous world, replete with wars, domestic violence, institutionalized racism and sexism, increasing rates of stress and anxiety, decreasing public investment in the building blocks of society, and sharply increasing wealth inequalities. But these are not the causes of our electoral and referendum results, they are simply indicators that there is something which continues to be very wrong in our world order. It is this more abstract yet ostensibly more fundamental of problems that I focus on in this book, and in a few specific ways.

The first of these is an examination of politics, and of how the current failings in our political systems are indicative of a liberal myth about what politics is about. In this discussion, I argue that the liberal myth of the origins of politics—our compact or contract that sets up the modern state—is a lie, and that as a consequence we have been looking for politics in all the wrong places.[30] Politics is necessarily conflictual, although this does not mean that the option has to be violence. The "Love Trumps Hate" slogan is nice, but hopeless if it is to inspire a political movement. The activity of politics is about change, about making the world we live in a better place. Doing so involves negotiations, compromise, and disagreement but also respect and responsibility.

Second, the way we conceptualize what counts as knowledge in the service of politics has become tainted because of the extent to which complex methodological positions have become caricatured into seemingly dichotomous options—which are then reflected in our political choices—and in a misguided faith in anything that can objectively be called science.[31] The significant errors in polling data in both the 2015 UK election and the 2016 US presidential election are not blanket indictments of the worth of positivist research, but are a serious indicator of how we understand such research, of the lack of reflexivity in such work, about how such research is used, and in how we have come to prioritize method over other forms of thinking. Debates about evidence are increasingly important in the public sphere, but they have taken on a new line, when evidence itself becomes irrelevant.

This approach has, it appears, been taken to new heights by Trump, although it was already in use elsewhere (including during the UK referendum when the Leave campaign regularly misled the public with, among other things, a complete lie about how much money the UK sends to the EU). As reported in *Esquire*, the Trump surrogate Scottie Nell Hughes, while speaking on the *The Diane Rehm Show*, "illustrated a defining principle of Trumpism: There's no longer such [a] thing as fact, because anything is true if enough people believe it."[32] In her words:

> Well, I think it's also an idea of an opinion. And that's—on one hand, I hear half the media saying that these are lies. But on the other half, there are many people that go, "No, it's true." And so one thing that has been interesting this entire campaign season to watch, is that people that say facts are facts—they're not really facts. Everybody has a way—it's kind of like looking at ratings, or looking at a glass of half-full water. Everybody

has a way of interpreting them to be the truth, or not truth. There's no such thing, unfortunately, anymore as facts.

And so Mr. Trump's tweet[s], amongst a certain crowd—a large part of the population—are truth. When he says that millions of people illegally voted, he has some—amongst him and his supporters, and people believe they have facts to back that up. Those that do not like Mr. Trump, they say that those are lies and that there are no facts to back it up.[33]

The article went on to point out just how shocking this claim is:

This is an astounding claim. It's an attack not on Trump's detractors, but on the idea of objective reality. Modern society is built on the idea we can observe things in the world, use the scientific method to verify them and form a consensus that a certain set of things are true. This set of things constitutes the reality in which we live. Hughes, Trump, and his campaign have set out to undermine all of that in order to claim that the truth is anything they want it to be right now—as long as enough of the people who support them believe it.[34]

The authors at *Esquire* are right to be concerned, but they miss the point that focusing on method will not resolve the problem. Methods are never politically neutral. The debate here is not about the scientific method, but about methodology. This is, in some ways, a more complicated topic, but without exploring the significance of how knowledge production works, we cannot have a political conversation about what facts are and about their relationship to political decision-making.

Third, now that we have the results of the election and referendum, what are we to make of them? Much energy is being invested in trying to interpret who voted for what and why. But all of this analysis is for naught if we have not provided a narrative in which to understand the results. What the results tell us is that there is something wrong with our politics, our elites, and our public discourse (our political culture). I suggest that we can interpret the results of the Trump victory and of Brexit as a vote for nothing. I am not suggesting that those who voted for either did not think they were voting for something, but rather that there was nothing upon which to base a reasoned decision to vote for because of the vacuous nature of the campaigns. There certainly could, for example, be a case made against the EU (the EU Commission has a lot to answer for in its democratic deficit and lack of transparency and accountability), but this was never done, and there was no clear argument for what to do if Leave won because there was no idea of what to do should Leave win. That voting Leave could, for example, threaten the UK was not contemplated, nor was the status of all the EU workers in the UK, nor how to overcome lost access to the Common Market. It was all about telling people that everything will be fine (hence the whole "project fear" rhetoric from the Leave side, when the real fear was coming from them). The Trump campaign was just as bad, if not worse. I take issue with how the role of identity politics has come to provide the lens though which to understand these results and of how democracy has changed in ways that can undermine itself. I suggest that the role of identity in politics is being misunderstood. It is not multiculturalism or egalitarian liberalism or political correctness that are the issue, although they are all important. Rather, we need to look at the role of the state, and how the state is failing us.

In the final chapter, I explore where we can find politics, or rather how. There are, I suggest, three elements to politics: the relationship between knowledge and power, with a particular emphasis on the role of interpretation; political responsibility or the politics of responsibility; and the significance of narratives or meaning (hermeneutics). What I do not address in this chapter is the question of political space, but I will make a few points about this now.

It is a mistake to place our faith in the state as the final political space of significance. The state and its accompanying normative narrative of sovereignty is easily understood as being at the top level of our political spaces (other than perhaps the international).[35] However, the thing is that, for most of us, the politics that we are most likely to encounter are much more local, and the means by which we can participate in politics reflect as such. This is why movements such as the various Occupy ones are so important. They demonstrate that it is through local actions that our political voices can be heard most loudly, most of the time. Students often study International Relations because they think that it is in state capitals and in the halls of international organizations where our political futures reside. They have a point in that these are important places. But they depend on how what they do matters for people and, in this regard, it is in our daily lives, which happen locally, that we encounter the consequences of their decisions. I am not suggesting that we need to think globally and act locally, although that often makes sense. Rather, I am suggesting that we need to be open to the possibility that there are different kinds of political spaces that we need to take seriously. These can be a city square (like Tahrir Square in Cairo),[36] a street (like Wall Street),[37] or even a farm (think of the Slow Food movement).[38]

Before we begin, I want to add one last thing. This book is a response to what I take to be a serious political crisis. What this means is that the book has largely been the process of my working through how to find a world when I feel lost in the present one, as the forces of populism, nativism, xenophobia, misogyny, and parochial nationalism appear to be the currency of the day. Because the stakes are so high, there will no doubt be many commentators, academic and otherwise, who feel the need to step into the fray and provide some explanation of what went wrong, why Clinton lost and Brexit won. Many will also no doubt work on identifying and explaining the specific causes of Brexit and of Trump winning and Clinton losing. This is not that kind of a book.

First, in regard to the causal question, causality is a complicated concept in large part because it is not necessarily clear what we mean by the term "cause."[39] It is a term that gets thrown around by neo-positivists and scientists who study the relations between variables, trying to identify why a particular event or result occurs. But the danger in many of these studies is that they end up simplifying a set of complex relations into a linear one. We see this approach every time some news report surfaces about a study pointing out the latest food that will either kill us or save us, as if isolating a miracle nutrient

makes sense for how our bodies function, which is absurd.
No such miracle food or nutrient exists, although there is
a lot of money to be made if people can be convinced that
they do.[40]

There can be all sorts of different ways of understanding
what a cause "is,"[41] and of the different types of knowledge
that underlie what appear to be causal outcomes.[42] Causes
can be understood in linear ways but also as a varied set of
conditions that provide the basis for something to happen,
but do not preclude alternatives from also happening.

One of the arguments of the book is that the Brexit and
Trump results are a consequence of a series of failures. There
has been a failure of politics in multiple senses: the failure
of understanding the ground and thus legitimacy of modern
politics; the failure of political practice in its being overwhelmed
by the logic of global capital; the inability of the state and its
political institutions to manage the forces of global capital
for the benefit of the majority of society, thus encouraging a
further distancing and alienation from politics; and the failure
to acknowledge a close relationship between methodology and
politics. These various failures have demonstrated themselves
not just in the narrow electoral success of the Leave vote in
the UK and the presidential election of Trump, but also in
the ways that the politics of identity have come to frame both
these electoral victories and the responses to them. However,
I do not suggest that these conditions had to have caused the
results of the EU referendum or Brexit.

Instead, most of the argument in the book is not about
identifying the specific conditions that contributed to Brexit
and Trump but is rather a critique of existing, as well as
potential, responses to these events, and how we understand
these events. Thus, whereas we might turn to some kind of
social contract argument to explain the conditions for justice
and thus identify a response to Trump or Brexit in these
lines, I argue that such a path would be wrong. In addition,
I argue against the claim that somehow the post-structuralist
turn has created the conditions for a post-truth world.[43] I also
argue about the importance of identity, responding to claims
that identity politics could be what got us into this mess.

Too much of our political and scholarly discourse continues to make what I consider to be basic errors, and it is time to stop, rethink, and start to think differently.

Subsequently, what concerns me is that the Trump election and the Brexit result are indicative of a much deeper problem within Western society that is by no means new (or possibly even unique), which became exceedingly evident in how Trump appeared to have "tweeted" his way into the White House, and how Leave won on an argument completely devoid of any evidence. The problem at issue is one about the relationship between knowledge and politics, and it gets to the heart of some thorny philosophical and political debates, including the science wars of the 1990s about relativism and post-modernism, the role of higher education, the connection between politics and economics, the nature of facts and evidence, the place of interpretation in our political discourse, and the ability to deploy normative arguments in a world where evidence is less important than narrative and identity. The method of this book is thus a combination of political theory and public commentary. Interwoven throughout the book's more theoretical discussions and engagements with academic debates are references and quotes from popular statements of politicians, other public figures, and news reports, as these are the sources where we find our information that helps shape our political views. Consequently, it seems only logical to use them as important source material.

The structure of this book is, thus, mildly eclectic. I jump in and out of philosophical discussions and engagements with a range of source material. The purpose is to demonstrate how political philosophy can help us in these difficult times, but in a way that speaks to what we encounter in our everyday dealings. This is about making philosophical debates meaningful and accessible, and, hopefully, providing a voice, or at least an argument, that progressives like myself may find useful.

Notes

1 Francis Fukuyama, "The End of History?," *The National Interest*, no. 16 (1989): 3.

2 David Remnick, "An American Tragedy," *The New Yorker*, November 9 2016.

3 Michael Moore, "5 Reasons Why Trump Will Win," http://michaelmoore.com/trumpwillwin/. Accessed January 27 2017.

4 Naomi Klein, *The Shock Doctrine: The Rise of Disaster Capitalism* (New York: Picador, 2015).

5 Wendy Brown, *Undoing the Demos: Neoliberalism's Stealth Revolution* (New York: Zone Books, 2015).

6 Some examples of this literature include Noam Chomsky, *Profit Over People: Neoliberalism and the Global Order* (New York: Seven Stories Press, 1998); Philip Mirowski, *Never Let a Serious Crisis Go to Waste: How Neoliberalism Survived the Financial Meltdown* (London: Verso, 2014); Robert Pollin, *Contours of Descent: US Economic Fractures and the Landscape of Global Austerity* (London: Verso, 2005). See also William Davies, *The Limits of Neoliberalism: Authority, Sovereignty and the Logic of Competition* (London: Sage, 2017); Pierre Dardot and Christian Laval, *The New Way of the World: On Neoliberal Society* (London: Verso, 2014); Philip Mirowski and Dieter Plehwe, eds, *The Road from Mont Pèlerin: The Making of the Neoliberal Thought Collective* (Cambridge, MA: Harvard University Press, 2009).

7 Ilan Zvi Baron, "Jews Were Europeans Even before the EU. That's Why U.K. Jews Should Vote 'Remain'," *HaAretz*, June 20 2016.

8 Arlie Russell Hochschild, *Strangers in Their Own Land: Anger and Mourning on the American Right* (New York: The New Press, 2016).

9 This is the conclusion found in Thomas Frank, *What's the Matter with Kansas?* (New York: Henry Holt and Company, 2005). I would like to thank Brian Black for helpful discussions on this point.

10 Noam Chomsky, *World Orders Old and New* (New York: Columbia University Press, 1996).

11 Thomas M. Holbrock and Aaron C. Weinschenk, "Campaigns, Mobilization, and Turnout in Mayoral Elections," *Political Resarch Quarterly* 67, no. 1 (2014); Colin Rallings and Michael Thrasher, "Local and Police and Crime Commissioner Elections" (Plymouth: Elections Centre, Plymouth University, 2016). See also BBC, "Elections 2017 Results: Tories Win Four New Mayors," www.bbc.co.uk/news/election-2017-39817224. Accessed May 6 2017.

12 A classic that explores and tries to explain this detachment or disconnect is Robert D. Putnman, *Bowling Alone: The Collapse and*

Revival of American Community (New York: Simon & Schuster, 2000).

13 Luke Heigton, "Revealed: Tony Blair's Worth a Staggering £60m," *The Telegraph*, June 12 2015.

14 John Solomon and Matthew Mosk, "In Private Sector, Giuliani Parlayed Fame into Wealth," *The Washington Post*, May 13 2007.

15 Ben Tobin, "One in Three Middle-Class Brits Would Struggle to Pay a £500 Bill," YouGov, https://yougov.co.uk/news/2016/06/08/third-middle-classes-would-struggle-pay-sudden-500/. Accessed January 24 2017.

16 Pew Research Centre, "America's Shrinking Middle Class: A Close Look at Changes within Metropolitan Areas" (Washington D.C.: Pew Research Centre, 2016), 5.

17 Pew Research Centre, "The American Middle Class is Losing Ground: No Longer the Majority and Falling Behind Financially" (Washington D.C.: Pew Research Centre, 2015), 5.

18 Michael W. Doyle, "Kant, Liberal Legacies, and Foreign Affairs," *Philosophy and Public Affairs* 12, no. 2 (1983); "Kant, Liberal Legacies, and Foreign Affairs, Part 2," *Philosophy & Public Affairs* 12, no. 4 (1983).

19 Steven Pinker, *The Better Angels of Our Nature: A History of Violence and Humanity* (New York: Penguin, 2012), 836.

20 Ibid., 4.

21 Wesley Lowery, "Aren't More White People Than Black People Killed by Police? Yes, but No," *The Washington Post*, July 11 2016.

22 Anne Case and Angus Deaton, "Rising Morbidity and Mortality in Midlife among White Non-Hispanic Americans in the 21st Century," *PNAS* 112, no. 49 (2015): 15078. Since publication, Gelman and Auerbach have contested the findings on the grounds of aggregation bias. Case and Deaton have acknowledged that the consequences of age-adjusted mortality rates do yield a difference for women in the 45–54 age group, but outside of this difference they stand by their findings. Andrew Gelman and Jonathan Auerbach, "Age-aggregation Bias in Mortality Trends," *PNAS* 113, no. 7 (2016), "Letters." Anne Case and Angus Deaton, "Mortality and Morbidity in the 21st Century," *Brookings Papers on Economic Activity*, BPEA Conference Drafts, March 23–24 2017.

23 Case and Deaton, "Rising Morbidity," 15081.

24 Dan Jones, "Seeing Reason: How to Change Minds in a 'Post-Fact' World," *New Scientist*, November 30 2016.

25 I am not suggesting that the structural conditions that existed prior to the rise of fascism in Europe are repeating themselves. But there are some similarities that should give us cause for concern.

26 There are too many examples here to mention, but which could start with the Whitewater scandal (or non-scandal) in the 1990s, and the more recent refusal to support President Obama's pick for the US Supreme Court. But perhaps the most famous internationally significant examples are the 2011 and 2014 crises over the US debt-ceiling, where Congress risked the US government not paying its debt.

27 "2016 Election Exit Polls," *The Washington Post*, November 29 2016.

28 "Après Brexit et cette élection, tout est désormais possible. Un monde s'effondre devant nos yeux." Anthony Bond, "French Ambassador to the US Says the 'World is Collapsing' as Donald Trump Looks Set to Become President," *Mirror*, November 9 2016. Harriet Agerholm, "Donald Trump Wins: French Ambassador to the US Reacts by Posting Tweet Declaring the End of the World," *Independent*, November 10 2016. (The Twitter post was subsequently deleted.)

29 These are the final lines of Emma Lazarus's sonnet, and can be found inscribed on a plaque at the pedestal of the Statue of Liberty in New York. See the US National Parks Service website: https://www.nps.gov/stli/learn/historyculture/emma-lazarus.htm. Accessed September 25 2017.

30 There are many criticisms of the social contract tradition—too many to mention here—but one that shares some similar features with the account I will advance can be found in Samuel Chambers' book *Bearing Society in Mind*. See in particular his discussion on pages 21–22 where he argues against the liberal idea of individuals creating a political order, and the accompanying assumption of an apolitical order existing out of which a political one can emerge. Samuel A. Chambers, *Bearing Society in Mind: Theories and Politics of the Social Formation* (New York: Rowman & Littlefield, 2014). One important philosophical critique of the social contract is Stanley Cavell, *The Claim of Reason: Wittgenstein, Skepticism, Morality, and Tragedy* (Oxford: Oxford University Press, 1979). I will return to Cavell via Havercroft in a subsequent chapter. See also the discussion of Cavell in Andrew Norris, "Political Revisions: Stanley Cavell and Political Philosophy," *Political Theory* 30, no. 6 (2002). An important feminist critique of the social

contract is Carole Pateman, *The Sexual Contract* (Cambridge: Cambridge University Press, 1988).

31 Even an academic professional association has got into this game. See Jeffrey C. Isaac's writings about APSA and DA-RT: Jeffrey C. Isaacs, "Further Thoughts on DA-RT," www. the-plot.org/2015/11/02/further-thoughts-on-da-rt/. Accessed Janury 27 2017; "For a More Public Political Science," *Perspectives on Politics* 13, no. 1 (2015).

32 Jack Holmes, "A Trump Surrogate Drops the Mic: 'There's No Such Thing as Facts'," *Esquire*, December 2 2016.

33 Ibid. See (or rather, listen) also to *The Diane Rehm Show* of November 30 2016 (especially from minute 14:40 onwards): Diane Rehm, *How Journalists Are Rethinking Their Role Under a Trump Presidency*, podcast audio, *The Diane Rehm Show*, 49:072016, http://thedianerehmshow.org/audio/#/shows/2016-11-30/how-journalists-are-rethinking-their-role-under-a-trump-presidency/ 114095/. Accessed Janury 27 2017.

34 Holmes, "A Trump Surrogate Drops the Mic."

35 See, for example, Richard Ned Lebow, *A Cultural Theory of International Relations* (Cambridge: Cambridge University Press, 2008); Kenneth N. Waltz, *Man, the State, and War: A Theoretical Analysis*, revised ed. (New York: Columbia University Press, 2001). I have, however, questioned this view: Ilan Zvi Baron, "The Continuing Failure of International Relations and the Challenges of Disciplinary Boundaries," *Millennium: Journal of International Studies* 43, no. 1 (2014). See also Warren Magnusson, *The Search for Political Space* (Toronto: University of Toronto Press, 1996).

36 Jeroen Gunning and Ilan Zvi Baron, *Why Occupy a Square: People, Protests and Movements in the Egyptian Revolution* (London: Hurst & Company, 2013).

37 Carlo Petrini, *Slow Food Nation: Why Our Food Should Be Good, Clean, and Fair*, trans. Clara Furlan and Jonathan Hunt (New York: Rizzoli Ex Libris, 2007). In addition to the farm, the kitchen can be treated as an important location of politics, on both feminist grounds and for wider reasons pursuant to the consequences of our food choices.

38 David B. Grusky et al., eds, *Occupy the Future* (Cambridge, MA: MIT Press, 2013).

39 For a discussion of causality in the social sciences see Patrick Thaddeus Jackson, *The Conduct of Inquiry in International Relations:*

Philosophy of Science and its Implications for the Study of World Politics (London: Routledge, 2011); "Causal Claims and Causal Explanation in International Studies," *Journal of International Relations and Development* (2016).

40 See Marion Nestle, *Food Politics: How the Food Industry Influences Nutrition and Health* (Berkeley and Los Angeles: University of California Press, 2013); Julie Guthman, *Weighing In: Obesity, Food Justice, and the Limits of Capitalism* (Berkeley and Los Angeles: University of California Press, 2011).

41 See, for example, Stephen Kern, *A Cultural History of Causality: Science, Murder Novels, and Systems of Thought* (Princeton: Princeton University Press, 2004).

42 See, for example, Patrick Thaddeus Jackson, "Must International Studies Be a Science?," *Millennium* 43, no. 3 (2015).

43 Helen Pluckrose, "How French 'Intellectuals' Ruined the West: Postmodernism and its Impact Explained," *Areo* (March 27 2017).

1
The end of politics

Introduction

At the end of the Cold War, American intellectuals proffered lofty proclamations about the strength of American ideals, represented most generally in the Western values of liberal democracy and capitalism. In addition to Fukuyama's end of history thesis,[1] there was Charles Krauthammer's argument on behalf of the *Unipolar Moment*[2] where he predicted a greater risk of war despite how, "The center of world power is the unchallenged superpower, the United States, attended by its Western allies." This glamorization of American power and values was similarly articulated in the phrase, "the indispensable nation," which was used by the Secretary of State, Madeleine Albright. One of the authors of that phrase, Sydney Blumenthal, recalled that it was meant to convey how "Only the United States had the power to guarantee global security: without our presence or support, multilateral endeavors would fail."[3] While these ideological convictions were largely directed at presenting an image of America within the context of its international ambitions and foreign policy capabilities, they also spoke directly to domestic concerns about the values that America represents and of American identity.

This synergy between an externally facing image and an internally assumed one is recognized by scholars. David Campbell's 1998 book, *Writing Security*, provides one of the earlier instances of highlighting this intimate relationship between the construction of a state's foreign policy and the idea of the national identity.[4] This synergy has been taken up more explicitly in the ontological security literature, including

Brent J. Steele's 2010 book, *Defacing Power*, which further explores this interrelationship involving a nation-state's self-image and its politics. One of Steele's conclusions is how events that can undermine this self-image can lead a state to act in ways that may be contrary to its own interests as the state seeks to uphold its sense of self, regardless of either the undermining consequences of doing so or any contradictions involved.[5]

This conclusion finds extensive support across political philosophy. Politics can undermine itself, but being able to identify this possibility is possible only if we change the way we think about the world. This point was suggested by the political theorist Max Horkheimer, one of the founding fathers of the Frankfurt School and the author of its core methodological essay, *Traditional and Critical Theory*.[6] The Frankfurt School mainly comprised a group of Jewish Marxists, influenced also by Freud, who had to flee the Nazis and set up shop in the US. One of Horkheimer's points is that there are different types of theory. There is theory which seeks to simply explain the current status of things. This kind of traditional theory works in the service of the prevailing social order but does not help people to liberate themselves from the oppressive nature of this order. Horkheimer calls this Traditional Theory. Critical Theory is different. It seeks to transform the social order. Importantly, one does not have to be a Marxist to recognize that Horkheimer was on to something that remains relevant and deeply important.

Horkheimer points out that if we judge Critical Theory by the standards of Traditional Theory, Critical Theory will always come up short. This is because the standards used to judge which types of knowledge matter are rarely able to recognize, and often dismiss, knowledge that operates from fundamentally different premises. Being able to dismiss forms of knowledge which may have as their goal upending the social structures contributes to giving Traditional Theory its legitimacy and its edge. Ironically, while Horkheimer was making this argument from the left, Trump frequently made a similar point in his denial of polling data, of how polls are rigged. In the UK, we find a similar expression from Michael Gove, the former Secretary of State for Justice and member of the Conservative Party, who said during the referendum campaign that "People in this country have had enough of experts."[7] What they all share is a rejection of the traditional forms of knowledge that have been used in the service of entrenching the interests of the status quo—or at least, the appearance of this rejection in the case of Trump and Gove. For these two, their anti-intellectualism was used to help sustain their own political ambitions. Horkheimer, as an intellectual and a Jewish Marxist deeply troubled by the linkage between the Enlightenment and the rise of fascism, had different and more important concerns.

Horkheimer recognized that data does not function simply as an accumulation of facts, but rather exists within a social system. As a Marxist, he saw this structure in traditional class terms. But he also knew that a consequence of this link between knowledge and society is that for knowledge about society or politics to have any emancipatory potential, it cannot be judged according to the methodological criteria established within this same social structure. A similar non-political version of this argument was advanced by the historian of science, Thomas Kuhn. In Kuhn's case the point was not about emancipatory knowledge, it was that within any given paradigm, most knowledge production functions according to the traditions and conventions of this research community, and that a radical break constitutive of a new research programme is akin to a revolution. It is revolutionary because the new paradigm cannot make sense according to the terms for research set out in the old paradigm. Hence the idea of incommensurability, of how different paradigms are incapable of making sense within the frames of reference of the other.

If we are to mount a real critique to the seemingly prevailing order where Donald Trump can become President of the US, and the UK can turn its back on the institution created with the intention to help foster greater international openness and co-operation and prevent war, we need a very different way of thinking. Current modes of thinking are not working. There are at least two reasons for this failure, as discussed in this and the next chapter. Both of them are already apparent in Horkheimer's argument about Traditional and Critical Theory. One of these, the focus of this chapter, is about understanding what politics is about. The second, the focus of the next chapter, is about the relationship between methodology and emancipatory knowledge.

Political theory and the end of politics

It seems illogical to suggest that political theory or political philosophy as a tradition has for most of its history actually been about the end of politics. Yet it could be argued that this is exactly what the tradition of Western thought has been about. To understand how this could be is especially important because it provides us with an opening into trying to work out what exactly politics ought to be about. For those of us who identify with the left, but whose political values appear to be under attack from the forces of xenophobia, ideological nativism, parochialism, and nationalism, we need to explore how some of the fundamental ways by which the Western political tradition has theorized about politics have contributed to undermining our future. Doing so helps not only to find a place in which to think clearly and creatively, it also helps us to understand something significant but otherwise hard to grasp about the contemporary political order of Brexit and Trump.

For those who study political philosophy, the idea of the social contract is a fairly traditional one, linked to such philosophers as Rousseau, Hobbes, Locke, and Rawls. The basic idea is fairly simple, that there exists a condition whereby people are unable to live safe and productive lives. This condition, which we call a state of nature, needs to be escaped from, as there can be no justice in such a state. Thus, we all enter into a fictional contract whereby the people give up some of their freedoms in exchange for certain rights, along with a sovereign to protect such rights. Contract theorists do not presume that there is an actual contract, or a specific moment in time when the contract is signed—hence the idea of tacit consent—but rather use the contract as a heuristic device. Nevertheless, even though "a hypothetical contract is not simply a pale form of contract; it is no contract at all,"[8] the idea of the contract remains an especially powerful way of setting óut a method by which to interpret the condition and character for a just political community. The contract is one of the fundamental stories in political philosophy. The logic of agreement that underpins the moral force of the contract has even been used in the literature to explain why people obey the law,[9] when in reality for most of us, most of the time, there is no real choice. The normative power in contract thinking is appealing, as it ostensibly allows for an objective position in which to explore justice. However, what if the actual effect of this type of theoretical argument is not the creation of politics, but the exact opposite and, consequently, that the foundations of our liberal ideals of the modern state are built on a major deception. What if the very idea of the contract and its heuristic purpose is not about justice and politics at all, but is a delusion? To see how this can be the case let us turn back the clock and start with the source of most Western philosophy, Plato and Socrates.

There already exists with Socrates the original idea of the social contract. He presents this idea when, after his trial and impending execution, he argues with his friend Crito against escaping and for remaining to accept his punishment.[10] Part of Socrates' argument is based on the idea that he chooses to remain and to live in Athens, and as such he has no right not to accept the laws as they apply to him, even should the court decide that he will be executed by his own hand. This choice to remain serves as the equivalent of a contractual duty to obey the decision of the court and the authority of the polity over him. He has chosen to obey the law by deciding to live his life there. The consequence of his remaining was his execution.

The modern political theorist Hannah Arendt provides an innovative critique of the political philosophy of Plato as a response to the death of Socrates. Relying on one of her preferred methodologies, anamnesis (a critique based on the forgetting of past heritage) Arendt returns to both Ancient Greek thought and the political theory tradition that starts with Plato and Aristotle. She argues that we find there what became the traditional paradox of political theory, in which the purpose of political theory becomes the removal of politics: "Thus our tradition of political philosophy, unhappily and fatefully, and from its very beginning, has deprived political affairs, that is, those activities concerning the common public realm that comes into being whenever men live together, of all dignity of their own."[11] Amazingly, Arendt appears to be claiming that political philosophy has no tradition of politics because political philosophy originally sought to remove actual participation in politics from the concern of political philosophy.

In her interpretation, political philosophy was concerned with being able to remove the philosopher from politics. Even Aristotle does this: "In Aristotelian terms, politics is a means to an end; it has no end in and by itself. More than that, the proper end of politics is in a way its opposite, namely, non-participation in political affairs."[12] The consequence of this approach to politics (and political philosophy) is that politics is ultimately concerned with escaping from itself: "Politics, in other words, is derivative in a twofold sense: it has its origin in the pre-political data of biological life, and it has its end in the post-political, highest possibility of human destiny."[13] This paradox is especially evident in the thought of Karl Marx, who sought to explain politics with the ultimate goal of escaping from a condition of politics defined in terms of class struggle.

Arendt argues that the death of Socrates represented a major threat to philosophy, and set in motion an intellectual tradition whereby the pursuit of political thought is directed toward its own demise to be achieved by escaping or ending politics. By killing Socrates, the city (i.e. politics) proved that it was against philosophy and thus posed an existential danger to the very practice of philosophical enquiry. Plato was thus tasked with a seemingly impossible problem to resolve: how to protect

philosophy from politics. Socrates, however, also demonstrated
that the role of the philosopher is to participate in public life
and engage in public discussion, and that in our choices of
where to live we are involved in accepting our membership
in a political community. For Socrates, philosophy was not a
private affair, it was something to be done out in the open,
with others, in the city. In this sense, to be a philosopher was
to be a public intellectual, someone who participated in open
and public debate and discussion as a member of a political
community, which meant having some contact with, if not
outright participation in, politics. Moreover, this activity,
because of its open and public nature, was itself a form of
politics. However, for Plato this philosophical outlook could
not be divorced from the public decision to execute Socrates.
Hence the problem. Socrates was not against politics, but
politics appeared to be against Socrates.

Plato's solution to this aporia was for philosophers to become
politicians, sort of. This is the point at which Plato introduces
the idea of the philosopher kings—leading intellectual lights
who have superior knowledge and are able to use this knowledge
to steer the ship that is the city (or state). Philosophers had
to protect themselves from the city, but the only means to do
so was for them to co-opt the city into the service of philosophy,
and the only way to do this was to take political control of
the city. This is one of the lessons from *The Republic:* "Unless
the philosophers rule as kings or those now called kings and
chiefs genuinely and adequately philosophize, and political
power and philosophy coincide in the same place ... there is
no rest from ills for the cities ... nor I think for human kind."[14]
What Arendt takes from this argument is that the solution to
protect philosophy is to become active in politics, but the
paradox that this move entails is that ultimately the goal of
politics is the end of politics through the protection of
philosophy.[15]

Moreover, even if we follow Plato's logic and the turn
to philosopher kings, philosophers are no longer able to
function as philosophers. They cannot pursue knowledge of
things in themselves, but become tied to having to care for

the city. It is unlikely that philosophers would in fact rule, but even assuming this, if philosophers do not themselves rule they are still necessary for politics. Only philosophers are able to discover knowledge impartially in the pursuit of justice. Others cannot, due to their short-sighted and partial interests. Thus, politics requires philosophy but philosophy then ends up serving politics. However, the goals of politics and of philosophy are not the same. In politics what matters is care for the city, but in philosophy it is genuine curiosity for knowledge. If philosophy does serve as the handmaiden for politics, it loses itself. The same is true for politics, for once philosophers are able to exert power in politics, politics is no longer primarily based on care for the city, but on protecting philosophy. Consequently, the solution for the survival of philosophy becomes the end of politics, as the aim of politics is its demise in the protection of philosophy. The end of politics, if it is to protect philosophy, also inevitably requires its own demise.

The Socratic critique that most of us have heard in some fashion is that without philosophical intervention, which over time became transformed into intervention by superior agents—technocrats, princes, kings, political rulers, etc.— politics will be unable to pursue its normative aims for the good of the city. However, underpinning this critique is the notion that politics is the enemy of philosophy. When modern political theorists in the social contract tradition argue for finding politics through the contract, they are simply providing their own riff on this Socratic position. Except for them, the contradiction is not between politics and philosophy, it is in how the contract is itself the 'end of politics.

Modern political thought in the social contract tradition continued to search for a solution to this paradox identified by Plato and of the danger posed by politics. The great innovation of the social contract thinkers was really a bait and switch tactic. Instead of starting with the danger posed by politics, they claim that the danger is posed by the absence of politics, but the solution remains the same as before: an escape from politics.

We see in the social contract tradition an attempt to continue this rescue mission of politics from itself. What is so ironic about this tradition of political thought is how people at first are treated as the enemy of politics, and then are only able to enter into a political relationship and a political community through a process of giving up something that seemingly defines them. Social contract thinking assumes that human subjectivity universally requires the contract, but that once the contract exists our subjectivity changes. Or, put another way, prior to the contract we exist as one type of being, and after the contract a different type. In addition, the social contract tradition transforms politics into a kind of administrative tinkering that undermines its political purpose.

Habermas makes a related argument when he questions the ability of the contract as a liberal idea to resist the absolutist tendencies in the sovereign order it creates.[16] This tension is expressed by Habermas when he notes that "The rationale for Hobbes' absolutist state ... is a liberal one."[17] Habermas, building on and contributing to the continental tradition of Critical Theory, argues that political thought has become less concerned with politics than with control, and that this change owes its origins to the methodological shift in political thought from philosophy to science: "On the road toward science, social philosophy has lost what politics formerly was capable of providing as prudence."[18] The argument here is clearly different but the conclusion is similar in its emphasis on the removal of politics from political thought.

If we assume that the contract is the most prevalent of political metaphors by which we understand the normative potential and conditions of our political order, then it does follow that our political imagination is failing us. Although within political theory there exists considerable debate about contract thinking, this debate seems to exist largely in isolation among political theorists. Yet three important recent books about the failings of politics and how people are voting against what would appear to be their self-interest all fall back in some way on the idea of a contract as the normative bargain that underpins the state and our relation to it. Both Thomas

Frank's *What's the Matter with Kansas?* and Arlie Hochschild's *Strangers in Their Own Land* repeatedly refer to how the state (or government—the two get conflated) is not providing *for* the citizenry, even when the citizens do their part (or at least, feel that they are).[19] David Ricci, in *Politics Without Stories*, similarly refers back to the contract, even if the issue at stake is a rejection of the existing contract or political order.[20] The logic of the contract remains a powerful device by which to imagine the normative character of our relationship to the state.[21]

However, so long as the idea of contract carries currency in our political imagination, it remains the case that politics ends the moment the contract is (metaphorically) signed. Where politics could exist in this metaphor is in the production and agreement of the contract. It is irrelevant here that no contract is ever in fact signed. The thinking device that the social contract serves leads to the same conclusion. Think about coming up with a contract: it involves a negotiation. Negotiations are ultimately political, at least in the obvious sense of them being about exchange and compromise, and even more so when they take place across different relations of power in order to come to a mutual agreement. All of that is political. However, once the contract is signed, all of this ends (unless the contract is broken or challenged), and along with it so too does politics. The politics end the moment the contract takes effect because politics only really make any sense in the negotiations for the contract. Post-contract, our lives are not about debate, negotiating, or compromise. Rather, our lives become about adhering to and interpreting where necessary the meaning or intention of the contract. In this sense, post-contract politics is not just about control it is about ensuring hierarchical relations that sustain the contract. The meaningful form of politics that gave rise to the contract is viewed instead as a destabilizing form of activity, not politics but something else that poses a threat to the existing order. The politics that the contract enables, a process of ensuring control, is a remarkably less significant activity than the actual creation and agreement of the contract itself. The contract is the end of politics and the beginning of administration. The idea of the contract as a heuristic device is, as such, inherently against people participating in politics.[22]

Modern politics is seemingly built on this destructive idea—that the state provides some kind of security (or other benefits) for its citizens and in return we agree to abide by the law and respect the institutions of state by giving up those freedoms that inhibit the successful implementation of governmental rule. The conventional wisdom in this view is that politics is what happens inside the state, made possible by the social contract.

However, politics in this liberal tradition is not really about politics at all. So why then has this tradition become so resilient? The idea of the contract appeals to the liberal tradition because of its simultaneous emphasis on the individual and on rationality. The contract works to the extent that we emphasize the importance of the individual and of individual freedom. Liberalism's great appeal is the value it places on the human being as an individual endowed with rights. The logic of liberalism necessarily requires that we place the idea of the rights-based human being central in our political imagination. As a consequence, any theories of state that justify relinquishing certain rights and freedoms needs to accord the individual the option to freely chose to do so.

Note, for example, that Hobbes is in many ways an extreme egalitarian. Other than physical abilities, Hobbes recognizes people to be fundamentally equal, although it is because of the differences among us that this equality ends up posing a challenge. This equality, nevertheless, is necessary for the contract to make sense. The contract works because people are viewed as agents who have the political power or will to enter into the contract or compact. Without this underlying view of human beings, the idea of a social contract is morally dubious. In this sense, our ability to enter into the social contract is a sign of our underlying (universal) equality.

Yet there are many criticisms of this kind of liberal thinking, including from within the liberal tradition. Throughout his work, Michael Walzer has repeatedly argued for the importance of taking seriously the character and values of the community, as opposed to starting from some blank slate of what could be appropriate for anybody, anywhere, anytime.[23] Membership, or at least the ability to think as if one were a member, is central to any social criticism or political critique. His point, which is elaborated in a short book about social criticism,[24] is that normative critique of society or politics has to make sense to the people whom the critique is intended to benefit. In other words, as members of society, we all have different ways of understanding what is most important for us, and without being able to speak to that shared understanding, the critic's argument will fall on deaf ears. The critic does not have to be a member in the strict sense, but does need to understand the normative discourses of that society and be able to articulate a position that can be *heard*.

Walzer's main point here is that identity matters, and that it is a mistake to treat people as empty shells with rights or freedom. Rights or freedom are meaningless if we do not have a context in which to understand them. Another critique about the importance of identity and context is taken up in two different ways by the post-colonial theorist Gayatri Spivak in her Marxist essay "Can the Subaltern Speak?," and by Hannah Arendt in her comment about the right to have rights.

Spivak's argument on this point, in what is a now largely dated essay, is that any normative argument is irrelevant if it cannot be *heard*.[25] One way to interpret her argument is to note that even in discourses of rights, if the rights-language functions according to a set of normative concerns and values that are foreign or opposed to indigenous political discourse, language can still serve to discriminate and enforce a colonial apparatus or rule. The significance is that what is said is meaningless if it is not also heard, but that what it is possible to hear is contingent on context. In her argument, those who are not heard are the subalterns, and not those who control the apparatus of rule for whom the words of the subaltern cannot be heard. The same point is advanced by Jonathan Havercroft in his discussion of Stanley Cavell and Ibsen's play *A Doll's House*. As Havercroft explains, "In Cavell's reading of this play Nora is unable to voice her sense of injustice in terms that her husband Thorvald finds intelligible."[26] The point is that it is not always possible to be able to explain an injustice, even when there is one. The ability to make intelligible an injustice requires that the injustice can be recognized as such by others who are in hierarchically superior positions. However, they are not always able to hear in this way, and appeals to the idea of a shared institution does not remedy this problem—this is Cavell's critique against Rawls. As Havercroft explains, "From Cavell's perspective, the model of consent that is at the base of Rawls' social contract theory creates a situation in which claims of injustice such as Nora's cannot be heard."[27] The reason is that in Rawls, and in most traditional contract theories, justice and injustice can only be addressed according to the terms of the "previously consented ... principles of justice."[28] In this original position, all forms of difference that matter specifically when there is injustice are ignored and thus render the ability to communicate injustice potentially unintelligible. In Nora's case, the point is not only that her husband does not understand, but that he is incapable of understanding or appreciating her position, and thus is unable to hear her plight. This argument is significant in that it highlights how hierarchies can condition the terms for how our normative communication functions. People who are disenfranchised or discriminated against can be further harmed by the inability to hear their concerns. Sensitivity to experience and context matter, otherwise we force people to speak in languages that are foreign and further entrench hierarchies of discrimination and oppression.

Whereas Cavell advances this argument in the abstract, the distinction between what is said and what is heard is demonstrated in a different context in the ethnographic writings of Harold Garfinkel, who highlights that a conversation about one thing can also be a conversation about something else that is not being articulated explicitly.[29] The example he gives is of a student recording a conversation between a husband and wife, where the content of the discussion refers to a set of other concerns that are not in fact spoken about. Many of us have, at one point or another, no doubt been involved in such a conversation, where discussing where to go out for dinner, for example, is actually a state of the union discussion about the relationship. The distinction between what is heard and what is said matters greatly in politics, as it provides a means to communicate and simultaneously discriminate. Debate about voter fraud in the US is one such example, where there is no clear evidence of voter fraud, but the consequences of debating it end up discriminating against minority populations and their ability to vote. Similarly, debates about minority rights, and the Black Lives Matter movement, speak to a particular set of historical and cultural experiences that are not always understood or recognized by those who are insensitive to them—hence the reaction against Black Lives Matter by Blue Lives Matter or All Lives Matter. Each of these is saying one thing that is not being heard by another group.

This distinction between speaking and hearing, of being heard, is important politically, and normative political theory ignores this significance when it focuses on universal abstractions without taking into account the relevance of how the normative inferences from these abstractions are experienced and/or understood by the group in question. When we do this we are guilty of focusing on what is said, but not what is heard.

Arendt's critique about the right to have rights raises a similar point, but in this case it is how the Enlightenment liberal ideal of rights did not take seriously that there needs to be a right to have rights if the idea of universal rights is to mean anything. Imperial (colonial) policies, and the horrors of totalitarianism and the Holocaust are the evidence. Both colonialism and totalitarianism came out of the same soil of Enlightenment liberalism, and while they are not consistent with its underlying normative ideals this does not mean that they are completely devoid of the political discourses from the Enlightenment tradition.

In this case, the fatal flaw was the ability to conceive of a people for whom rights are not applicable. We have seen this kind of logic across political thinking in regard to gender, and the way that political, social, and economic features have ensured a patriarchal system at the expense of gender equality. That women were finally granted the vote across Europe only in the late twentieth century (in federal elections women could not vote in Switzerland until 1971, and it was 1991 when they had the right to vote in all local elections) should help remind us that the progress of rights discourse is not only slow, it is often hypocritical when we protect the enfranchisement of certain groups at the expense of others.

Arendt's critique about rights was a response to the political processes whereby an entire people became viewed as not having any rights, but that when such a creature was created it was not immediately apparent. The Universal Declaration of the Rights of Man of 1789 appears to be universal, but it is lacking in a central respect. The Declaration was approved by the National Assembly of France on August 26 1789, and contained 17 articles:

1. Men are born and remain free and equal in rights. Social distinctions may be founded only upon the general good.
2. The aim of all political association is the preservation of the natural and imprescriptible rights of man. These rights are liberty, property, security, and resistance to oppression.
3. The principle of all sovereignty resides essentially in the nation. No body nor individual may exercise any authority which does not proceed directly from the nation.
4. Liberty consists in the freedom to do everything which injures no one else; hence the exercise of the natural rights of each man has no limits except those which assure to the other members of the society the enjoyment of the same rights. These limits can only be determined by law.
5. Law can only prohibit such actions as are hurtful to society. Nothing may be prevented which is not forbidden by law, and no one may be forced to do anything not provided for by law.
6. Law is the expression of the general will. Every citizen has a right to participate personally, or through his representative, in its foundation. It must be the same for all,

whether it protects or punishes. All citizens, being equal in the eyes of the law, are equally eligible to all dignities and to all public positions and occupations, according to their abilities, and without distinction except that of their virtues and talents.

7. No person shall be accused, arrested, or imprisoned except in the cases and according to the forms prescribed by law. Any one soliciting, transmitting, executing, or causing to be executed, any arbitrary order, shall be punished. But any citizen summoned or arrested in virtue of the law shall submit without delay, as resistance constitutes an offense.

8. The law shall provide for such punishments only as are strictly and obviously necessary, and no one shall suffer punishment except it be legally inflicted in virtue of a law passed and promulgated before the commission of the offense.

9. As all persons are held innocent until they shall have been declared guilty, if arrest shall be deemed indispensable, all harshness not essential to the securing of the prisoner's person shall be severely repressed by law.

10. No one shall be disquieted on account of his opinions, including his religious views, provided their manifestation does not disturb the public order established by law.

11. The free communication of ideas and opinions is one of the most precious of the rights of man. Every citizen may, accordingly, speak, write, and print with freedom, but shall be responsible for such abuses of this freedom as shall be defined by law.

12. The security of the rights of man and of the citizen requires public military forces. These forces are, therefore, established for the good of all and not for the personal advantage of those to whom they shall be intrusted.

13. A common contribution is essential for the maintenance of the public forces and for the cost of administration. This should be equitably distributed among all the citizens in proportion to their means.

14. All the citizens have a right to decide, either personally or by their representatives, as to the necessity of the public

contribution; to grant this freely; to know to what uses it is put; and to fix the proportion, the mode of assessment and of collection and the duration of the taxes.

15. Society has the right to require of every public agent an account of his administration.

16. A society in which the observance of the law is not assured, nor the separation of powers defined, has no constitution at all.

17. Since property is an inviolable and sacred right, no one shall be deprived thereof except where public necessity, legally determined, shall clearly demand it, and then only on condition that the owner shall have been previously and equitably indemnified.[30]

This important document is one of the foundations of modern rights discourse, and it is worth noting a few points in it.

Note that whereas Article 1 provides a universal reference point, the actual content of the rights in Article 2 provides some limits. The rights only exist within a political association (the document provides indirect reference to contract or compact in Articles 3 and 6). Thus, if you are outside of such an association you have no rights. This is what modern conventions about refugees address. The point for our immediate purposes is that there is already the opening here for a condition in which it is possible for a person not to have any rights—should they be stateless or deemed not to belong to the political association. Article 6 similarly locates rights within citizenship, and locates the legitimacy of the limits imposed on our freedoms by law according to the General Will (a now outmoded and fairly vague term that was used in eighteenth-century political thought). Thus, we find yet again an instance of limiting the conditions in which rights can be understood to function. That the idea of the General Will is notoriously difficult to operationalize does not help. Rousseau distinguished the General Will from the Will of All, which is more like mob rule, but it was clear that he noted the difference between what any group of people, even a majority, may want and what is best for the society.

The distinction between the General Will and the Will of All was intended to identify and resolve this problem. Finally, Article 17—which is very Lockean in its emphasis on private property—provides yet another problem. Private property exists in no small measure, if not exclusively, by the graces of the state. It is the state and its system of laws and enforcement that enables and protects private property. But what the state protects it can also take away, and this Article recognizes as such in its reference to "public necessity." Although the example here is one of property and compensation, there is a greater principle at work here, which is that while the rights of some can be protected, there exists no right to property, merely the right to have your existing ownerships protected, but that even in such cases property can be taken away if the public necessity demands it. In other words, the right of property functions only so long as it is within the interest of the public good, and by extension rights in general also function in the same way.

This critique is important, not because of how we understand property, but rather because it highlights that rights are largely contingent on the political association, and what this association "decides" is in the public interest. There is nothing here about the inviolability of people's rights. There is, in short, no right to have rights.

Arendt writes that "We became aware of a right to have rights (and that means to live in a framework where one is judged by one's actions and opinions) and a right to belong to some kind of organized community, only when millions of people emerged who had lost and could not regain these rights because of the new global political situation."[31] In short, we did not take seriously the idea that Universal Rights could allow for the removal of rights. Yet when we create a class of people who are deemed not to belong to the nation, and by extension to the political association, we create precisely such a class of people.

The political theorist Seyla Benhabib helps explain the difference between the two different understandings of rights that Arendt invokes in her "right to have rights" phrase. There is, Benhabib notes, an asymmetry between the two different rights:

> The first use of the term "right" is addressed to humanity as such and enjoins us to recognize membership in some human group. In this use of the term "right" evokes a *moral imperative*: "Treat all human beings as persons belonging to some human group and entitled to the protection of the same." What is invoked here is a *moral claim to membership* and a *certain form of treatment compatible with the claim to membership.*[32]

The second use of the term right

> is built upon this prior claim of membership. To have a right, when one is already a member of an organized political and legal community, means that "I have a claim to do or not to do A, and you have an obligation not to hinder me from doing or not doing A." Rights claims entitle persons to engage or not in a course of action, and such entitlements create reciprocal obligations. ... In this usage, "rights" suggests a triangular relationship between the person who is entitled to rights, others upon whom this obligation creates a duty, and the protection of this rights claim and its enforcement through some established legal organ, most commonly the state and its apparatus.[33]

The asymmetry between the first and second "rights" is one of duty and membership: "The duty to recognize one as a member, as one who is protected by the legal-political authorities and as one who is to be treated as a person entitled to the enjoyment of rights."[34] This distinction is important because it highlights how within the liberal tradition there are very serious absences that are easy to miss and gloss over.

The Universal Declaration of the Rights of Man seems to provide a foundation for a universal conception of rights for all people, but it also provides for the opening of an interpretation where such rights can be taken away. This is entirely consistent with the liberal deception discussed above. There is always something left out from our political discourses that has to be left out in order for the discourse to function. Whether it is rights or something else, our political imagination is based on acknowledged discriminations that can lead to perverse

positions whereby what appears to be an argument on behalf
of rights or politics ends up being the same logic that enables
the removal of rights and the destruction of politics. Arendt's
concern about the right to have rights was clearly advocated
in response to the Holocaust, but this does not mitigate that
there remains the potential relevancy for exploring what we
understand to count as politics in our contemporary world,
which rights we prioritize and protect, and at the expense of
what other rights or opportunities.

The what and how of political theory

If we are to take the previous critique of political theory seriously, it suggests a fairly radical rethinking of how we ought
"to do" political theory. It is not as though political theory
(or political philosophy—I am using them interchangeably)
has necessarily been focused on the wrong questions, but
rather has been going about trying to answer these questions
incorrectly. It is the role of the political theorist to highlight
the discriminations that enable our societies to function, to
highlight the consequences of these discriminations, and to
argue for how to overcome them, but if we reject the starting
place for such discussions as contract and a universal logic
of rationality (which is what Kant argues for), what are we
to do? Political theorists rarely engage in discussions about
methods, although there are some exceptions,[35] but there has
been considerable methodological debate within political
theory.[36] How we do political thought is to enquire into the
methodological debates about how we understand political
theory to function. Central to this is the ability to differentiate
political theory as a form of philosophical knowledge from
other forms of knowledge.

The philosopher William Blattner notes that philosophy has
a history of trying to define itself in distinction from other
sciences:

> The idea of philosophy as a separate discipline, distinct from
> physics, theology, and psychology for example, is a relatively
> new innovation. The writings of the major philosophers from

the time of ancient Greece up until the nineteenth century covered a range of topics that would not be considered philosophical today. Indeed, natural science was called "natural philosophy" until the end of the eighteenth century.[37]

There is a tradition of philosophy having to define itself in contrast to other sciences. However, by the twentieth century, as methodological issues became increasingly important within academia, this tradition took on an exceedingly extremist form, with the rise of an almost ideological methodism (more on this below), and the subject of politics became treated as if it were a natural science. This development ostensibly begins during the methodological debate between the behaviouralists and political theorists in the middle of the twentieth century. Yet, even with the passage of time, contemporary questions about methodology and political theory are still shaped by this debate for the simple reason that the naturalist scientific model of research has become the gold standard in the hierarchy of evidence, and thus is presumably what political theory needs to contrast its methodological positions against. Arguing against the behaviouralists required that political theorists defined their own methodological terrain. It is, consequently, worth returning to that debate.

One of the classic works that set out the promise of the empiricist methodological approach to political science is Robert Dahl's article, "The Behavioural Approach in Political Science," published in 1961. As he argues, the behaviouralist approach was a "protest movement" against humanities-style methodologies used in politics research.[38] This protest was so successful that he saw it as becoming conventional within political science, which while not rejecting historical knowledge, methodologically was increasingly grounded on empirically based science. Dahl's definition was influenced by a short essay published a decade earlier, in 1951, by David Truman.

The same year that David Truman published his seminal work on behaviouralism, "The Implications of Political Behaviour Research," David Easton published "The Decline of Political Theory." The contrast between these two texts clearly outlines a problem that remains important when determining what we understand methodology to mean. More extensive political theory critiques of the behaviouralist turn are provided by Wolin and Taylor,[39] who I will return to later, but the publication of these two texts in 1951 provides a shared moment in time in which to begin.

Truman's argument is nuanced in an important way. His argument is not a precursor to the kind of "Freakonomics" approach to social research, where it is not the subject that is important but the method.[40] Truman is clear: "The essential training," he writes, "must be in terms of significant problems in political behaviour, not techniques in general or theory unrelated to empirically researchable questions."[41] His argument is equally clear in its methodological focus:

> Research must be systematic if it is to identify the patterns of relationships which work through, or in spite of, the formalities of government to define the operating political system. This means that research must grow out of a precise statement of hypotheses and a rigorous ordering of evidence which will permit: (1) the identification of behavioural uniformities and of the conditions under which they are to be expected; (2) the validation of findings through successive research; and (3) the accretion of knowledge reflected in concepts of increasing power and generality.
>
> In the second place, research in political behaviour must place primary emphasis upon empirical methods.[42]

This statement is largely a social scientific adoption of the basic elements underlying a naturalist scientific method: empirical observation, generalizable conclusions, a process to test the conclusions, and improved knowledge being that which has greater explanatory power.[43]

Contrast this view to Easton's four-part distinction of what comprises traditional political theory (and which is based on Locke). Easton acknowledges the significance of empirical knowledge and allows for causal theory. Political theory involves four different types of propositions. Easton writes:

> We can conveniently identify this variety of propositions by calling the descriptive statements, factual statements; the assumed

relations between facts, pure or causal theory; the inter-related statements of preferences, value theory; and the propositions designed to apply facts and implicit causal theory to the fulfilment of given ends, applied principles.[44]

Any similarity with the empirical-based research programme advanced by Truman and Dahl is, however, incidental, because Easton is specifically targeting the historical approach to political theory that seeks "to concentrate on the relation of values to the milieu in which they appear rather than on the task of attempting to create new conceptions of values commensurate with men's needs."[45] Not mincing his words, "As it is has been practiced by the majority, the historical approach has managed to crush the life out of value theory."[46] Easton goes on to argue that insofar as values are important to the work of political theorists, the "task of defining the situation in value terms must be considered an art rather than a science."[47] Values, he argues, are "personal responses fixed by our life-experiences."[48] He continues to argue that values are important in framing much empirical political research, but instead of focusing on the art of value-creation, empirical researchers circle around this art.

There are a few key points of contrast here. In the empiricist camp, research is about problem-solving: it is historically informed, but it is restricted to either a description or explanation of related phenomena in its ability to create knowledge, and it is focused on empirical research that can be subject to scientific standards (Truman mentions verification, but we could substitute falsifiability and still end up with the same general idea—Easton mentions both). Easton, on the other hand, focuses on the production of values, i.e. normative theory, that is produced via a different methodological position akin to "art" but which is mildly reflexive, certainly reflective, makes use of empirical evidence, and also assumes a variety of causal relations by which normative positions can be applied to a specific end. In more ways than one this contrast is remarkably similar to that between Traditional and Critical Theory, as explained by Horkheimer in the 1930s.[49]

Easton is no Critical Theorist. Nevertheless, this similarity is interesting precisely because the Lockean basis of Easton's analysis is inconsistent with both the content and the aims of Critical Theory. Easton's conclusions are not the same as those of Horkheimer. Easton wants political theory to serve as a kind of foundational sub-field in political science by "attempting the ... massive task of elaborating a usable conceptual framework for the whole body of political science."[50] He wants political theory to assimilate into the "main current of empirical research in political science, and thereby revive itself after the unrewarding historical study to which it has been devoted in the last fifty years."[51] Horkheimer is, of course, more radical in wanting Critical Theory to serve a revolutionary purpose in highlighting and then overcoming the conditions of oppression in a capitalist society. Moreover, Horkheimer is not so sanguine about the verification or falsifiability test for theory as Easton is, arguing instead that "There are no general criteria for judging the critical theory as a whole, for it is always based on the recurrence of events and thus on a self-reproducing totality."[52] Nevertheless, there are some underlying similarities that remain relevant when thinking about how to conduct political theory.

The focus on values and on normative theory, as well as some of the means by which normative theory is conducted, are noteworthy, albeit general, points of similarity: using empirical claims and assuming the existence of empirical causal relations, and applying values in their analysis in order to then advance a normative argument, are largely all consistent across both arguments. Of course, the actual content of how they understand empirical knowledge (and thus their ontological framing of the thinking subject) are dramatically different. Yet it is worth reflecting for a moment that as political theorists, there are general methodological points we share that enable the field to function, even if most of the time we focus on the differences, but even then the contestation reveals an important shared methodological concern across the field.

One of these shared points of contestation is ontological. In this vein, Horkheimer's attack against positivism and traditional theory was tied to his suspicions about objective and ostensibly neutral social knowledge. His hostility to this kind of theorizing is expressed in various ways, one of which relates to the values and identity of the thinking subject. He notes how the "subject is ... a definite individual in [a] real relation to other individuals and groups, in ... conflict with a particular class, and, finally, in the resultant web of relationships with the social totality and with nature."[53] In short, we can never escape our socio-political and economic conditions: they matter. Horkheimer is also advancing an ontological argument, one which is a significant challenge to the traditional thinking subject.

> The subject is no mathematical point like the ego of bourgeois philosophy; his activity is the construction of the social present. Furthermore, the thinking subject is not the place where knowledge and object coincide, nor consequently the starting-point for attaining absolute knowledge. Such an illusion about the thinking subject, under which idealism has lived since Descartes, is ideology in the strict sense, for in it the limited freedom of the bourgeois individual puts on the illusory form of perfect freedom and autonomy.[54]

If we leave aside the admittedly important Freudian commentary and the idea of a bourgeois philosophy, there is a superficial similarity to some of the underlying methodological points that we will discover feature strongly in Martin Heidegger's philosophy, insofar as both critique the traditional Cartesian subject/object distinction.

For now, however, the point I want to emphasize is how values and context are so clearly central to the idea of Critical Theory. Intriguingly both Easton and Horkheimer recognize the importance of context, either (for Easton) in the ability to develop value-propositions or (for Horkheimer) in understanding the current conditions that Critical Theory questions and reveals. Both are necessarily engaged in making ontological claims about the role of context and of the empirical world of study, and of the identity of the subject. Just because both have dramatically differing ontological worldviews does not mitigate the fact that they recognize its methodological importance. Moreover, both Easton and Horkheimer acknowledge the significance of either reflection or reflexivity. This is another important shared point of contestation, one whose significance seems to have been missed by Easton. He is not entirely clear in what he means by values involving "personal responses fixed by our life-experiences." At first glance this could be a rearticulation of Max Weber's argument about the importance of appreciating the identity of the scholar.[55] However, this is unlikely as Easton clearly has a different agenda in mind than Weber did (significant for our purposes, Easton was also critical of the hermeneutic move rooted in the work of Dilthey because of its historicism).[56] Instead, the point raised by Easton about personal responses is evidence of Locke's influence on his work, but it also speaks to a more general and very important question about the detached critic, and what personal experience actually means for the conduct of political theory and of interpretation.

Michael Walzer addresses this issue in his book on social criticism.[57] In this text, Walzer provides a methodological argument for the conduct of normative political theory. As has been mentioned already, his argument of relevance is to question the idea of the detached critic. Walzer takes aim at the traditional position in much analytic political theory that normative judgements and moral arguments are best developed from a set of abstract and preferably universal principles. Instead, argues Walzer, the social critic, i.e. the political theorist or moral philosopher, needs to be invested in the issue at hand. Easton seems to be raising this same question—that the identity of the theorist is somehow important in being able to develop a position from which to advance value-laden judgements. Yet, whereas Easton seeks, in the words of Michael Gibbons, "greater scientific purchase of political theory,"[58] Walzer's argument is influenced by Gramsci and post-Marxist thought. There is an important difference here that also represents a shared point of concern within political theory.

Easton's recognition about context is restricted to the positionality of the scholar, in the sense that personal knowledge of living at a particular time and place provides the empirical grounding for the theorist's worldview. He writes, "Locke makes observations of political facts that rest on his knowledge of history and of his own time, and, therefore, we do not need to dwell on the factual statements."[59] Walzer is making a different point. This kind of positionality remains important, but for a different reason. Walzer is responding to the argument that too much positionality renders the theorist inherently conservative, insofar as the critic will not be able to step outside of the normative framework in which they reside and thus cannot offer a truly transformative moral argument. For Walzer, like Gramsci and the post-Marxist Critical Theorists, the idea of the detached moral critic is unintelligible. Not only is it not possible to be detached in this way, it is unfathomable, as it removes one's investment in the normative project.

Moreover, one could argue that detached moral critics are rarely as detached as one might think. Barry Schwartz provides such an argument in his book, *The Battle for Human Nature*, where he points out how seemingly revolutionary ideas about the human condition that have been so transformative in history, such as Darwin's biological theory and subsequent reinterpretation via Spencer into social Darwinism, are influenced by assumptions about society, identity, and values that are products of their time.[60] The point I want to take away from this discussion is that identity and positionality, and the contexts or worlds in which the theorist resides, are as important as the narratives that accompany both. How they all matter is debated, as is which identity, context, and narrative are deemed most important (age, gender, class, profession, parent, child, citizen, resident of which country, religion, etc.), but that they matter is clear.

Yet these are methodological concerns that have not seemed to shape how we interpret political data—not only that, the opposite has been the norm as humanities-style knowledge production becomes increasingly devalued within the social sciences. There is something decidedly odd about this, since ontologically it makes much more sense to turn to the humanities in how we come to interpret the human condition, as opposed to using tools that have been honed to make sense of objectively observable causal relations in the natural world. Narratives, the stories we tell about ourselves and about others, and how we interpret each other's stories, seem to be much more sensible as a way to think about politics than has been commonly assumed.

The importance of narratives, however, is easily overlooked, perhaps because they are so ubiquitous. As Roland Barthes remarks:

> The narratives of the world are numberless .... [N]arrative is present in every age, in every place, in every society .... All classes, all human groups have their narratives, enjoyment of which is very often shared by men with different, even opposing, cultural backgrounds.[61]

Narrative, he notes, "is international."[62] Similarly, Carole Pateman begins her feminist critique of the social contract by writing that "Telling stories of all kinds is the major way that human beings have endeavoured to make sense of themselves and their social world."[63]

Recently, the political theorist Jade Schiff, in her book *Burdens of Political Responsibility*, provides an important contribution to understanding how narratives serve as a methodological vehicle for political theory. In her argument, narratives provide the vehicle by which to cultivate responsiveness for political responsibility. In the narrative turn in political theory, narratives become "a site for the cultivation of ethical and political inclinations toward solidarity, inclusion, and the enlargement of our moral sensibilities."[64] In Alice Crary's work, the narratives found in literature offer a "fertile source ... of moral thinking."[65] For Crary, engaging with literature involves emotional responses, which in turn contribute to our ability to make rational understanding moral. Martha Nussbaum makes a similar point in her *Poetic Justice*.[66] Literature, and by implication narratives, can serve a methodological function in working out our normative commitments. Relatedly, in Richard Rorty's work, narrative is what the theorist does: "How can one be a theorist—write a narrative of ideas rather than people—which does not pretend to a sublimity which one's own narrative rules out?"[67]

In the above reading of methodological debates within political theory I have tried to demonstrate that there are some interesting shared assumptions across political theory that can help us to understand how to approach normative political questions. I am not suggesting that there is a unified methodology within political theory or that there ought to be. Rather, I am claiming that across political theory it is possible to discern critiques that set out the various ways in which we can evaluate normative theorizing on its own terms. It is vital that we appreciate this for two reasons. First, political "science" is not a science in any naturalist sense. There is a very large interpretive difference between being able to explain the natural properties of water and thus predict its effects, and anticipating voting results through polling. Second, the role of context, identities, of being reflexively aware, and of narratives is important. Multiple political theorists from across a range of political theory approaches are in general agreement on this.

Conclusion

There are a few important conclusions to take from this critique. The first is that the liberal tradition has been trying to use the wrong tools and in doing so has suggested that we look for politics in the wrong places. By creating an argument about politics where the ultimate end is in fact the removal of politics, mainstream political theory provided us with the wrong normative language to address some of our most pressing challenges. To be sure, there have been successes, and the tradition remains intellectually influential and important. However, if we are to provide real normative solutions to the challenge of living in a post-truth world where it is becoming harder and harder to see a positive place for politics, the delusion needs to be acknowledged.

The election of Donald Trump and the vote to leave the EU were the result of many different social, political, and economic forces. But what both events share is their indebtedness to a politics that can function in a post-truth world, and

in a failure to understand what politics is. If we are to respond
to these events as progressives, we need to start thinking
differently. To put this another way, the failure of politics can
be understood as the correlate to the liberal delusion of politics
being a contractual exercise, and of basing our normative
aspirations on the search for universal rules. There are a few
points that need further explanation. One is to further unpack
this distinction between methodology and political knowledge.
In this chapter, I have started this conversation by exploring
debates about methodology and political theory, and about
the importance of context and thus of narratives. This critique
is as yet unfinished, and it now turns to the debate about
scientific knowledge and of the close and problematic relationship between what we understand as facts and how they
function in politics.

Notes

1 Francis Fukuyama. *The End of History and the Last Man* (London:
   Hamish Hamilton, 1992).
2 Charles Krauthammer, "The Unipolar Moment," *Foreign Affairs*
   70, no. 1 (1990/1991).
3 Sidney Blumenthal, "The Clinton Wars," in *The Clinton Wars*
   (New York: Farrar, Straus and Giroux, 2003), 155.
4 David Campbell, *Writing Security: United States Foreign Policy and
   the Politics of Identity*, rev. ed. (Manchester: Manchester University
   Press, 1998).
5 Brent J. Steele, *Defacing Power: The Aesthetics of Insecurity in
   Global Politics* (Ann Arbor: University of Michigan Press, 2010).
6 Max Horkheimer, *Critical Theory: Selected Essays* (London:
   Continuum, 1975), 188–243.
7 Henry Mance, "Britain Has Had Enough of Experts, Says Gove,"
   Financial Times, June 3 2016.
8 Ronald Dworkin, "The Original Position," in *Reading Rawls:
   Critical Studies on Rawls'* A Theory of Justice, ed. Norman Daniels
   (Stanford: Stanford University Press, 1975), 18.
9 Margaret Gilbert, *A Theory of Political Obligation: Membership,
   Commitment, and the Bonds of Society* (Oxford: Clarendon Press,
   2006). See also Horton for an overview of the literature: John

Horton, *Political Obligation*, 2nd ed. (Basingstoke: Palgrave Macmillan, 2010).

10 Plato, *The Last Days of Socrates: Euthyphro, Apology, Crito, Phaedo*, trans. Hugh Tredennick and Harold Tarrant (London: Penguin Books, 2003).

11 Hannah Arendt, *The Promise of Politics*, ed. Jerome Kohn (New York: Schocken Books, 2005), 82.

12 Ibid., 82–83.

13 Ibid., 83.

14 Plato, *The Republic of Plato*, trans. Allan Bloom (New York: Basic Books, 1986), 153 (473d).

15 Or its corollary, that politics makes philosophy possible. This is Hobbes' and Spinoza's argument as interpreted by Jonathan Havercroft when he writes how for them, "sovereignty [becomes] the necessary precondition of any political philosophy." Jonathan Havercroft, *Captives of Sovereignty* (Cambridge: Cambridge University Press, 2011), 136.

16 Jurgen Habermas, *Theory and Practice*, trans. John Viertel (Cambridge: Polity, 1973), 41–81.

17 Ibid., 67.

18 Ibid., 44.

19 Frank, *What's the Matter with Kansas?*; Hochschild, *Strangers in Their Own Land.*

20 David Ricci, *Politics Without Stories: The Liberal Predicament* (Cambridge: Cambridge University Press, 2016).

21 Iris Marion Young suggests in her feminist critique of the US government's reactions to 9/11 that the relation of exchange that characterizes the social contract is especially significant when populations feel under threat. Iris Marion Young, "Feminist Reactions to the Contemporary Security Regime," *Hypatia* 18, no. 1 (2003).

22 For Stanley Cavell, the contract serves a series of purposes which coalesce around, as Jonathan Havercroft argues, calling society into question. Havercroft, *Captives of Sovereignty*, 168. See Cavell, *The Claim of Reason.*

23 Michael Walzer, *Politics and Passion: Toward a More Egalitarian Liberalism* (New Haven: Yale University Press, 2004); *Spheres of Justice: A Defense of Pluralism and Equality* (Oxford: Basil Blackwell, 1983); *Thick and Thin: Moral Argument at Home and Abroad* (Notre Dame: University of Notre Dame Press, 1994).

24 Michael Walzer, *Interpretation and Social Criticism* (Cambridge, MA: Harvard University Press, 1987).

25 Gayatri Chakravorty Spivak, "Can the Subaltern Speak?," in *Marxism and the Interpretation of Culture*, ed. Cary Nelson and Lawrence Grossberg (Urbana and Chicago: University of Illinois Press, 1988).

26 Havercroft, *Captives of Sovereignty*, 180.

27 Ibid., 181.

28 Ibid.

29 Harold Garfinkel, *Studies in Ethnomethodology* (Englewood Cliffs, New Jersey: Prentice-Hall, 1967).

30 National Assembly of France, "Declaration of the Rights of Man," http://avalon.law.yale.edu/18th_century/rightsof.asp. Accessed February 28 2017.

31 Hannah Arendt, *The Origins of Totalitarianism* (London: André Deutsch, 1986), 296.

32 Seyla Benhabib, *The Rights of Others: Aliens, Residents and Citizens* (Cambridge: Cambridge University Press, 2004), 56. Emphasis in original.

33 Ibid., 57.

34 Ibid., 58.

35 Note the following textbook: David Leopold and Marc Stears, eds, *Political Theory: Methods and Approaches* (Oxford: Oxford University Press, 2008).

36 I am using methods to refer to the tools or the actual means by which research is carried out, whereas methodology pertains to the philosophical justification or basis upon which knowledge production itself is understood or recognized. In other words, methods are what you do, methodology is why doing it that way works. For a more detailed discussion see chapter 2 note 5.

37 William D. Blattner, *Heidegger's Being and Time: A Reader's Guide* (London: Bloomsbury, 2006), 25. See also Stephen Gaukroger, *The Emergence of a Scientific Culture: Science and the Shaping of Modernity 1210–1685* (Oxford: Clarendon Press, 2006).

38 Robert Dahl, "The Behavioural Approach in Political Science: Epitaph for a Monument to a Successful Protest," *The American Political Science Review* 55, no. 4 (1961): 766.

39 Charles Taylor, "Interpretation and the Sciences of Man," *The Review of Metaphysics* 25, no. 1 (1971); "Neutrality in Political Science," in *Philosophical Papers: Philosophy and the Human Sciences*, ed. Charles Taylor (Cambridge: Cambridge University Press,

1985). Sheldon S. Wolin, "Political Theory as Vocation," *The American Political Science Review* 63, no. 4 (1969).

40 Steven D. Levitt and Stephen J. Dubner, *Freakonomics: A Rogue Economist Explores the Hidden Side of Everything*, rev. and expanded ed. (New York: William Morrow & Co., 2006). As a side note, I would suggest that this kind of methodological approach contributed to the intellectual foundations that enabled the sub-prime mortgage crisis to occur, as statisticians were tasked with creating financial products—it was the method that mattered and not so much what was being done with these methods or the normative consequences therein.

41 David B. Truman, "The Implications of Political Behaviour Research," *Items (Social Science Research Council)* 5, no. 4 (1951): 39.

42 Ibid., 38.

43 For an overview of the scientific method, see A.F. Chalmers, *What is This Thing Called Science?*, 3rd ed. (Buckingham: Open University Press, 1999).

44 David Easton, "The Decline of Modern Political Theory," *The Journal of Politics* 13, no. 1 (1951): 38.

45 Ibid., 40.

46 Ibid.

47 Ibid., 49.

48 Ibid., 47.

49 Horkheimer, *Critical Theory*, 118–243.

50 Easton, "The Decline of Modern Political Theory," 58.

51 Ibid.

52 Horkheimer, *Critical Theory*, 242.

53 Ibid., 211.

54 Ibid.

55 Max Weber, *The Methodology of the Social Sciences*, trans. Henry A. Finch and Edward Albert Shils (London: Transaction Publishers, 2011 (1949)).

56 See David Easton, *The Political System: An Enquiry into the State of Political Science* (New York: Knopf, 1953). See also the discussion in Michael T. Gibbons, "Hermeneutics, Political Inquiry, and Practical Reason: An Evolving Challenge to Political Science," *The American Political Science Review* 100, no. 4 (2006).

57 Walzer, *Interpretation and Social Criticism*.

58 Gibbons, "Hermeneutics, Political Inquiry, and Practical Reason," 564.

59 Easton, "The Decline of Modern Political Theory," 39.

60 Barry Schwartz, *The Battle for Human Nature: Science, Morality and Modern Life* (New York; London: Norton, 1986).

61 Roland Barthes, "Introduction to the Structural Analysis of Narratives," in *Image, Music, Text,* ed. Stephen Heath (London: Fontana Press, 1977), 79.

62 Ibid.

63 Pateman, *The Sexual Contract,* 1.

64 Jade Larissa Schiff, *Burdens of Political Responsibility: Narratives and the Cultivation of Responsiveness* (Cambridge: Cambridge University Press, 2014), 21.

65 Alice Crary, *Beyond Moral Judgment* (Cambridge, MA: Harvard University Press, 2007), 128.

66 Martha C. Nussbaum, *Poetic Justice: The Literary Imagination and Public Life* (Boston, MA: Beacon Press, 1995).

67 Richard Rorty, *Contingency, Irony, and Solidarity* (Cambridge: Cambridge University Press, 1989), 108.

2
Unlearning how we think

Introduction

One of the main functions of a higher education degree is to teach the ability to develop an argument to suit a position you hold. In fact, most written work in the UK university system is based on this model. The strength of this system is that it teaches thinking and communication skills, how to construct an argument so that you are able to persuade others to see things as you do, but also enables you to differentiate between strong and weak arguments, and recognize flaws in your own argument. In this sense, the process of constructing an argument reflects one of the underlying requirements for democracy, which is the ability to publicly debate and defend your position, but also to be prepared to change your mind when confronted with a superior argument.

Martha Nussbaum advances a similar claim in her book in support of the humanities:

> Education is not just for citizenship. It prepares people for employment and, importantly, for meaningful lives. ... All modern democracies ... are societies in which the meaning and ultimate goals of human life are topics of disagreement among citizens who hold many different religious and secular views, and these citizens will naturally differ about how far various types of humanistic education serve their own particular goals. What we can agree about is that young people all over the world, in any nation lucky enough to be democratic, need to grow up to be participants in a form of government in which the people inform themselves about crucial issues they will

address as voters and, sometimes, as elected or appointment officials. ... Without support from suitably educated citizens, no democracy can remain stable.[1]

Her argument confronts the increasing tendency across universities to treat a degree not as a part of helping develop citizens but rather as producing consumers—a tendency that should be resisted. But her argument also helps affirm an underlying democratic ideal upon which a liberal arts education functions— that a key skill it teaches is a methodological one about being able to engage thoughtfully in the production and critique of knowledge.

However, there are also political downsides to an approach that prioritizes the best argument. How we recognize and evaluate the deployment of specific knowledge claims is not a neutral activity. There are methodological stances that prejudice how we are able to differentiate across strong and weak arguments. The stronger argument is not necessarily the one that has more facts to back it up, nor is the simpler and more elegant theory that relies on few variables but is able to explain a lot. Nor is the stronger argument necessarily the one that is the easiest to follow or which provides a novel explanation in a counter-intuitive way. There exist a wide range of ways by which to evaluate what constitutes a strong or weak argument, but all of them rely on methodological premises about the purpose of theory and how we understand knowledge production to function.

Another downside to focusing on the skill of the argument is that this way of thinking can reward rhetorical skill and solipsistic thinking. The more we prioritize our abilities to persuade, the less we are able to participate in meaningful discussion where opposing views need to be taken seriously and respectfully. If the priority is to persuade others to come to our own conclusions, knowledge becomes less about developing improved understandings of the contexts in which we find ourselves and contribute toward, and becomes more closely linked with power and the ability to emphasize our own views at the expense of others. Knowledge production in this sense is evaluated on its ability to encourage others to think—and perhaps even to do—what we want them to.

These methodological issues need to be addressed in further detail as they are important for understanding current concerns about the role of facts and evidence in the public sphere. It is becoming increasingly important for the sake of public debate and the integrity of our democratic life—including making our political leaders accountable—to recognize that there are political consequences in how we understand what counts as scientific knowledge, that is to say, knowledge that is not opinion, along with how we evaluate normative arguments, and how we understand the deployment of particular knowledge claims for partisan purposes. Central to these issues is understanding methodology and the relationships that exist between the production of knowledge and politics.

When we emphasize the superior argument as an indicator of intelligence or at least intellectual skill (which is what most liberal arts education involves in some measure, either directly or indirectly), we are recognizing something worthwhile: that being able to effectively deploy information at our disposal is important. However, there is more at stake here than the deployment of information. There are complications in emphasizing the superior argument without also realizing that how we recognize what counts as a better argument is itself based on an often-unaddressed set of knowledge claims.

Most of the time we deploy arguments to suit our predisposed normative positions. Call this confirmation bias or something else, it is rare for anybody to seriously question that which they know. Most research is similar. To borrow from Thomas Kuhn, most work is normal science, work that sustains the paradigm by contributing to it.[2] Questions that challenge the paradigm are most likely open not just to criticism but hostility because they deviate from established wisdom. Universities now tend to teach students to think in a similar way. We are not so much interested in creative thinking, but rather in training students to have whatever transferable skills governments or business leaders expect. Students in this world are not treated as intellectual beings able to think creatively, but as consumers who need to tick a series of boxes so they can communicate effectively in their post-degree professional careers.

There are many consequences to this kind of intellectual trajectory, one of which is that it becomes all too easy to think that people who do not think "like us" and who cannot come to the same conclusions "that we do" are not thinking properly. This conclusion is possible for the very simple reason that our education system and universities have become less about learning and more about degree production. This is not an indictment of our universities, although one would hope that our institutions of higher learning should know better. Rather, universities (and schools) exist as part of society and as such they have come to reflect and respond to the wider societal and political pressures linked to consumerization and professionalization.

Universities have largely become degree factories, where students enroll not necessarily for the sake of intellectual curiosity, of becoming better people and better citizens, but rather out of economic concerns—to land that high-paying job. It is a shame that we tend to view these as either/or choices, politics and society versus economics. In the case of the latter, the idea of an education has come to be framed as being about transferable skills and entrepreneurship. The importance of learning how to think, how to communicate effectively, and how to find (relevant) information has become lost amid concerns over what our private sectors need. Instead of thinking about thinking, we treat the activity of thinking, and the skills involved in finding and analysing information, as tools that we deploy to serve specific goals.

We do not take seriously that it is difficult to judge the action or activity of thinking. Instead, we have come to emphasize the application of tools as opposed to the activity of thinking. There are a few different ways to explain this point, as it is complex and controversial. To explain what I am trying to get at, I am going to advance this argument from a few different directions, starting with debates in political science and political theory that pertain to when we started to emphasize method over methodology, before moving to a discussion of the Sokal hoax, when a physicist attacked what he saw as relativist nonsense in post-modern or post-structural research. The Sokal hoax is interesting because Alan Sokal got one point right—that not resorting to falsifiable and persuasive evidence in the deployment of political arguments can be a problem—but he got another wrong—that interpretive knowledge is relativist and harms a progressive normative agenda.

Methodology and political knowledge

In his 1969 article, "Political Theory as Vocation," the political theorist Sheldon Wolin noted that "American political scientists, for the most part, have not only generally supported the traditional American diffidence toward theories, but they have elevated it to scientific status."[3] What he means by this is the turn away from theory, or for that matter philosophical reflection on the conduct of social science, toward method. He refers derogatorily to this obsession about method at the expense of theory and philosophy as methodism. This focus on methods, which are in effect problem-solving skills, remains powerful but should be viewed with scepticism. Indeed, even in the early days of American political science moving toward a greater focus on methods and seemingly more "scientific" approaches to knowledge, there were warnings from its early advocates of not focusing on methods as such, but rather on problems requiring research.[4]

One consequence of the success of the scientific method in the natural sciences has been a fallacy of authority in regard to research in other disciplines. The fallacy of authority is when an authority on one subject is treated as an authority on an entirely different subject, one in which they are, in fact, not an authority. The idea that the social sciences ought to emulate the natural sciences is a kind of fallacy of authority. The fallacy is that one methodology, which is appropriate for a particular type of research programme, is deemed appropriate for other research programmes. The authority figure in this case is not a person, but a methodology. This is not to say that a range of fundamentally different types of questions could not be addressed by recourse to the methodology of the natural sciences, but it is a fallacy to presume that all can.

The corollary, that questions which cannot be addressed by naturalist methods have no place in the social sciences, is grounded in this fallacy. However, many within the social sciences have accepted this fallacy, even when challenging it. It is in this context that we find what I would describe as a kind of methodological paranoia. If social scientists do not sound scientific—so goes this psychosis—they are not doing science. What is meant by science in this context is a variant of an empirically grounded positivism that tries to replicate naturalist methods, and if we are to sound scientific we need a suitably scientific-sounding language.[5] Brian Fay made a similar argument in 1996, in the opening to his methodological book, *Contemporary Philosophy of Social Science*:

> Throughout much of its history, the basic question in the philosophy of social science has been: is social science scientific, or can it be? Social scientists have historically sought to claim the mantle of science and have modelled their studies on the natural sciences. Consequently, the philosophy of social science has traditionally consisted in assessments of social science's success in this regard, of the ways social science is like and unlike natural science.[6]

Similarly, the philosopher Hubert Dreyfus writes, "There is, indeed, something wrong with our culture's worship of natural science, as if what science tells us about the fundamental particles has fundamental importance for all aspects of life."[7]

In qualitative social science, one side-effect of this scientism has been an attempt to replicate the sciences by making use of our own jargon in order to sound scientific. The result has been methodological inflation, what Charles Taylor describes as an "epistemological bias" or an "obsession" that follows from "the progress of natural science."[8] An example of this kind of methodological inflation is when social scientists turn to philosophy for methodological terminology to describe something that is (1) not necessarily methodological and (2) involves repurposing philosophical terms that denote particular philosophical problems or methodologies for non-philosophical meanings. It has become common to throw around philosophical language, using terms such as ontology, phenomenology, and hermeneutics, in order to provide gravitas to qualitative research as though we need to compete with scientists and their scientific jargon.[9] I want to reject this assumption about the unimpeachable merits of the scientific method for the simple reason that political theory, and by implication normative political research, should be understood on their own terms.

Part of the problem here is that we regularly and repeatedly fail to appreciate that there are fundamentally different ways of knowing. Martin Heidegger, in *Being and Time*, suggests that the natural sciences and philosophy exist in different worlds; both do their own thing, they do not answer each other's questions, and they should not drive each other's methodologies or research programmes.[10] As he writes:

> In suggesting that anthropology, psychology, and biology all fail to give an unequivocal and ontologically adequate answer to the question about the *kind of being* which belongs to those entities which we ourselves are, we are not passing judgement on the positive work of these disciplines. We must always bear in mind, however, that these ontological foundations can never be disclosed by subsequent hypotheses derived from empirical material, but that they are always "there" already, even when that empirical material simply gets collected.[11]

Debates about philosophy, science, and methodology are clearly not new, and are rarely conclusive. Famously, Paul Feyerabend went so far as to argue that there is no single method that defines science.[12] Moreover, Heidegger's views about science changed by the time he wrote his essay about technology, at which point he called into question his previous views about there being space for both scientific and philosophical methodologies.[13] In the social sciences, debates about what methodology provides the grounding for social knowledge are not new, and can be traced back to Hume, Weber, Parsons, and many others.

In political science, the key debate about methodology in political theory or political philosophy pertains to a set of methodological positions that started to gain prominence in the 1950s and 1960s. Some points from this debate between the behaviouralists and those in political theory have been addressed in the previous chapter. In what follows I build on that discussion by elaborating on the points of similarity, not between the political theorists and the behaviouralists, but among the political theorists. These similarities are interesting because although they do not suggest a unified methodology or unitary direction of purpose within political theory, they do suggest that there are some very general methodological positions that cut across political theory, some of which are consistent with hermeneutic phenomenology. Noting these similarities helps demonstrate the importance of interpretation in the conduct of normative political research.

As political theorists sought to fight back and defend their place in political science, guiding statements were crafted that remain insightful about what political theory is and how it is done. In making their case for political theory, certain similarities emerged. These similarities provide a shared point of reference so that what might seem to be controversial can actually be read as one reasonable answer that follows from a set of shared general assumptions about how to approach thinking about knowledge production as a political theorist. Central to this issue is the argument against forms of knowledge that can be dismissed as relativist and overly contextual, and the ways in which each of us construct and respond to meaning in different ways. The methodological target in such anti-relativist arguments is usually some version of continental philosophy, including hermeneutic phenomenology and any post-Heideggerian philosophy (post-structuralism, post-modernism).

The tendency to dismiss hermeneutic phenomenology, for example, as a source for political knowledge can be found in the extent to which such a methodology is understood to be inherently relativist because it is fundamentally based on interpretation, without foundational moral principles to serve as a framework for normative analysis. In his discussion on this issue, Hubert Dreyfus quotes Evelyn Fox who highlighted just how serious the stakes of this debate are: "if truth is relative, if science is divorced from nature and married instead to culture then the privileged status of that authority is fundamentally undermined."[14] The extent by which this culture or science war spread across the academy was evident in the infamous Sokal hoax, when Alan Sokal, a physicist, published a hoax article in *Social Text*, and he has since gone on to argue at great length about the political dangers of conducting any social research on non-naturalist-grounded methods.[15]

This debate is, however, problematic if taken at face value, for two reasons. First, it assumes a hegemony of methods, and thus seeks to assess all knowledge production according to a single standard with no room for alternatives. Second, it misses the key insight that is of significance, which, in the words of Hubert Dreyfus, is that "it would be sufficient to demonstrate that although natural science can tell us the truth about the causal powers of nature, it does not have a special access to ultimate reality. This is exactly what Heidegger attempts to show."[16] For our purposes, what matters is that the science of interpretation can be addressed methodologically on its own terms. The question at issue, consequently, is what these terms are. It is in this regard that the shared points of similarity across political theory are significant. They point out a frame of reference in which to appreciate and evaluate our own methodology.

Any discussion of methodology and political theory needs to be cautious not to fall into the trap of trying to defend political theory as though the point of contrast is natural science. It was in response to the behaviouralist revolution that Sheldon Wolin wrote about the importance of theory.[17] The turn away from theory (or for that matter philosophical reflection on the conduct of social science) toward method remains powerful in the social sciences, as evident in the

classic methods textbook, *Designing Social Inquiry*.[18] Recent
monographs in IR on causality provide a useful counter to
this kind of methodism,[19] and the related work of Hidemi
Suganami has been an important reminder not to forget the
role of philosophical reflection for methodology (his primary
interest is causation).[20] Nevertheless, Wolin's point remains
important in no small part because it is crucial for any methodological discussion within political theory (or political
philosophy) to function in terms of their own research
programmes.

Wolin's critique is additionally insightful because of how
methodism dismisses what he terms "tacit political knowledge."[21] Tacit political knowledge, Wolin writes, "accrues over
time and never by means of a specified program in which
particular subjects are chosen in order to produce specific
results."[22] Tacit political knowledge is "rooted in knowledge
of the past and of the tradition of theory."[23] This kind of
accumulated knowledge is related to daily know-how and is
not something that relies on the application of a formula or
proposition, but is largely interpretive and rests on our ability
to decipher connotations and meanings that matter. This is a
type of knowledge that political research rarely takes seriously,
although it should because addressing the normative conditions
of political life, i.e. a human life, requires an engagement
with how people understand the conditions that they find
themselves in.

Central to this endeavour is the ability to interpret these
conditions. Charles Taylor provides a methodological explanation of this kind of knowledge, which he classifies as falling
under the science of hermeneutics. The defining criteria of
this science is interpretation: "the criteria of judgement in a
hermeneutical science" come down to "successful interpretation."[24] Of course, this sounds rather circular, and it raises the
question of what counts as successful interpretation. Taylor is
not as clear as one would like on this point. His answer, which
is decidedly Heideggerian, is that it unveils something that is
otherwise hidden. But this answer provides no moral standpoint
from which to judge which interpretation is normatively better.

However, this absence is only a problem if we require a moral standpoint or some suitably objective set of moral principles, and if we require this then the interpretation is not consistent with hermeneutic phenomenology.

The methodology of hermeneutics

> [w]ould not be founded on brute data; its most primitive data would be readings of meanings, and its object would have three properties: the meanings are for a subject in a field or fields; they are moreover meanings which are partially constituted by self-definitions, which are in this sense already interpretations, and which can thus be re-expressed or made explicit by a science of politics. In our case, the subject may be a society or community; but the intersubjective meanings ... embody a certain self-definition, a vision of the agent and his [her] society, which is that of the society or community.[25]

Taylor is here invoking the hermeneutic circle, which has come to play an important part in social theory.[26] The hermeneutic circle is explained by Taylor as the unavoidability of an "ultimate appeal to a common understanding of the expressions, of the 'language' involved."[27] The general idea is that in order to help someone else understand our own position, we can only do so in terms that they themselves understand. Providing his own account of the hermeneutic circle, Anthony Giddens writes, "All understanding demands some measure of pre-understanding whereby further understanding is possible."[28] Giddens' definition of the hermeneutic circle is from Heidegger via Gadamer.

The hermeneutic circle seems to me to be a fairly conventional experience that we all share, although it is not a method insofar as it is "the ontological process of human discourse in operation, in which, through the mediation of language, 'life mediates life.'"[29] As Michael Gibbons writes, "According to the Gadamer-Taylor position, our appropriation of the world, at both the intellectual and practical levels, always takes place within a linguistic-historical tradition from which we cannot fully extricate ourselves."[30] Indeed, it is only possible to explain an argument when all the interlocutors are able to understand the language in which that argument is conducted.[31]

If we reject the need for a fixed moral point for critique, and instead accept the inevitability of the hermeneutic circle, even for moral criticism and political theory, is there something that stands in place of foundational rules? The answer is no, sort of. There is not so much a replacement as a different way of thinking about our place in the world. It is useful here to recall that for Heidegger, the hermeneutic circle is by itself not a problem, provided that we enter it the right way. The same could be argued about normative interpretation. The absence of a fixed normative principle is not a problem, provided that we enter into the interpretation—into the hermeneutic circle—the right way. And this entry point involves a very important ontological move. Whereas detached critics ostensibly design their arguments by way of fixed moral standards, this approach only works if we also accept a separation between subjects and objects. The separation is needed in this case because without it there can be no moral position that is independent of the subject.

This approach is what Heidegger argues is wrong in the history of Western philosophy because it treats the human condition as just another type of being like any other entity or substance, when it patently cannot be. To presume that there exist normative foundations that are independent of human beings is to presume that human existence is similar to that of any other creature. Moral rules do not, in this view, live among us but exist externally to us, for us to discover. The alternative ontological stance is explained in Taylor's philosophy as intersubjectivity.

Intersubjectivity is the ontological basis for a few things, including understanding our condition of interpretation in the world. In explaining intersubjectivity, Taylor writes:

> But what we are dealing with here is not subjective meaning, but rather intersubjective meanings. It is not just that the people in our society all or mostly have a given set of ideas in their heads and subscribe to a given set of goals. The meanings and norms implicit in these practices are not just in the minds of

the actors but are out there in the practices themselves, practices which cannot be conceived as a set of individual actions, but which are essentially modes of social relations, of mutual action.[32]

Another way to think of the intersubjective condition is to recognize that there are structures in the social world (the world that we create) that we come into contact with, which shape our experiences, interpretations and thus understanding of this world. However, these structures do not exist independently of us, we construct them and are shaped by them. When we interact with the world we do so by coming into contact with elements of a socially constituted reality. This reality is an intersubjective one, as it cannot exist independently of our meanings and norms. If we take this argument and apply it to questions of a normative nature, such as rules of acceptable conduct, it is not that everything is relative so much as that our normative understandings are produced intersubjectively. I will return to ethics later, but for now, one way to appreciate this point is that it is rare to find anybody who acts in a manner that is consistent all the time with an unchanging moral code. If that was the case, we would not need to come up with such terms as cognitive dissonance. Similarly, as one recent report noted (and as most of us can probably relate to), depending on the context the same person can interpret the same information in completely different ways.[33] Assuming an unchanging moral foundation or grounding does not help us very much when having to address the ways by which people engage in their lives as intersubjective beings.

Indeed, people rarely act consistently to the extent that we presume, and those who do would most likely appear to be a little odd. Rather, humans are creatures of their world, they are creatures of habit but also of context, and while there may be patterns of behaviour, such patterns do not mean we operate according to a determined set of principles all the time. Barry Schwartz's book about human nature provides a compelling and straightforward critique against a universal ontological view of the human condition, arguing that some of the objective views we hold about human nature, such as rationality, are often self-fulfilling and thus cannot be treated as objective and independent universal truths.[34] The absence of foundations does not, however, negate that people operate according to normative beliefs, and the absence of a universal law for conduct does not mean that we are all nihilists or relativists. We are, instead, intersubjective beings, based in and shaped by our worlds of human interaction. As I address in the next section, Sokal did not take this option seriously, and to be fair, neither do many political scientists, who find it much more comfortable to focus on methods and choose not to engage in the more abstract philosophical questions upon which their methods reside.

The limits of science

The US election and UK referendum results suggest that people who voted for Remain or Leave, or for Trump or Clinton, appeared to be acting upon dramatically different views of the world. In the US it was a choice between one unpopular but highly qualified candidate, and another who may well be the most unqualified and unsuitable candidate for President in the country's history. In the UK, the referendum favoured populist and nativist romantics who dream of the Empire, with little respect for the values of internationalism and the underlying anti-war reasons for the establishment of the EU. Both the election and referendum were won or lost on the strengths of the stories the different sides told.[35] In the US, an establishment millionaire told an anti-establishment story, furnished with a Twitter account where he could seemingly provide his credentials as someone who could tell it like it is, without the filter of a career in Washington D.C. In the UK, the trio of Gove, Johnson, and Farage provided a story based on fear of immigrants and concerns about jobs and globalization. Their populist story of xenophobia and parochialism, built on an imaginary notion of sovereignty, was and is delusional, but contributed to people fearing that their country was lost and its legislative powers were being taken away by EU membership. The hostility of the anti-EU press in the UK appears to be based on nothing but sheer opportunism and cynicism. Even Boris Johnson noted how it was not accuracy but sensationalism that drove (his) EU news stories;[36] at one point *The Sun* called for the reintroduction of the old blue colour of UK passports, clearly reflecting the real priority of the Leave camp as symbolism rather than substance.[37] Both votes were all about narratives. The Leave side knew this very well when they admitted that focusing on immigrants was the only story they had that could win it for them,[38] as they had no evidence to justify their wildly unrealistic claims about a post-EU UK.

What was clear on both sides of the Atlantic is that what matters to win a referendum or an election is not evidence (i.e. facts) but *meaning*, and especially which meanings carry greater currency.

The story for those of us who lost is traumatic. At least that is how it feels. Those who voted to leave the EU made a decision against the values of inclusivity and of being a part of the world, of being connected to the world, not divorced from it. Those who voted for Trump voted for a racist, misogynist, narcissist bully, who lies pretty much about everything and anything when it suits him, and who relies on *ad hominem* assaults and threats of lawsuits as the means to conduct his affairs. However, these are caricatures. They contain an element of accuracy, but they also gloss over a more foundational problem which is less about either Brexit or Trump and more about the role of knowledge production and the relationship between knowledge and politics. Central to this is the role of fake news and of what the comedian Steven Colbert refers to as "truthiness."[39] One complication in all of this concern about facts, evidence, or "truthiness" is that it is not clear what the opposite is. The dichotomy seems to be between facts and post-facts, as though if only people listened to the evidence it would all be alright. Unfortunately, this position is flawed because it keeps the debate on the terms of the "scientists," ignores the political consequences of how falsifiability or the related testable requirements of scientific research methods contribute to the meanings of scientific conclusions, and ignores the power of narratives and of meaning. Put another way, the longer we argue for more accurate facts, the harder it becomes to understand the power of interpretation and the less likely it becomes to be able to counter the forces that led to both electoral results.

There is some irony here worth exploring, which is perhaps most easily understood by turning to an infamous moment in academia. In 1996 the journal *Social Text* published the article "Transgressing the Boundaries: Towards a Transformative Hermeneutics of Quantum Gravity," in their Spring/Summer issue (46/47, pp. 217–52). The article, which in order to be published underwent the usual peer review process, was written by the physicist Alan Sokal and was, in fact, a parody or hoax. After the article was published, Sokal sent another submission to *Social Text*, claiming that the article was nonsense and explaining why he submitted it in the first place. This second article was rejected by *Social Text* but versions of it were published in various places, including *Dissent* (43 no. 4, Fall 1996, pp. 93–96), *Philosophy and Literature* (20, no. 2, Winter 1997, pp. 107–10) and in the book *Beyond the Hoax*. Sokal defends the hoax article as a response to the science wars between scientists and post-modernists. As he writes in his defence:

> But why did I do it? I confess that I'm an unabashed Old Leftist who never quite understood how deconstruction was supposed to help the working class. And I'm a stodgy old scientist who believes, naively, that there exists an external world, that there exists objective truth about that world, and that my job is to discover some of them.[40]

Furthermore, he continues,

> my main concern isn't to defend science from the barbarian hordes of [literary criticism] (we'll survive just fine, thank you). Rather, my concern is explicitly *political*: to combat a currently fashionable postmodern/poststructuralist/social-constructivist discourse—and more generally a penchant for relativism—which is, I believe, inimical to the values and future of the Left.[41]

In other words, Sokal felt that the trend in academia rooted in post-Heideggerian philosophy, concerned less with objective facts and more with interpretation and meaning, was politically damaging. The more we argue that everything comes down to interpretation, so his view goes, the less it becomes possible to clearly identify specific causes for inequality (for example) and thus how to overcome them. In short, if everything comes down to interpretation and meaning, there is no objective basis upon which to advocate normative political positions.

The hoax was a blatant violation of academic integrity in the sense that it was a deceptive submission to an academic journal.[42] It is not quite the same thing as submitting false research, but it might as well be. The point of getting the article published was more about sensationalism than anything else, although he did go out of his way to repeatedly stress the political and normative reason for the hoax article—as though a good intention justifies a bad deed. This good intention was about the need to deploy empirical evidence in support of normative claims: How could you argue in support of redistribution policies if there is no evidence of an unfair distribution of wealth or resources? His argument rests on the need to provide firm empirical evidence that could be used to identify proof of injustice and to support normative policy proposals. If, as he argues, we view all evidence as somehow subjectively generated then there can be no ground upon which to defend political positions: it all just becomes about personal belief or ideological conviction. We might as well govern by astrology.

Importantly, in the philosophy of science it was a similar argument that led Karl Popper to claim that the basis of the scientific method is falsification.[43] Fields like astrology, argue Popper, could never be proven wrong. The theory could always be modified to suit specific purposes or conclusions. A similar argument could be made in regard to classical Marxism—which was one of Popper's targets. As this argument goes: just because the revolution did not happen in an industrial society but in Russia, which was largely agrarian when compared to more industrial economies like those of England or Germany, did not mean that Marxism was wrong. The theory can be changed to suit the facts. It was precisely this kind of thinking that Popper challenged, arguing that for any theory to adhere to the standards of scientific knowledge it needs to be falsifiable. If a theory cannot potentially be proven wrong, it cannot be treated as scientific and might as well be the equivalent of personal opinion or even superstition.

Sokal was trying to make a similar point in regard to what he saw as the potential side-effects of a post-modern relativism. He has a point. There are certainly areas in which being able to wield empirical evidence in support of demonstrating that injustices are real is of crucial importance. Having an evidence-base is important. But he was wrong to see the problem of relativism and its political consequences as a problem for the political left—it actually became the methodological mantra of the right, where evidence no longer matters—and he was wrong to argue that other forms of political enquiry are damaging because they are not "scientific" according to the methods and philosophical assumptions that lie behind the natural sciences. Moreover, it is wrong to claim that the political right's turn toward post-facts is a consequence of left-wing post-modernism.[44] If anything, this intellectual barb is about deflecting responsibility from the right and the alt-right for their political application of "truthiness." The intellectual connection here from post-Heideggerian thought to the right's adoption of "truthiness" could be a continuation of Leo Strauss's response to Nietzsche and Heidegger.[45] However, even if this is the case, it does not abrogate the responsibility of any "post-facters" and it does not mean that there can be no ethics in post-Nietzschean philosophy.

Nietzsche's philosophical critique of morality[46] notwithstanding, the political issue at hand is about how normative claims can be deployed in response to empirical arguments. It is this connection that animated Sokal and which is behind our condemnation of the political application of truthiness by our politicians.

In response to Sokal's defence of the hoax, Stanley Aronowitz, one of the founders of *Social Text*, wrote in *Dissent*, that Sokal

> believes that reason, logic, and truth are entirely unproblematic. He has an abiding faith that through the rigorous application of scientific method nature will yield its unmediated truth. According to this doctrine there are "objective truths," because the earth revolves around the sun, gravity exists, and various other laws of nature are settled matters. So Sokal never interrogates the nature of evidence or facts, and simply accepts them if they have been adduced within certain algorithms that bear the stamp of "science."[47]

This is a point that Sokal rejects, and in fact finds hard to understand—but understanding Aronowitz's point is crucial. Sokal's response was to write:

> The trouble isn't just that Aronowitz distorts my own positions; it is that much of his essay is based on setting up and demolishing straw opponents. Who nowadays claims that culture has nothing to do with economic injustice or that funding sources have no effect on scientific work? Who denies the value of sociological and political study of science and technology or of the philosophical analysis of epistemological problems? My point is a modest one: that such investigations need to be conducted with due intellectual rigor.[48]

Similarly, he has argued that his target was a "new and more radical breed" of critique "which aims at the scientific *method* itself."[49] "It seems to me," he writes in another essay, "that truth, reason and objectivity are values worth defending no matter what one's political views; but for those of us on the Left, they are crucial—without them, our critique loses all its force."[50] And finally, in another of his multiple defences of his hoax:

> What concerns me is the proliferation, not just of nonsense and sloppy thinking *per se*, but of a particular kind of nonsense and sloppy thinking: one that denies the existence of objective realities, or (when challenged) admits their existence but

downplays their practical relevance. At its best, a journal like *Social Text* raises important questions that no scientist should ignore—questions, for example, about how corporate and government funding influence scientific work. Unfortunately, epistemic relativism does little to further the discussion of these matters.

In short, my concern over the spread of subjectivist thinking is both intellectual and political. Intellectually, the problem with such doctrines is that they are false (when not simply meaningless). There *is* a real world; its properties are *not* merely social constructions; facts and evidence *do* matter. What sane person would contend otherwise? And yet, much contemporary academic theorizing consists precisely of attempts to blur these obvious truths—the utter absurdity of it all being concealed through obscure and pretentious language.[51]

Yet, as we know full well, facts apparently no longer matter. Both Trump and Brexit have demonstrated as much. What Sokal fails to understand is that while the tools of the natural sciences and its ontological assumptions about the existence of a real, objective, independent world may work perfectly fine for the natural sciences, it is a massive leap of faith to then presume that they should also work for a socially constructed world. This is a key part of Aronowitz's argument and one that Sokal repeatedly goes out of his way to avoid. It is also an argument that has become more important over time.

In much contemporary discussion, what gets conflated is a methodological question about how to interpret empirical evidence (or what counts as empirical evidence), and the political contexts in which we deploy knowledge claims. There is, to be sure, a need for empirical studies to demonstrate that there are conditions which may violate or come into conflict with our normative values. However, it does not follow that just because evidence matters we cannot assail the veracity of facts—which is exactly what the populist right has been doing, hence, truthiness. I will return to this question of evidence deployment and post-facts or truthiness later. In order to get us there we need to see the consequences of an unquestioned faith in scientific knowledge production.

There are at least two consequences. The first of these is that what Sokal marginalizes in his discussions is that even within the scientific community, facts and evidence can be treated with suspicion and challenged. There is, for example, the infamous case that linked vaccines to autism, which was subsequently retracted by the journal that published the research.[52] Another example is how women are ignored in medical research, thus contributing to false diagnoses of medical conditions and mis-interpretations of symptoms when the patients are not men.[53] It could be argued that in both of these examples the problem is merely that the studies were not carried out properly (that was certainly the case in the vaccine study). However, there is another issue which is that there may be underlying un-articulated bias (what is often called implicit bias) that undermines the possibility of there ever being a truly objective social science. If such bias can exist in the natural sciences, it would logically be compounded in the social sciences where the objects of study are always of an intersubjective character.

Part of the issue here is that the public is not always able to interpret scientific findings or understand how the scientific method works (or appreciate that within academic training we learn to constantly question each other's conclusions, but this does not necessarily diminish the strength of research findings), so when a study is challenged, it lends credibility to the popular view that facts are only good until the next one comes along that replaces or debunks the previous one. This process is related to what the political theorist Stephen Welch refers to as one of the features of hyperdemocracy.[54]

A second consequence is that when we conduct our research, context and identity matter. They shape the types of questions we ask, who participates, who conducts the studies, the interaction between the researchers and the participants, and how the findings are then reacted/responded to and interpreted. Ever since Max Weber emphasized the importance of positionality,[55] and scientists became aware of how the act of studying something can alter the object of study (known most commonly as the Heisenberg uncertainty principle), researchers have

tried to control for these kinds of methodological factors that
can negatively impact research. For American listeners of
NPR, this issue was commonly raised in the programme Car
Talk, when Click and Clack would question the integrity of
how laboratory studies rarely translate into practice in the
world outside the controlled environment of the lab. Theorists
have been wise to this characteristic of research for years, with
feminist and post-colonial scholars being especially important
in this regard by highlighting how research can be inherently
sexist or can reflect racist discourses.[56]

However, before either feminist or post-colonial theory
became more recognizable as part of Western academia, Max
Horkheimer noted in the 1930s that there needs to be a distinction between the social and political contexts in which we are
able to produce a type of knowledge that can be deployed as
a fact, and a methodological awareness about how we value
different types of knowledge.[57] He identified how research
cannot be divorced from the conditions in which it is
produced.

People filter knowledge, and no pretending about some
objective universe of facts can overcome this characteristic of
human beings. Consequently, it is unsurprising that public
debate turns on identity claims instead of ostensibly objective
factual ones.[58] To debate social facts is consequently to engage
in a debate about how identity informs our interpretation of
the world, and of the function of identity in our social and
political world. It is through identity claims that we navigate
across competing interpretations of events, which is partly how
we can understand the difference between proportionality and
total sums when it comes to the experiences of minorities.

In the case of Black Lives Matter versus Blue Lives Matter,
the facts are in a sense the same: the number of deaths caused
by police. What changes is which number carries greater
significance, and this comes down to interpretation. In public
debate, this matter of interpretation ends up being framed
through the politics of identity (for example, multiculturalism
or egalitarian liberalism). What such debates reveal is that if
you are unable to understand the grounds upon which facts
are undermined or determined, you cannot provide an

argument in which facts matter. Similarly, using facts to advocate political change is meaningless if they cannot be located within a narrative in which these facts make sense. In other words, the veracity of facts within the sciences cannot be divorced from the culture of knowledge within which the sciences operate. This conclusion does not lead to the opposite, that there are no facts outside of this world (which is what Sokal thinks). Rather, it points to the limits of how far we are able to deploy what count as facts, and to the very real significance of how our narratives help us to interpret the social reality that we are faced with. There is still the possibility to deploy empirical evidence in pursuit of normative goals. What matters here is that we are cautious in how evidence is used but also that we acknowledge that it simply does not matter how many fallible studies one conducts if the research cannot be located within a narrative whereby it makes sense. Scientists already do this; they just pretend that they don't.

Political theorists, and not just those from the Frankfurt School, have been aware of the problematic nature of treating facts or research findings about politics as if they are the equivalent of the same type of knowledge produced in the natural sciences—and the more we pretend that this is the case, the more we undermine our potential to develop normative arguments in politics. Hannah Arendt was equally concerned on this matter, writing that

> Instead of indulging in such old-fashioned, uncomputerizable activity, they [scientifically minded brain trusters in the councils of government] reckon with the consequences of certain hypothetically assumed constellations without, however, being able to test their hypotheses against natural occurrences. The logical flaw in these hypothetical constructions of future events is always the same: what first appears as a hypothesis ... turns ... into a "fact," which then gives birth to a whole string of similar non-facts, with the result that the purely speculative character of the whole enterprise is forgotten. Needless to say, this is not science but pseudo-science, "the desperate attempt of the social and behavioural sciences," in the words of Noam Chomsky, "to imitate the surface features of sciences that really have significant intellectual content."[59]

Political theorists have long been aware of the political significance contained in methodological decisions, and of what happens when we ignore methodological awareness and instead concentrate on methods. This is both Sokal's concern and his mistake. He was correct to highlight that there is a relationship between knowledge production and politics. However, he was wrong to presume that the solution lay in uncritically replicating the assumptions within the natural sciences about the scientific method. It is not as though facts do not exist, or that social scientists should dismiss the scientific method. Rather, the point is that an approach that emphasizes facts unproblematically cannot account for the other fact, which is that people interpret the world in a variety of different ways, and that an appeal to factual, ostensibly objective knowledge is ultimately meaningless when the knowledge fails to make sense according to how we understand the world. To put it more pragmatically, it does not matter whether there is or is not an objective real world of facts out there if we don't accept the knowledge that describes this world as valid.

The naturalist response to this critique is that there is only one world, and that social scientists need not engage in metaphysical speculation about context. However, this is also to fall foul of Horkheimer's crucial observation, which is that it is patently illogical and unreasonable to take one epistemological position and evaluate all others according to this same standard because it makes it impossible for alternatives to present themselves.

Whatever the reason, the methods have largely won (for evidence see *Freakonomics*),[60] even when they lose (see Trump and Brexit). The more we constantly try to get our data right at the expense of all other forms of knowledge production, the less we are able to question those conditions under which we assume that such data can tell us what we want it to. Thus, instead of "thinking," we treat people and problems like puzzles where the boundaries are clear and easy to find, and all we need to do is put the rest together. With such a dismal view of the human condition, is it any wonder that people have turned away from facts and embraced truthiness?

Between thinking and knowing

Enquiring into our understanding of the sources of morality, Friedrich Nietzsche asks in *On the Genealogy of Morality* "how is such forgetting possible?"[61] Indeed, this is also the question we should be asking ourselves. But it is not clear what exactly we have forgotten. During the science wars of the 1990s against the post-modernists, we find a self-appointed spokesperson for the Traditional Left arguing that facts matter and that the relativist tendencies among academics pose a danger to progressive politics. Today, we find those who might be on the left, at least those who supported Clinton or did not support Trump and those who voted for the UK to remain in the EU, arguing that it is the populist right who have turned their backs on evidence. It is an odd convergence of claims. First it was the left that was guilty and now it is the right. That both left and right would eventually have to deal with debates about facts is a sign not that there are no facts, or that facts cannot be tested, but rather that we have forgotten what exactly facts are.

Facts exist as part of a wider scheme in which knowledge is produced. It is not necessarily which facts are accurate or true that is at issue, but rather the philosophical and political character of facts as pieces of knowledge. There are political consequences in this forgetting, or, if it is not forgetting, dismissing knowledge about the nature of facts as irrelevant. The Critical Theorist Max Horkheimer knew of this danger all too well. In his critique against Traditional Theory he rightfully noted that facts are produced and that the production of facts serves a purpose in enabling a form of scientific knowledge to function:

> In traditional theoretical thinking, the genesis of particular objective facts, the practical application of the conceptual systems by which it grasps the facts, and the role of such systems in action, are all taken to be external to the theoretical thinking itself. This alienation, which finds expression in philosophical terminology as the separation of value and research, knowledge and action, and other polarities, protects the savant from the

tensions ... and provides an assured framework for his
activity.[62]

One of the points he is making is that facts are socially produced
and produce (in turn) a social function. This does not mean,
however, that there can be no recourse to evidence-based
argument.[63] Rather it means that we need to understand how
knowledge is produced as knowledge, and why this form of
knowledge production carries the kind of significance that
means we ought to take it seriously. Most of the time, we do
not ask ourselves this question and instead have fallen on to
the treadmill of questioning the use of facts—as though we
can manipulate them to suit our purposes.

Indeed, it is possible to manipulate data. Politicians, corporations, and on occasion academics, have all done so, but to
focus on this possibility is to forget the key point here, which
is that we no longer take seriously underlying questions about
knowledge production. We focus instead, like Sokal, on
methods, ignoring that the methods themselves have to come
from somewhere and, crucially, that there are different ways
of understanding and interpreting the world, but that this
does not amount to relativism. What it does amount to is
having to return to questions about how people as self-
interpreting beings make sense of the world they find themselves
in. This is not a question about facts but about interpretation
and thinking.

In her essay, "Thinking and Moral Considerations," Hannah
Arendt offers a provocative distinction that can serve to help
summarize some of the points made so far. The distinction
is between thinking and knowing. She writes, "We owe to
Kant the distinction between thinking and knowing, between
reason, the urge to think and to understand, and the intellect,
which desires and is capable of certain verifiable knowledge."[64]
Thinking, Arendt tell us, is always concerned "with objects
that are absent, removed from direct sense perception."[65]
Thinking is not only concerned with that which is invisible;
it too is invisible, "lacking all the outside manifestation of

other activities."[66] Arendt goes on to emphasize this aspect of thinking:

> when I am thinking, I move outside the world of appearances, even if my thought deals with ordinary sense-given objects and not with such invisible concepts or ideas, the old domain of metaphysical thought. In order to think about somebody, he must be removed from our senses; so long as we are together with him, we don't think of him—though we may gather impressions that later become food for thought; to think about somebody who is present implies removing ourselves surreptitiously from his company and acting as though he were no longer there.[67]

It is in thinking that we find our moral faculties. The trajectory of much philosophy, however, has not been concerned with thinking but rather with knowledge. Knowledge, we can infer from the above description, pertains to the world of appearances, is observable, or at least can be treated as though it were observable. The pursuit of knowledge is, therefore, about being able to develop some understanding of this observable world, even when we are unable to observe it.

In facing this distinction Arendt also notes that "if it is true that thinking deals with invisibles, it follows that it is out of order because we normally move in a world of appearances in which the most radical experience of *dis*appearance is death."[68] Consequently, she adds that "the question is unavoidable: How can anything relevant for the world we live in arise out of so resultless an enterprise? An answer, if at all, can come only from the thinking activity, the performance itself, which means that we have to trace experiences rather than doctrines."[69] Thinking, she is telling us, is an experience. To conceptualize thinking as an experience might seem obvious (think about the activity of thinking and it is clear that thinking is a kind of experience) but her point is in opposition to the traditional philosophical view that distinguishes the body from the mind and that provides part of the philosophical justification for being able to treat bodies and material objects as objectively given in the world.

What, however, does this distinction mean? Where are we to turn in understanding what thinking is? As Arendt notes, "The trouble is that few thinkers ever told us what made them think and even fewer have cared to describe and examine their thinking experience."[70] For those who are familiar with Arendt's work, it should come as no surprise that she turns to Socrates for help. One of the conclusions she draws is that there is something paralysing about thinking. This paralysis suggests a connection between thinking and the world of appearances and of knowledge: "The paralysis of thought," she writes, "is twofold: it is inherent in the *stop* to think, the interruption of all other activities, and it may have a paralyzing effect when you come out of it, no longer sure of what had seemed to you beyond doubt while you were unthinkingly engaged in whatever you were doing."[71] This is an especially significant point because what Arendt is ultimately suggesting is that thinking can be deeply discomforting in the sense of how it can destabilize our previously held beliefs. It also provides another direction by which to view ourselves as intersubjective beings. Thinking involves encountering and discovering ourselves in the world.

What we have witnessed in recent political events has been the removal of thinking from the public sphere, or at least the stigmatization of it within the public sphere. What has come to be treated as "thinking" are soundbites, statements on Twitter, rejections of anything that does not fit within a preconceived worldview, and a rejection of any kind of expert analysis that is complicated. The idea of parsimony may well have set up the stage for valuing the ability to simplify above the ability to think. Instead of thinking we turn to whatever confirms that which we want confirmed, ignorant of how narratives contextualize evidence in a world where thinking is increasingly being removed from the public sphere. Thinking, and thus the ability to be challenged on intellectual grounds has been lost, as facts and confirmation bias have taken hold instead. However, thinking, in this Arendtian sense, is crucial for any successful politics—which is why authoritarian and totalitarian regimes fear free thinking so much—and it is currently at risk in our democracies.

Most public debate about facts and evidence pertains to the ability to deploy particular knowledge claims in support of specific political goals, or, alternatively, to dismiss facts and evidence because they inhibit specific political goals. But to focus on facts is to miss the point, and it is to forget that facts cannot exist in isolation. We set up all sorts of procedures so that it becomes theoretically possible to recognize certain pieces of evidence as more persuasive and more representative or accurate than others. Such methods can work, but when we prioritize this kind of knowledge over others we make it impossible to contest the narratives that enable fake news and lead to someone bringing a gun to a pizza parlour.[72] What has been forgotten is not only that knowledge and power are related but rather that the ability to control a narrative or deploy one for a particular purpose is much more powerful because it speaks not to the evidence but to the conditions of possibility in which we can recognize something as evidence. The march to methods and forgetting the lessons of political theory have made this post-fact world possible. Sokal had a point, but he is also guilty of contributing to a situation where we do not take seriously that interpretations can be just as powerful a source of knowledge as other kinds. Consequently, for any traditional Old Leftist, what ought to matter is the ability to develop a narrative so that people are able to think about that narrative, to engage with it, and understand it, and only then does it become possible to discuss facts and how to interpret them. Considering that developing a narrative of history and future of emancipation was precisely what Marx and Engels did in the *Communist Manifesto*,[73] it is curious that as an Old Leftist Sokal seems to have missed this.

Conclusion

None of these concerns are new. In fact, they are as old as philosophy itself, and played a role in the history of creating a scientific method. This method, we should not forget, was

originally closely connected with philosophy, theology, and
political authority. Methods were never politically neutral, as
Galileo unfortunately experienced in his life. In this regard,
little has changed (we *have* forgotten). In the fifteenth and
sixteenth centuries, the Reformation and philosophical scepticism concerned themselves in no small part with the methodological basis upon which knowledge and authority were
connected. For Luther, the issue was one of authority and
tradition in being able to interpret scripture, and for the sceptics
the question was similarly about the grounds of knowledge.
Interestingly, one of the consequences of scepticism was
undermining what was, at that time, considered to be objective
truth. As Richard Popkins writes in his book, *The History of
Scepticism*, "each individual could appeal to his own conscience
and claim that what appeared to him was true. No effective
standard of truth would be left."[74] There is a striking similarity
between this concern and that of Sokal and others from the
science wars in the 1990s. Underlying debate about politics
and methods is that there is a "moral dimension" to how
scientific knowledge is about "formulating logical possibilities."[75] Again, there is nothing novel in being concerned about
the relationship between methodology and politics. For
example, as Jonathan Havercroft points out, both Thomas
Hobbes and Baruch (Benedict) Spinoza were "ethical sceptics,"
and "they both doubted the possibility of transcendental
normative principles. They believed that the consequence of
ethical scepticism was that individuals would be unable to
come to agreement on the meaning of morally evaluative terms
such as good and evil."[76] This concern, argues Havercroft,
contributed to their respective political thought that emphasized
the importance of sovereignty.

   In an example from the first half of the twentieth century,
Stephen Gaukroger describes in his history of scientific culture
how, "In the USA during the 1930s and 1940s ... scientific
values were contrasted with those of fascism, communism,
Catholicism, and McCarthyism in particular."[77] Gaukroger
also mentions how "the Yale social scientist Mark A. May was
proposing a 'morality of science' as a basis for world culture,

whereby everyone would eventually live by the code of the scientist, which consisted in a devotion to honest, free, critical, evidence-based enquiry."[78] There is no such world of open and honest facts where such things exist unproblematically—and there never has been one, although this has not stopped social scientists acting like Vladimir and Estragon as they wait for Godot to arrive. Moreover, if such a world of certain knowledge existed, it is quite likely that it would resemble a dystopian technocracy more than a democracy. Yet we operate as though such a world could exist, with the implication that such a world would be a good place to be ... where only evidence governed.

The consequence of this worldview has not only been an absence of thinking, but also its corollary, the inability to stop and think reflexively, which is to say, to ask ourselves what we think about what we are thinking. It is one thing to reflect, to ask who am I, but another to be reflexive and ask what do I think about who I am? As thinking necessarily requires the possibility that we might not like the answer, it rarely finds a place in our public sphere of certainty and all-too-often parochial narrow-mindedness. Hence, we find ourselves in the present situation of Trump and Brexit. Returning to the political point raised by Sokal, it is now possible to rephrase and respond to the questions about evidence, facts, and a normative political response from a different perspective, offering different critiques.

First, the more we treat questions about injustice (or justice) as rooted in scientifically objective data, the more we make it possible to remove the consequences of our own implication in such injustices. The reason is that objective knowledge requires that we remove ourselves from the equation (hence our inability to empathize with Trump or Clinton supporters, or Leave/Remain supporters). We may not want to agree with alternative views, but we need to recognize our own place in how these narratives are able to function. We are all implicated in some way in each other's narratives. Injustices are rarely as removed from our own deeds and decisions as we might like to think. However, we take for granted much that is necessary for injustices to happen in the first place, and we then demonize those whom we hold responsible for them. Yet in politics we need to be able to think and thus destabilize our own views in order to understand how different narratives feed off and respond to each other. A "facts only" position ignores our ability to reflexively think about the interpretations we hold of this world.

Second, the more we focus on facts, the more we fall into a dichotomous view of the world where things are either true or false. However, things are rarely so simple or so dichotomous. Referendums with their yes/no choice feed into and reinforce this tendency to see problems in either/or situations. The media does the same thing in assuming that there are always two sides to a story (it is rarely so simple). Similarly, the American two-party political system has the same consequence, as has the Labour/Conservative stronghold in the UK as the two only parties of significance (the Lib Dems are trying hard to counter this view). Such dichotomies end up entrenching polarized views of the alternative, as if there are only two choices even when both choices often end up looking so similar, which has been one of the longstanding criticisms against New Labour, that it looked suspiciously like the Conservatives. When President George W. Bush said in November 2001 "You're either with us or against us," he was not only feeding into this dichotomous view of the world, he was reflecting a world where not being on whatever our side happens to be is viewed as dangerous.

The danger in this kind of methodologically dichotomized worldview is not just that most issues we face are more complicated and defy dichotomous classification; it is that this view inhibits any clear reflexive critique. We become immune to identifying our own complicity in the injustices experienced or felt by others and unable to recognize how others interpret our own decisions, actions and beliefs. Instead, it is not us who are the problem, it is someone else, something else, someplace else. Rural vs urban, religious vs secular, white vs black, straight vs gay, us vs them. False consciousness reigns: whereas we get it, they are the racist bigots; or those people in the city don't understand what life is really like. I was told by one man shortly after the EU referendum something about "the everyday man" who politics ignores—his point was not just that the political class ignores them (whomever they are—and I asked him about the "everyday woman"), it was also a commentary intended to dismiss my knowledge as an expert, and to question the value of my life experiences as a non-blue-collar working-class professional. We all feed into a cognitive map by which we navigate our normative political engagements, such that it starts to make sense to us that people in the city don't understand what life out here is really like, or that rural voters are racist hicks. These kinds of representations occur all the time, and both of them are ugly discriminations.

In the UK, the EU referendum clearly fed into this kind of angry dichotomous worldview, except, of course, that multiple dichotomies were at play simultaneously. Consequently, it became possible for both working-class Labour voters to side with more right-wing Conservative voters as they both were able to tap into a logic whereby their narratives of the EU and interpretation of the slogan "Let's take back control" actually made sense—even though the reality is quite different.

The former Prime Minister Gordon Brown argued during the referendum that by leaving the EU, the UK may be able to take back some control, but it will also lose the greater control it has as a member of the EU to push back against a globalized marketplace, where most states appear unable or unwilling to forcefully fight back against the forces of neoliberal capitalism without self-harm.[79] This may or not may be true but it does plausibly address how through forces of our own making, we live in a globalized world with economic and political consequences.

The political success of both Tony Blair and Bill Clinton was built on this recognition, although I would argue that while they got the question right, they ended up with very wrong answers. What they failed to grasp was that it was not that the traditional left had no persuasive answers to the forces of economic globalization, it was that there were very serious consequences of buying uncritically into the neoliberal economic agenda that seemed to correspond to rising economic fortunes. Clinton and Blair did not adequately perceive that the role of state governments is even more important in a neoliberal economic age, as are those of our international institutions. It is up to these institutions to fight back against the international forces of global capitalism and the neoliberal agenda, and thus enable the state to function for the benefit of its inhabitants. Blair and Clinton gave up on the need to sustain and protect something of the physical economy (the economy that produces goods and services, as opposed to the financial sector of speculation), to provide services necessary for societies to function, and to provide protection from the forces of financial speculation and corporate greed. I am not suggesting that alternative options from the Republicans or the Conservatives would have been any better, but our major political parties appear to have failed to grasp the challenges of economic globalization and international mutual dependence, and instead have brought us to the brink being led by snake-oil charmers like Boris Johnson, who presented a completely false story of "taking back control" and was believed. The very idea of control in this worldview assumes a kind of isolated mentality, where we remain separated from whoever they are who are threatening our ability to control our own futures. Again, it is a dichotomy that sets up the structure in which such normative arguments work.

The same us/them frame clearly also shaped the American election, as it is hard to understand American polarization without buying into a methodological duality whereby one clearly very capable, albeit flawed, candidate is viewed as a criminal, while the other, who has no qualifications whatsoever and is clearly a narcissist, becomes a reasonable candidate. Our candidate against yours. There is no other plausible choice, as independents have no real chance of electoral success at this level. That senior Republican and former President George W. Bush left his ballot blank and did not vote for either Trump or Clinton is evidence of precisely this problem, except that now he could not choose which side to be on, he had no side.

Third, the more we prioritize the scientific method above all else, the easier it becomes to view moral arguments as relative. The argument goes something like this: if there are no clear moral rules of any kind, then the logical consequence is that all morality is relative. However, this view is to work within a false dichotomy that only works on its own terms. We rarely appear able to seriously consider the conditions by which *only* a universal moral law is acceptable for our moral language, and of what kind of consequences follow from this philosophical position.

Part of the reason why our moral reference points seem to work within this philosophical worldview is the need to recognize that there are certain types of acts that are just wrong. Into this list we place murder and genocide, rape, extortion, theft, and so on. However, when dealing with our ideological or normative convictions about what type of society or country we (want to) live in, it is not in response to such issues that our normative framework rests. Our ability to conceive of future dystopias is illustrative of precisely this point. We recognize a dystopia because of the everyday values, because it represents the opposite world where the extreme situation becomes the norm. However, these are the types of issues that rarely characterize our daily political debates or struggles (even if it might seem like they do): that is why they are dystopias; the craziness serves to emphasize the point that it is possible to recognize morality in situations of daily life without needing a foundational moral norm that underlines the world. Within the dystopia, whether it is George Orwell's classic *1984*[80] (although Philip Roth's *The Plot Against America*, Margaret Atwood's *The Handmaid's Tale*, or Sinclair Lewis's *It Can't Happen Here* might be more appropriate to contemporary politics), or Hollywood action films like *The Running Man, Escape From New York, Blade Runner, The Matrix*, or the *Hunger Games* series (of movies and novels), the protagonists *within* the dystopias are able to identify moral positions that are in opposition to the normative rules of the wider world they find themselves in. That they are able to do so, and to act on them, even when it places them in danger, reveals a few things. First, that there can be moral demands that we hold and that contradict the society we find ourselves in. Second, nevertheless, these moral demands matter precisely because they are in contrast to the society. They do not come from the world that they pertain to, but are still able to emerge out of it. Third, the moral demands are not representative of the dystopic society, nor do they emerge from some external source, but rather are reactions to the value of human interactions and relations within particular contexts. In other words, the normative values are produced intersubjectively.

This is not to say that there have not been places in our societies that have appeared to be like a dystopia—crime-ridden, burned-out, inner-city neighbourhoods perhaps, parts of Detroit over the years, or sections of New York in the 1980s. Yet even in the more dangerous areas there can still exist important experiences that shape positive cultural and normative engagements with the world. That this is possible is not because there exists a universal law of right and wrong, but because as human beings we are able to interact with a world of our own making through our own interpretations of this world, and in this way we bring our normative views into the world. Even in war there are codes of conduct.[81] We embed this world with meanings, meanings that come from our experiences and from the narratives we use to make sense out of an often senseless world. These narratives in turn shape how we develop our normative commitments. It is not rules that shape our morality, it is our ability to find ways to make sense out of the world that we find ourselves in that does, and our ability to *think*. That we can communicate these normative views with others is evidence that we do not live in a relativist world, but an intersubjective one

It is not surprising that urban and rural voters might have very different belief-systems that shape their normative political commitments, and that they will come into conflict. They do live in different worlds, worlds that produce different meanings based in different narratives. But this does not mean that we are descending into some kind of murky relativism, nor does it mean that one narrative is more moral than the other. To think that way is to fall back into a mode of cognition where there are objective moral rules that shape all of our human engagements. Since this world does not exist, we might as well get used to the world we've got.

Notes

1 Martha C. Nussbaum, *Not for Profit: Why Democracy Needs the Humanities* (Princeton: Princeton University Press, 2010), 9.

2 Thomas S. Kuhn, *The Structure of Scientific Revolutions*, 3rd ed. (Chicago: Chicago University Press, 1996).

3 Wolin, "Political Theory as Vocation," 43.

4 A brief but good overview of the naturalist or positivist turn in political science is Stephen Welch, *The Theory of Political Culture* (Oxford: Oxford University Press, 2013), 17–21.

5 I am distinguishing here between methods and methodology. Michael Crotty defines methods as "the techniques or procedures used to gather and analyze data related to some research question or hypothesis"; whereas methodology is defined as "the strategy, plan of action, process or design lying being the choice and use of particular methods and linking the choice and use of methods to the desired outcome." Michael Crotty, *The Foundations of Social Research: Meaning and Perspective in the Research Process* (London: Sage, 1998), 3. Sheldon Wolin offers a historically informed explanation. Method used to be understood as a way of doing things, and it was with Descartes that method included the idea of "the progression of knowledge," and, importantly, that the rational method was about discipline or control in order to compensate for the "unfortunate proclivities of the mind." The consequence was that method, in the Cartesian sense, was also tied to his "fear of disorder." Wolin, "Political Theory as Vocation," 1067, 1068. The distinction between method and methodology is often unclear, as method cannot be understood outside of its political context. For our purposes, I am concerned with methodology, which I understand as philosophical knowledge about how knowledge is produced—including an appreciation

of the socio-political dynamics of knowledge production—and which shapes the decisions we make about what we do in the production of knowledge.

6 Brian Fay, *Contemporary Philosophy of Social Science* (Oxford: Blackwell, 1996), 1.

7 Hubert L. Dreyfus, *Being-in-the-World: A Commentary on Heidegger's Being and Time* (Cambridge, MA: MIT Press, 1991), 252.

8 Taylor, "Interpretation and the Sciences of Man," 9.

9 I am no doubt just as guilty as others in doing this on occasion.

10 See, Dreyfus, *Being-in-the-World*, 206, 51–65. Martin Heidegger, *Being and Time*, trans. John Macquarrie and Edward Robinson (Oxford: Blackwell, 1999 [1962]), 194–95.

11 Heidegger, *Being and Time*, 75.

12 Paul Feyerabend, *Against Method*, 3rd ed. (London: Verso, 2010).

13 Martin Heidegger, "The Question Concerning Technology," in *Technology and Values: Essential Readings*, ed. Craig Hanks (Oxford: Wiley-Blackwell, 2010).

14 Quoted in Dreyfus, *Being-in-the-World*, 252.

15 Alan D. Sokal, *Beyond the Hoax: Science, Philosophy and Culture* (Oxford: Oxford University Press, 2008).

16 Dreyfus, *Being-in-the-World*, 252.

17 Wolin, "Political Theory as Vocation."

18 Gary King, Robert O. Keohane, and Sidney Verba, *Designing Social Inquiry: Scientific Inference in Qualitative Research* (Princeton: Princeton University Press, 1994).

19 Milja Kurki, *Causation in International Relations: Reclaiming Causal Analysis* (Cambridge: Cambridge University Press, 2008). Jackson, *The Conduct of Inquiry in International Relations: Philosophy of Science and its Implications for the Study of World Politics*.

20 Hidemi Suganami, "Bringing Order to the Causes of War Debates," *Millennium: Journal of International Studies* 19, no. 1 (1990); *On the Causes of War* (New York; Oxford: Oxford University Press, 1996); "Stories of War Origins: A Narrativist Theory of the Causes of War," *Review of International Studies* 23, no. 4 (1997); "Agents, Structures, Narratives," *European Journal of International Relations* 5, no. 3 (1999).

21 He borrows this term from Polanyi. Wolin, "Political Theory as Vocation," 1070.

22 Ibid., 1071.

23 Ibid.

24 Taylor, "Interpretation and the Sciences of Man," 5.

25 Ibid., 45.

26 See, Anthony Giddens, *New Rules of Sociological Method: A Positive Critique of Interpretive Sociologies* (New York: Basic Books, 1976).

27 Taylor, "Interpretation and the Sciences of Man," 6.

28 Giddens, *New Rules of Sociological Method*, 63.

29 Ibid.

30 Gibbons, "Hermeneutics, Political Inquiry, and Practical Reason," 567.

31 This bears a similarity to Thomas Kuhn's idea of a paradigm. Kuhn, *The Structure of Scientific Revolutions*. Dreyfus, in his discussion of Heidegger, draws multiple parallels between some of the claims made by Heidegger in *Being and Time* and Kuhn's argument about paradigms and science. See, Dreyfus, *Being-in-the-World*.

32 Taylor, "Interpretation and the Sciences of Man," 27.

33 Jones, "Seeing Reason."

34 Schwartz, *The Battle for Human Nature*.

35 A recent book emphasizes the significance of stories in politics, although the argument in that book is different from the one presented here. See Ricci, *Politics Without Stories*.

36 Henry Mance, "Bashing Brussels is Boris Johnson's Brand Not Conviction, Friends Say," *Financial Times*, February 22 2016. Bethan McKernan, "A Journalist Has Shared a Story About Boris Johnson That Completely Undermines His Authority on the EU," *Independent*, https://www.indy100.com/article/a-journalist-has-shared-a-story-about-boris-johnson-that-completely-undermines-his-authority-on-the-eu-bkoHJPBuVZ. Accessed Janury 24 2017. The original Facebook page post, which was posted on June 17 2016 (and was still available as of February 2 2017) is: https://www.facebook.com/martin.fletcher.3998/posts/10154422902371062.

37 Tom Wells and Jonathan Reilly, "Blueprint for Britain: It's Time to Bring Back the Famous Dark Blue UK Passport as a 'Symbol of Our Independence' after Brexit," *The Sun*, August 1 2016.

38 Nicholas Watt, "EU Referendum: Vote Leave Focuses on Immigration," www.bbc.co.uk/news/uk-politics-eu-referendum-36375492. Accessed September 25 2017. Richard Hall, "How the Brexit Campaign Used Refugees to Scare Voters," https://www.pri.org/stories/2016-06-24/how-brexit-campaign-used-refugees-scare-voters. Accessed January 24 2107. See also Aalia Khan, "Four

Ways the Anti-Immigration Vote Won the Referendum for Brexit,"
New Statesman, July 7 2016.

39 Ben Zimmer, "Truthiness," *The New York Times Magazine*, October
13 2010. Abraham Riesman, "Stephen Colbert is Pissed at the
Oxford Dictionary, Says 'Post-Truth' is Just a Rip-Off of 'Truthiness'," *Vulture*, November 18 2016.

40 Sokal, *Beyond the Hoax*, 94.

41 Ibid., 95.

42 He admitted as much in a paper he published on his NYU
website: "A Physicist Experiments with Cultural Studies" (1996).

43 Karl Popper, *The Logic of Scientific Discovery* (London: Routledge,
2002 [1959]).

44 Pluckrose; Peter Pomerantsev, "Why We're Post-Fact," *Granta*,
July 20 2016.

45 Aggie Hirst, *Leo Strauss and the Invasion of Iraq: Encountering the
Abyss* (London: Routledge, 2016).

46 Friedrich Nietzsche, *On the Genealogy of Morality*, ed. Keith
Ansell-Pearson, trans. Carol Diethe (Cambridge: Cambridge
University Press, 1994).

47 Stanley Aronowitz, "Alan Sokal's 'Transgression'," *Dissent* 44,
no. 1 (1997): 107.

48 Quoted in "Alan Sokal Replies," in ibid., 111.

49 Sokal, *Beyond the Hoax*, 118.

50 Ibid., 107.

51 Alan D. Sokal, "A Physicist Experiments with Cultural Studies,"
Lingua Franca (1996).

52 The Editors of *The Lancet*, "Retraction: Ileal-Lymphoid-Nodular
Hyperplasia, Non-Specific Colitis, and Pervasive Developmental
Disorder in Children," *The Lancet* 375, no. 9713 (2010); A.J.
Wakefield et al., "Retracted: Ileal-Lymphoid-Nodular Hyperplasia,
Non-Specific Colitis, and Pervasive Developmental Disorder in
Children," ibid. 351, no. 9103 (1998). David Gorski, "The
General Medical Council to Andrew Wakefield: 'The Panel is
Satisfied That Your Conduct Was Irresponsible and Dishonest',"
Science-Based Medicine, Februrary 1 2010.

53 Dustin Y. Yoon et al., "Sex Bias Exists in Basic Science and
Translational Surgical Research," *Surgery* 156, no. 3 (2014);
Cari Romm, "Where Are All the Female Test Subjects?,"
The Atlantic, September 4 2014. Amy Westervelt, "The
Medical Research Gender Gap: How Excluding Women from

Clinical Trials is Hurting Our Health," *The Guardian*, April 30 2015.

54 Stephen Welch, *Hyperdemocracy* (London: Palgrave Macmillan, 2013).

55 Weber, *The Methodology of the Social Sciences*.

56 Intentionality does not matter for this point. Some examples from this literature include: Judith Butler, *Gender Trouble: Feminism and the Subversion of Identity*, 10th anniversary ed. (London: Routledge, 1999); J. Anne Tickner, "You Just Don't Understand: Troubled Engagements Between Feminists and IR Theorists," *International Studies Quarterly* 41, no. 4 (1997); Edward W. Said, *Orientalism*, Penguin Classics (London: Penguin, 2003); Anne McClintock, Aamir Mufti, and Ella Shohat, *Dangerous Liaisons: Gender, Nations, and Postcolonial Perspectives*, Cultural Politics; V.11 (Minneapolis: University of Minnesota Press, 1997); Ania Loomba, *Colonialism/Postcolonialism*, 2nd ed. (London: Routledge, 2005); Frantz Fanon, *Black Skin, White Masks* (New York: Grove Press, 1967).

57 Horkheimer, *Critical Theory*.

58 As in Jones, "Seeing Reason."

59 Hannah Arendt, *On Violence* (New York: Harcourt Brace, 1970), 6–7.

60 Levitt and Dubner, *Freakonomics*.

61 Nietzsche, *On the Genealogy of Morality*, 13.

62 Horkheimer, *Critical Theory*, 208–09.

63 On the contrary, we are all too aware of how evidence can harm political ideology. How else are we to understand the previous Canadian Conservative government's cancellation of the long form census—a decision that the current Liberal government has changed—but as a way to prevent the accumulation of data that could be used for policy purposes. If there is no evidence, ideological conviction has little to run up against. There is an obvious similarity here to the Brexit and Trump approach to knowledge.

64 Hannah Arendt, "Thinking and Moral Considerations: A Lecture," *Social Research* 38, no. 3 (1971): 422. The essay was reprinted in *Responsibility and Judgment*, ed. Jerome Kohn (New York: Schocken Books, 2005), 159–91 (see p. 63).

65 Arendt, "Thinking and Moral Considerations: A Lecture," 423; *Responsibility and Judgment*, 165.

66 Arendt, "Thinking and Moral Considerations: A Lecture," 433; *Responsibility and Judgment*, 175.

67 Arendt, "Thinking and Moral Considerations: A Lecture," 423–24; *Responsibility and Judgment*, 165.

68 Arendt, "Thinking and Moral Considerations: A Lecture," 425; *Responsibility and Judgment*, 167.

69 Arendt, "Thinking and Moral Considerations: A Lecture," 426; *Responsibility and Judgment*, 167.

70 Arendt, "Thinking and Moral Considerations: A Lecture," 427; *Responsibility and Judgment*, 168.

71 Arendt, "Thinking and Moral Considerations: A Lecture," 434; *Responsibility and Judgment*, 176.

72 Cecilia Kang and Adam Goldman, "In Washington Pizzeria Attack, Fake News Brought Real Guns," *The New York Times*, December 5 2016.

73 Karl Marx and Friedrich Engels, "The Communist Manifesto," in *Karl Marx: Selected Writings*, ed. David McLellan (Oxford: Oxford University Press, 2000 (1848)).

74 Quoted in Havercroft, *Captives of Sovereignty*, 56.

75 Gaukroger, *The Emergence of a Scientific Culture*, 13.

76 Havercroft, *Captives of Sovereignty*, 77.

77 Gaukroger, *The Emergence of a Scientific Culture*, 13.

78 Ibid.

79 This is from a personal account of hearing Gordon Brown speak in Newcastle (Gateshead) on June 9 2016 at a Remain campaign event during the EU referendum.

80 It is interesting to note that *1984* became a surprise sellout in the wake of Donald Trump's election. Charlotte England, "George Orwell's *1984* Sells Out on Amazon as Trump Adviser Kellyanne Conway refers to 'alternative facts'," *Independent*, January 27 2017.

81 This is what the Just War Tradition or Just War Theory presumes, and there also exist the relevant international laws. I have explored the role of political authority and obligation in the ethics of war in Ilan Zvi Baron, *Justifying the Obligation to Die: War, Ethics and Political Obligation with Illustrations from Zionism* (Lanham, MD: Lexington, 2009). For works on Just Theory or the ethics of war more generally see, for example, Michael Walzer, *Just and Unjust Wars: A Moral Argument with Historical Illustrations*, 3rd ed. (New York: Basic Books, 2000); *Arguing About War* (New Haven: Yale University Press, 2004); James Turner Johnson, *Just War Tradition*

and the Restraint of War: A Moral and Historical Inquiry (Princeton: Princeton University Press, 1981); *Can Modern War Be Just?* (New Haven: Yale University Press, 1984); *Morality and Contemporary Warfare* (New Haven: Yale University Press, 1999); Yoram Dinstein, *War, Aggression and Self-Defence*, 4th ed. (Cambridge: Cambridge University Press, 2005).

3
Making sense of the results

Introduction

Sometimes I wonder, as a thought experiment, if there were intelligent life on other planets in the universe, and they were watching us, what would they think? I guess it all comes down to values. Perhaps they really like guns, hate men, and don't understand why we have elections instead of simply asking the tallest person in the room to lead. But, more seriously, I don't think I am alone in feeling deeply worried that something has been going very, very wrong and that whatever it is, it is finally starting to rear its ugly head.

But what exactly is going on? What is starting to show itself? If we listen to Michael Moore and many others on the left, the argument is generally about declining career prospects, working longer and harder for less money, lack of upward mobility, struggling to make ends meet on jobs that allowed people's parents to buy a house and go on holiday at least once a year. I think he's right. Yet it is actually quite hard to identify the reasons for how we vote. The votes for both Brexit and Trump involved people aligning themselves with some of the uglier sides of our society, which suggests that either everybody who voted in these ways actually agrees with such views, or is able to dismiss them as though they were entirely separate from the reasons for their vote. The problem with this latter view, however, is that it ignores how complicity functions and thus makes it easy to distance ourselves from political responsibility. There is an additional concern. While Trump won the electoral college with 62,979,636 votes (46.0%) compared to 65,844,610 votes (48.1%) for Clinton,[1] only

58.1% of eligible voters voted.[2] While this is not, contrary to media reports, a "twenty year low,"[3] it should still cause serious concern that slightly over 40% of eligible voters did not vote. This is deeply concerning as it suggests a democratic deficit and that a lot of people do not feel invested in the political system of their country. Electoral turnout is something to take seriously.

Voter turnout in the UK for EU elections is even worse. In 2014 only 35.6% of voters turned out for EU elections, with UKIP, the anti-EU party, getting the largest percentage of votes.[4] This by itself is concerning, suggesting that anger at the EU provided the greatest incentive to vote. Yet, for the EU referendum, turnout was 72.2%.[5] This disparity between those who engaged in the EU electoral process and the EU referendum can suggest many things, including that most voters do not feel invested in the EU political process and also most likely do not have a very strong grasp of what the EU does. It does not take a leap of judgement to note the potential irony here: that voters felt invested enough to detach themselves from a political institution that they knew little about and were hardly engaged with, most likely because of either apathy or ignorance. It seems entirely plausible that many people voted to leave the EU without really understanding very much about the EU at all. They voted to leave without knowing what they were leaving or even having been involved in the system that they were rejecting.

Much has been made about polling data recently, and about how the polls got it wrong. Nate Silver, of FiveThirtyEight, unsurprisingly defends polling data, telling CNN, "I think it's pretty irresponsible for people to blame the polls, though, when the conventional wisdom was so much more sure of itself than it should have been."[6] This is a disingenuous reply. Many of the polls supported the conventional opinion. What he fails to understand is that there is a very big difference from treating a poll as a snapshot in time that reflects only a probability with a margin of error, and how people act on polls.[7] The conventional wisdom was fed by polls. It is not as though they exist in different worlds. When polls point to a possible outcome, we have to act as though that outcome is going to happen. That is the political function of a poll. Silver, probably one of the most famous of poll analysts, demonstrates a colossal failure of reflexivity and self-reflection about how polls work politically, and thus how the public necessarily interprets them. It does not matter if the poll is only a probability, with 1 chance in 4 being good odds. It is that we have to act as though the 1 chance will actually happen, otherwise the poll is useless as a political tool. The way that polls work in public depends on us forgetting that they serve as probabilities and instead treating the conclusions as facts—this is identical to Arendt's concern about turning hypothesis into facts.[8]

The controversies about the polls, the increasing irrelevance of evidence, and the lack of public investment in our political institutions all point to political and methodological questions about how we are to understand the results of the Trump and Leave victories. In previous chapters I started this methodological discussion, and in this chapter I am going to develop it further by offering an interpretation of how to understand these electoral results. This discussion turns on the role of identity. When interpretation and narrative function as the means by which we engage with the world, identity is never far behind. Our narratives are necessarily linked with our identities. However, as identity politics has come to play an increasingly important role in the public sphere, we have lost sight of how identity functions and instead turned identity into a variable for conflict. This is the problem in many debates about multiculturalism, minorities, and diversity. They misrepresent the role of identity in politics. In this chapter, I explore the electoral results of Trump and of Brexit, offering an interpretation of what these results mean in the context of a post-fact world of identity politics. The chapter concludes by suggesting that the state is failing us, hence our turn to identity politics in which we misunderstand the failure of politics. As Groucho Marx once said, "Politics is the art of looking for trouble, finding it, misdiagnosing it and then misapplying the wrong remedies."

A vote for nothing?

In the UK, the younger you were, the more likely you were to vote Remain. Only 25% of Leave voters were between the ages of 18 and 24, and in the age demographics, it is only after the age of 50 that Leave voters become a majority. Education was another important factor, as 71% of Remain voters had a degree. The more "educated," the more likely you voted to remain. Party affiliation is mixed: 57% of Conservatives, 31% of Labour, 27% of Lib Dems voted to leave.[9] Or, as the British newspaper *The Guardian* reported:

> The decision for the UK to leave the European Union was overwhelmingly supported in parts of England with low income and education levels. Average educational attainment, median income and social class in English local authorities were the strongest predictors of how residents in that area voted in the referendum. The results indicate that the greater the proportion of residents with a higher education, the more likely a local authority was to vote to remain.[10]

There are many ways to read the data, depending on age, income, education, and geographical location. In the end, Leave had 17,410,742 votes compared to 16,141,241 Remain votes.[11]

In the US, if we turn to the exit polls as reported by *The Washington Post*,[12] two of the stronger variables were geography and demography: 61% of small city and rural voters voted for Trump; 57% of White, 8% Black, 28% Hispanic/Latino, 27% Asian and 36% other voters voted for Trump. The more educated you are, and the younger you are, the more likely you supported Clinton. On income levels the data is not especially conclusive: 53% of voters with an income under $50,000 voted for Clinton, compared with 41% for Trump; of those with an income between $50,000 and $99,999, 46% voted for Clinton, compared with 49% for Trump; 47% of voters with an income above $99,999 voted for Clinton, and the same percentage voted for Trump. *The New York Times* reported how the major shift was among white voters without college degrees. The real indicators in terms of identity-based factors were ethnicity, geographic location (rural or urban), party affiliation (obviously!), education (67% of white voters without a college degree voted for Trump), born-again or evangelical Christians (81% for Trump), military service (61% of those who served voted for Trump), and sexuality (78% of gay, lesbian, bisexual, or transgender voted for Clinton).[13] And, of course, Trump won the electoral college but he lost the national vote.

What each of these categories does is take a qualitative value about identity and geography and treat it as an explanatory cause for behaviour. Sometimes this kind of analysis works, sometimes it does not. Statistical analysis can provide useful descriptions but the causal explanations are more prone to philosophical critique. In either case, it is the value questions that provide the crucial information, such as what issues you care about the most, and whether or not you think the country is heading in the right direction. The statisticians will be going over this data, trying to find correlations across the value and identity indicators (although identity is also a value) so that identity or geography becomes a proxy for a set of values. While this data is certainly interesting and helpful, there are certain types of questions that it simply cannot address, and these are the big questions about values that become transformed into variables.

Central to my point here is that the data cannot address two very important questions. The first is about the ability to find common narratives across the divides, which in both the UK and the US were very close: 4 percentage points in the UK, even less in the US. These are not wide margins. They are images of fractured countries where slim majorities choose a path that is not so much a commentary or critique but a fundamental rejection. We are living in deeply polarized societies, and simply identifying the changes in who voted for whom cannot provide evidence of what is to be done when so many of us feel angry, hurt, upset, and deeply traumatized at having to suddenly live in a country that seems to want to reward values that are so very far from our own.

It could be argued that I am engaging here in some kind of liberal whingeing (thank you Boris Johnson), but this is to miss the point. Sure I, along with millions of others, am deeply shocked at recent political events, but on the other side (assuming for a moment it is clear who is on this other side), there was just as much alienation from the present political order. What is different and what is frightening is that in both the US and the UK the anger and frustrations that put the UK on course toward Article 50 (which was designed so that it would never be used), and in the US voted Trump into the White House, have accompanied and often manifested in very violent rhetoric: anti-immigrant, xenophobic, racist, sexist, nativist, and isolationist. It is not as if all voters who chose Trump or to leave the EU are racists. But they did align themselves with a group of people who are. Voting is not like picking some parts of what you like and some parts of what you don't, even if we rationalize it that way. You vote for the whole package. And this is what makes the results so traumatic, that so many people sided with those holding scary and frightening worldviews.

In the UK, the entire anti-EU argument was based on a series of lies (the biggest one was about how much money the UK sends to the EU), illegal campaign tactics (using the NHS logo on their campaign bus), and blatant xenophobic and anti-immigrant scaremongering, the likes of which we have not seen at this level in established democracies since the 1930s. In the US, well, Trump is an odious individual, who in his public persona appears to be incapable of empathy, is a bully, a liar, a cheat and a thief, a narcissist, an opportunist who had no qualms in using racist and sexist arguments during his campaign, not to mention a disdain for the US Constitution (of which he apparently has little knowledge).[14] Siding with either the Leave group or with Trump is to side with them, with all of it. I do not think it is unreasonable to feel shock and dismay that so many would do so. This is not about crying over spilt milk or whining because we lost. This is about witnessing millions of people finding it perfectly acceptable to align their political futures with the worst parts of our political past and the ugliest sides of our society. It does not seem possible that we can cross this divide. I will return to this problem later.

What is also important in this analysis is that it seems entirely plausible that our political leaders really have no idea what they are doing outside of getting into office.

Theresa May became Prime Minister because the existing one quit, and those who remained to vie for this office stabbed each other in the back. Whether she actually has any plan other than political survival is hard to tell, as there is little else one can take from her track record. During her tenure as Home Secretary, she was responsible for a whole series of fiascos. It was under her watch that the UK government sent out vans with billboards informing illegal immigrants that they needed to leave the UK—the so-called "Go Home" vans. There was the mistreatment of female asylum seekers at the Yarl's Wood Detention Centre, known, according to one account, for "endless reports of sexual abuse, hunger strikes and shocking healthcare."[15] One of her most publicly known debacles was her inability to cut back on immigration, and instead she oversaw an increase, when she was tasked with the reverse. As the British newspaper *The Spectator* noted:

And what of May's record on migration? During the last election campaign David Cameron took brickbats for the fact that net migration into the UK had actually increased from 244,000 in 2010 to 330,000 in 2014 rather than being brought down to less than 100,000 as he had committed. Mrs May, the cabinet minister actually responsible for making the government's commitment a reality, faced remarkably little criticism or even questioning about why this had failed.[16]

The same article concluded by saying that

As well as the buck passing that ensured that blame for all of the Home Office's failings fell onto junior ministers and civil servants, Mrs May and her staff put tremendous effort into ensuring that she rarely—if ever—faced a Paxman-style grilling. And so good were they at applying pressure on the media that remarkably few critical articles about her have ever been published.[17]

Another British newspaper, *The Guardian*, published a similar account of May's political success, which appears to be less about her accomplishments or competence than her survival.

One of her ideas for tackling political extremism was having "Ofcom vet British television programmes before they were broadcast."[18] Fortunately (though it was shocking that it was necessary), one of her own ministers, Sajid Javid, pointed out that such a policy would be state censorship. There are many examples of her incompetence and questionable judgement, but a few are worth noting and pertain to refugees, human rights, and her apparent rejection or dismissal of Parliamentary sovereignty.

As reported by *The Guardian*, she "pressed ahead with immigration policies that including [*sic*] splitting up an estimated 33,000 families in Britain because they don't earn enough and refused to put any time limit on the detention of immigration detainees."[19] May wants to remove the UK from the European Convention on Human Rights and has denounced the Human Rights Act, which would mean that "she is likely to go into the next election pledged to Britain's withdrawal from the European convention on human rights—which would leave Britain as the only European country in the same position as the pariah state of Belarus."[20] In regard to Brexit, the most she has been able to come up with is one of the most vacuous slogans conceived, "Brexit means Brexit," completely devoid of meaning or content (or at least it was until the next 2:00 am Twitter assault from Trump). In addition, she apparently holds the opinion that sovereignty resides not with Parliament, but with her office, as can be inferred from her contestation of the Supreme Court Case that Article 50 needs to be approved by Parliament and cannot be invoked by the Prime Minister's office.

May was not Prime Minister during the referendum, and she was on the Remain side. Nevertheless, fulfilling the mandate of the referendum—which is an admittedly slim mandate, although

this fact appears to have been forgotten—is now her remit as
Prime Minister. Just as the Leave campaign had no real clear
plans other than saying that everything would be great, she also
appears to have no clear plans, not to mention a shortage of
qualified personnel to conduct the Brexit negotiations.[21] The
absence of clear leadership working in the national interest is
shocking. In this sense the Leave vote was not a protest vote
against the EU or against globalization, neoliberalism, etc., it
was a vote for nothing, nothing being the absence of policy
and politics. The Trump electoral success can be understood
in the same way. He may well have won the electoral college
because he presented himself as an anti-establishment figure.

In the case of Donald Trump, there is no political record
of governance. Moreover, during the campaign he repeatedly
failed to provide any clear or detailed information as to his
policy proposals. His entire campaign appears to have been
run (and won) in no small part on his refusal to provide such
details and instead to run on slogans and verbal attacks via
Twitter. According to a widely reported claim by Michael
Moore, Trump's campaign was not about winning, but merely
gaining publicity to help with his TV negotiations.[22] Trump's
lack of qualifications led the periodical, *The Atlantic*, for only
the third time since its founding in 1857, to take an editorial
stance in the presidential election. It was against Donald Trump
and supported Hillary Clinton:

> Trump ... might be the most ostentatiously unqualified major-
> party candidate in the 227-year history of the American presi-
> dency. These concerns compel us, for the third time since the
> magazine's founding, to endorse a candidate for president. ...
>
> Donald Trump ... has no record of public service and no
> qualifications for public office. His affect is that of an infomercial
> huckster; he traffics in conspiracy theories and racist invective;
> he is appallingly sexist; he is erratic, secretive, and xenophobic;
> he expresses admiration for authoritarian rulers, and evinces
> authoritarian tendencies himself. He is easily goaded, a poor
> quality for someone seeking control of America's nuclear arsenal.
> He is an enemy of fact-based discourse; he is ignorant of, and
> indifferent to, the Constitution; he appears not to read.[23]

Donald Trump further defies any understanding of his policy positions since his Republican identity is actually fairly recent, having been a Democrat in the past, telling CNN's Wolf Blitzer in 2004 that he "probably [identifies] more as Democrat."[24]

It is, in short, surprisingly difficult to determine from past records what exactly the political positions of May and Trump are. The surprise is not that their policies are opaque, rather that it is not at all clear what they are or that they even have any. Trump's term in office has so far been, and will no doubt continue to be, a circus, a revolving door of performers and quick-change artistry of repeated contradictions. There is, unsurprisingly, no lack of public discussion about trying to figure out what precisely his policies are—which is something we would expect in a dictatorship, but not in a democracy. Equally concerning, in a democracy defined by a separation of powers and an independent judiciary, have been Trump's attacks against the judiciary as they ruled against his Executive Order barring immigration from select Middle Eastern countries. One of the ongoing scandals involves his firing of the FBI director James Comey, for reasons that either have to do with Comey refusing to pledge his loyalty to Trump and/or with the ongoing investigation into Russian meddling in the American presidential election. No doubt, other scandals will occur throughout his presidency (I suspect quite regularly). It is worth reflecting on how a person clearly so unsuited for elected office, especially the Oval Office, was able to win.

Michael Moore noted in his now famous prediction that Trump would win for five reasons.[25] The first reason is the "Midwest Math, or Welcome to Our Rust Belt Brexit." Moore argued that Trump would focus on the states that were harmed by NAFTA and related neoliberal global trade agreements:

> I believe Trump is going to focus much of his attention on the four blue states in the rustbelt of the upper Great Lakes—Michigan, Ohio, Pennsylvania and Wisconsin. ... He's said (correctly) that the Clintons' support of NAFTA helped to destroy the industrial states of the Upper Midwest. Trump is going to hammer Clinton on this and her support of TPP [Trans-Pacific Partnership] and other trade policies that have

royally screwed the people of these four states. When Trump stood in the shadow of a Ford Motor factory during the Michigan primary, he threatened the corporation that if they did indeed go ahead with their planned closure of that factory and move it to Mexico, he would slap a 35% tariff on any Mexican-built cars shipped back to the United States. It was sweet, sweet music to the ears of the working class of Michigan, and when he tossed in his threat to Apple that he would force them to stop making their iPhones in China and build them here in America, well, hearts swooned.[26]

Second, "The Last Stand of the Angry White Man." Here Moore argues that there exists a segment of society that holds deeply sexist and misogynistic views, and that they see a patriarchal world around them floundering. Writing sarcastically, Moore reports:

> Our male-dominated, 240-year run of the USA is coming to an end. A woman is about to take over! How did this happen?! On *our* watch! ... There is a sense that the power has slipped out of their hands, that their way of doing things is no longer how things are done. This monster, the "Feminazi," the thing that as Trump says, "bleeds through her eyes or wherever she bleeds," has conquered us—and now, after having had to endure eight years of a black man telling us what to do, we're supposed to just sit back and take eight years of a woman bossing us around? After that it'll be eight years of the gays in the White House! Then the transgenders! You can see where this is going. By then animals will have been granted human rights and a fuckin' hamster is going to be running the country. This has to stop![27]

Third, "The Hillary Problem." It is not only that Hillary Clinton voted for the Iraq War, which made many on the left deeply angry at her, it is that she is deeply unpopular:

> Our biggest problem here isn't Trump—it's Hillary. She is hugely unpopular—nearly 70% of all voters think she is untrustworthy and dishonest. She represents the old way of politics, not really believing in anything other than what can get you elected. That's why she fights against gays getting married one moment, and the next she's officiating a gay marriage. Young women are

among her biggest detractors, which has to hurt considering it's the sacrifices and the battles that Hillary and other women of her generation endured so that this younger generation would never have to be told by the Barbara Bushes of the world that they should just shut up and go bake some cookies. But the kids don't like her, and not a day goes by that a millennial doesn't tell me they aren't voting for her.[28]

Fourth, "The Depressed Sanders Vote." Here, and building on Clinton's lack of popularity, Moore suggests that the Sanders supporters are not excited by her candidacy and will not do much to help get out the vote:

The fire alarm that should be going off is that while the average Bernie backer will drag him/herself to the polls that day to somewhat reluctantly vote for Hillary, it will be what's called a "depressed vote"—meaning the voter doesn't bring five people to vote with her. He doesn't volunteer 10 hours in the month leading up to the election. She never talks in an excited voice when asked why she's voting for Hillary. A depressed voter. Because, when you're young, you have zero tolerance for phonies and BS. Returning to the Clinton/Bush era for them is like suddenly having to pay for music, or using MySpace or carrying around one of those big-ass portable phones. They're not going to vote for Trump; some will vote third party, but many will just stay home.[29]

Finally, "The Jesse Ventura Effect." The fifth point is that there is always an element of chance in any election and that many people may well decide to vote as a kind of mischievous protest vote against the status quo, just to see what will happen:

Finally, do not discount the electorate's ability to be mischievous or underestimate how many millions fancy themselves as closet anarchists once they draw the curtain and are all alone in the voting booth. It's one of the few places left in society where there are no security cameras, no listening devices, no spouses, no kids, no boss, no cops, there's not even a friggin' time limit. … millions are going to vote for Trump not because they agree with him, not because they like his bigotry or ego, but just because they can. Just because it will upset the apple cart and make mommy and daddy mad.[30]

Whether or not Moore was right in his explanations is not important. What is, and why I have quoted him at length, is that nowhere does he provide any indication of what exactly Trump stands for. As one of the few who early on recognized the tangible possibility of a Trump victory, it is worth taking his views here seriously, and he offers nothing about why someone would vote *for* Trump other than that doing so is a vote *against* something else. Thus, here as well we can read that the vote *for* Trump can be understood as a vote for nothing: no clear policy plans, no politics in any meaningful sense, just a protest without a plan.

Identity politics and democracy: hyperdemocracy, political correctness, and the politics of diversity

That people could consciously decide to vote for such vacuous slogans as "Make America Great Again" and "Let's Take Back Control" should not surprise anybody. While they are slogans, so we should not expect too much, these are pretty bad ones, since any content they did refer to was largely racist or sexist and possibly both. The slogans are, I suggest, illustrative of a development in democracy that the political theorist Stephen Welch describes as hyperdemocracy. He defines hyperdemocracy as "the phenomenon of democracy undermining itself," or "the reflexive undermining of democracy by the processes it itself unleashes."[31] Welch's definition owes some due to Alexis de Tocqueville, whose *Democracy in America* remains a classic work of democratic theory. De Tocqueville's analysis of democracy raises what Welch refers to as the reflexive paradox, which is when "out of the development of a condition emerges its contrary."[32] We see de Tocqueville raising this possibility when writing how within American democracy there exists a public intellectual life that is contrary to what we might find in an aristocracy, but which can nevertheless be profoundly undemocratic.

Addressing the dangers of the powers of the majority, de Tocqueville writes, "When it comes to examine what the exercise of thought is in the United States, then one perceives very clearly to what point the power of the majority surpasses all the powers that we know in Europe."[33] De Tocqueville is pointing out something that Arendt also notes in her essay on "Thinking and Moral Considerations," that the function of thinking (what Welch refers to as the cognitive dimension) is especially important for politics, although in de Tocqueville's case the point is about the role or function of the majority and of democratic governance. There is, however, a danger in this "tyranny of the majority"[34] for, as de Tocqueville writes, revealing more clearly the reflexive paradox:

> What I most reproach in democratic government, as it has been organized in the United States, is not, as many people in Europe claim, its weakness, but on the contrary, its irresistible force. And what is most repugnant to me in America is not the extreme freedom that reigns there, it is the lack of a guarantee against tyranny.[35]

The lack of security he has in mind is that the majority cannot be relied upon as a bulwark against tyranny. So long as public opinion remains the basis upon which democracy rests, it is conceivable that the public could turn to tyranny, as a majority is unique in its power:

> Thought is an invisible and almost intangible power that makes sport of all tyrannies. In our day, the most absolute sovereigns of Europe cannot prevent certain thoughts hostile to their authority from mutely circulating in their states and even in the heart of their courts. It is not the same in America: as long as the majority is doubtful, one speaks; but when it has irrevo-cably pronounced, everyone becomes silent and friends and enemies alike then seem to hitch themselves together to its wagon. The reason for this is simple: there is no monarch so absolute that he can gather in his hands all the strength of society and defeat resistance, as can a majority vested with the right to make the laws and execute them.[36]

This emphasis on thinking and its political character is some-thing I will return to in a discussion of Hannah Arendt, who also makes a connection between the act of thinking and its political character. However, for now, although the polarization of American politics suggests that de Tocqueville was not quite right in his estimation of the power of the majority, he was on to something. He was right to have concern about how the barrier against tyranny resides in thinking, and he also realized something counter-intuitive—that the power of the majority can also serve as a form of tyranny in its ability to silence alternatives.

> I do not know any country where, in general, less independence of mind and genuine freedom of discussion reign than in America .... In America, the majority draws a formidable circle around thought. Inside those limits, the writer is free; but unhappiness awaits him if he dares to leave them.[37]

De Tocqueville can be read here as foreshadowing what Fareed Zakaria refers to as the rise of illiberal democracy.[38] This is the idea that liberal democracy can give rise to illiberal forces.

While de Tocqueville's view might appear counter-intuitive in a society with the right to free speech, there is a rationale here to be taken seriously: that the public opinion of the majority comprises in a democracy the one and single authority, to which there can be no resistance. Rousseau held a similar concern, hence his distinction between the General Will and the Will of All. Arendt similarly noted this problem, hence her examinations of thinking and knowing, and of the distinction between politics and the activities of the mob.[39] Finally, however, and most pertinent in the information age, is de Tocqueville's warning in his chapter, "The Serious Attitude of Americans and Why it Often Does not Prevent Them from Ill-Considered Actions," of what happens when there is too much information available to society:

> There is a sort of ignorance that is born of extreme publicity. In despotic states men do not know how to act because one says nothing to them; in democratic nations they often act at random because one wanted to say everything to them. The former do not know, the latter forget.[40]

This seems to be a very accurate foreshadowing of Trump's entire media strategy, as well as that of the Brexiteers, who revelled in the absence of evidence and the proliferation of as many falsehoods as they could muster.

Within the discourses surrounding both Trump and Brexit was anger at a changing world, one that was changing not just economically but culturally. We see this issue raised in Michael Moore's second point about why Trump would win, "Last Stand of the Angry White Man," and in the conscious decision by the Brexit camp to focus on immigration. Peter Mandelson, one of the senior politicians of the British Labour Party, argued that during the referendum, as the Brexit camp's economic argument fell apart, they had nothing else to fall back on but xenophobia and immigration.[41] Owen Bennett, Deputy Political Editor of *The Huffington Post* UK, notes in his book, *The Brexit Club*, that Leave campaigners self-consciously took the anti-immigration rhetoric and deployed it for their own ends, even while some within that camp felt uncomfortable about the xenophobia that they were spreading.[42] The conclusion is that identity politics played a very strong role in the success of both Trump and Brexit.

While the identity politics in both cases focused on xenophobia and anti-immigrant rhetoric, this story relies on a long-standing debate across democratic societies about the relationship between nation (the identity group) and state (the political institutions and territorial unit). In the current context, this is a story in at least two parts. The first is about the relationship between identity politics and political correctness, and the second is about the politics of diversity, one that has played out across societies, including in universities.

Within the past few years, groups of students on both sides of the Atlantic started protesting the representative iconography of White Privilege. Notable targets included a statue of Cecil Rhodes at Oriel College at the University of Oxford, and the demand to remove the name of Woodrow Wilson from the School of Public and International Affairs from a residential college at Princeton.[43] These and many other incidents across university campuses, including Brown, Missouri, Yale, Harvard, Amherst, and Ithaca, are an interesting product of the combined forces of social justice and free speech. As summed up in the

British newspaper the *Independent*, "What happens when two of America's most hallowed principles, the fight against racism and intolerance and the right to freedom of expression, crash into each other on campus?"[44]

The issues here about identity, diversity, and justice have been explored at length in too many articles to note, but suffice to say the underlying concern has been with the increase of identity politics as a form of public discourse, of what Kenan Malik refers to in an article in *Foreign Affairs* as "The Failure of Multiculturalism," and which is neatly summed up by Mark Lilla in a recent op-ed in *The New York Times*:

> But how should this diversity shape our politics? The standard liberal answer for nearly a generation now has been that we should become aware of and "celebrate" our differences. Which is a splendid principle of moral pedagogy—but disastrous as a foundation for democratic politics in our ideological age. In recent years American liberalism has slipped into a kind of moral panic about racial, gender and sexual identity that has distorted liberalism's message and prevented it from becoming a unifying force capable of governing.[45]

Lila's message is that "It is at the level of electoral politics that identity liberalism has failed most spectacularly, as we have just seen. National politics in healthy periods is not about 'difference,' it is about commonality. And it will be dominated by whoever best captures Americans' imaginations about our shared destiny."[46] Malik makes a similar point, that the consequence of multiculturalism has been to affirm differences:

> As a political tool, multiculturalism has functioned as not merely a response to diversity but also a means of constraining it. And that insight reveals a paradox. Multicultural policies accept as a given that societies are diverse, yet they implicitly assume that such diversity ends at the edges of minority communities. They seek to institutionalize diversity by putting people into ethnic and cultural boxes—into a singular, homogeneous Muslim community, for example—and defining their needs and rights accordingly. Such policies, in other words, have helped create the very divisions they were meant to manage.[47]

In political theory, it is in Brian Barry that we find one of the more ardent critics of multiculturalism and the related politics of diversity. As he writes in his book, *Culture and Equality*, his "concern is with views that support the politicization of group identities, where the basis of the common identity is claimed to be cultural."[48] Moreover, in what might seem to be a prescient foretelling of events to come, he notes with concern that

> The proliferation of special interests fostered by multiculturalism is ... conducive to a politics of "divide and rule" that can only benefit those who benefit most from the status quo. There is no better way of heading off the nightmare of unified political action by the economically disadvantaged that might issue in common demands than to set different groups of the disadvantaged against one another.[49]

Barry develops a position that he calls egalitarian liberalism, which he suggests poses an alternative to a politics where any practice claimed to have cultural significance needs to be protected—as though, in his view, specific cultural practices can be treated as the equivalent of a cultural identity, so that having to change or stop one practice means losing one's culture, such as the fishing rights of First Nations peoples.[50] Barry views multiculturalism and its related identity politics as harbouring a kind of moral nihilism, where any cultural good or claim to protecting cultural practices or identity involves assuming that "the values of different groups are incommensurable."[51] Barry, unsurprisingly, refers repeatedly to the abuse of culture, as though groups consciously and mischievously deploy their claims to culture to take away the power, privileges, resources, or opportunities of others.

In his account of egalitarian liberalism it is empathy with the whole of society that is the goal. This solidarity can be "fostered by common institutions" and fair distribution of resources so that all are able to recognize their membership in society (so that they cannot buy themselves out).[52] Barry's position is that culture should not matter in how we approach questions of rights or equality. "Undoubtedly, the claim that

all *human beings* are entitled to equal respect is an assertion
of fundamental equality that lies at the heart of egalitarian
liberalism."[53] This is in opposition to an identity politics claim
where different peoples may have different rights, such as the
language rights debate in Quebec which protects the French
language (Barry then asks, what happens if in the future the
English language becomes potentially threatened ...).[54]

Barry targets Will Kymlicka, Charles Taylor, James Tully
(all three, incidentally, are Canadian), and Iris Marion Young,
among others, as some of the central theorists who represent
a multicultural position. In their various ways, these political
theorists all advance the claim that culture and identity matter.
What is so amazing in Barry's world, however, is that his
argument makes no sense unless we also accept a world where
culture and identity do not matter, which is patently absurd.
Identity clearly matters a great deal and something has gone
very wrong if we can presume that it does not. Moreover, and
thinking as a member of the academic community, if identity
did not matter, it would be hard to contemplate the significance
of the entire academic discipline of anthropology, and the
important debates within that discipline about the ethics of
ethnography.[55] However, and without having to venture into
the academic territory of dismissing a discipline's normative
worth, what Barry is unable to appreciate is that while his
argument might (*might*) make sense in a logical world devoid
of people, it is patently impossible to deploy in any meaningful
sense because, to put it bluntly: identity matters—why else
would even quantitative polling data include questions about
identity?[56]

Moreover, identity matters in situations where rights may
not necessarily be fought for (as they were by civil rights
and feminist campaigners in the 1960s, for example, or by
lawyers at airports in early 2017 fighting against President
Trump's ban on travellers from seven Middle Eastern and
predominantly Muslim countries) but are taken away. What
Barry forgets in his book of over 300 pages is that the state
used identity politics within its own institutions long before
there was discussion about multiculturalism. I have written

about this in regard to dual loyalty and the experiences of minority groups who, by virtue of their being of a different ethnic group than the majority, are deemed by the state to pose a security risk.[57] The most famous example was the internment of residents with Japanese ancestry in North America during the Second World War. However, there are further historical examples, such as that of French Jews who, in the mid-to-late 1800s, fought for the protection of Jews in Damascus who were being accused and persecuted on blood libel grounds. While French Jews were successful in helping the Jews in Damascus, the consequence in France was that the Jews were viewed as caring more for their kin abroad than for France.[58] As the political theorist William Connolly writes in his important book, *Identity/Difference*, "When 'identity politics' is attacked as impervious to the larger whole upon which it depends, a majority identity is implicitly invoked to characterize the whole. Even critics of identity politics participate, it seems, in the politics of identity."[59] The idea that multiculturalism has somehow given rise to identity politics in any negative sense is empirical and theoretical nonsense. Identity politics has always been present, both for good and for bad.

I am much more sympathetic with the positions advanced by critics of Barry, and the view, as expressed by Charles Taylor, that "The politics of difference is full of denunciations of discrimination and refusals of second-class citizenship."[60] Relatedly, although writing from a different perspective, Connolly emphasizes that "You need identity to act and to be ethical."[61] Consequently, "To be ethical is to put identity, to some degree, at risk."[62] Barry would no doubt not dispute the point about discrimination and citizenship, but he does prevent us from taking seriously that the politics of difference can enable a disputation against second-class citizens or that identity and ethics are closely related. Consequently, the debate we should consider more seriously is not one with egalitarian liberals who pretend that identity is irrelevant, but between theorists of difference because they are the ones that acknowledge the significance of identity for ethics (and politics).

I did not finish the sentence by Connolly in the above quote. After writing that we need identity to be ethical he continues: "but there is a drive to diminish difference to complete itself inside the pursuit of identity."[63] This "drive" is shared by many of us, which is what makes the politics of identity paradoxical.[64] In trying to secure our own identity claims, our ethics involve various degrees of trying to limit the differences that we come into contact with.[65] One of the reasons why identity politics is so often treated as a negative is because of this tendency to try to force difference into a unified whole so it is removed and we are all in some senses the same, thus belonging to the same community, sharing the same values, and desiring a similar political culture—all of which are also consistent with the ambitions of egalitarian liberalism. These ambitions, however, can never be met, precisely because of the points made by Connolly, that they require the diminishment of difference and find salvation in an identity that does not require difference (which is impossible). In this sense, even though the institutional norms in egalitarian liberalism are liberal, this imagination about identity has more in common with authoritarian or totalitarian fantasies. The challenge in the politics of identity is to avoid precisely this fantasy.

Part of what I take from Connolly is that it is not debates about either multiculturalism or the politics of diversity that we should be focusing on here. Rather, we need to take it for granted that identity matters, and that there will always be self/other claims made across and even within identity groups. Instead, the issue in our public discourse appears to be one about what has become a curious view about believing that there is a right not to be insulted. While it can be difficult to define what exactly this view is, the underlying narrative is one of trying to remove from our public spaces any viewpoint that we find distasteful. It is, in this view, better to silence critics than allow them to speak. The challenging nature of this political position is that although it is often waged by the discriminated, it is not that different in its form from extreme right-wing views toward censorship. What this debate does is focus on identity politics in zero-sums when the issue is really one of granting legitimacy to specific political positions by granting them public platforms.

To see how this is the case, note that at issue here is not personal safety. Instead, it is about how historical symbols and regional narratives become representations of cultural appropriations, sexism, repression, and exploitation. The issue is about ideational and iconographic representations of colonial and racist practices, which are (appropriately) recognized as symbols of violence. But because the target is largely one of symbols, they are easily countered as attempts to silence speech or erase a cultural legacy. I am not suggesting that the protests on these matters are unimportant. They are very important, and it is a mistake to think that we can create a safe present or future by erasing the past. It is also problematic when our identity politics, which are based on the importance of difference, try to silence (sometimes by force) opposing (and often distasteful) views. The issue in such situations ought to be about the politics of granting legitimacy through the offering of public platforms, not about silencing. Public debate is important. The more we try to silence debate, the more we veer away from the foundations of a free and open society. This does not mean that anything goes, but any discussion of the limits needs to be carefully done.

Removing symbols of oppression, racism, sexism, and other forms of violence is important. However, in our public spaces it is very likely that we will come into contact with views we do not like, and that so long as our identity claims matter for framing political narratives, we have to work out the challenging politics of how to address competing identity-narrative political claims. Many statues and other symbols probably should be removed, but perhaps we should also consider adding different statues that represent alternative histories, giving other historical narratives a place in the public sphere.

Returning to Connolly, one way to work through the tension here is to note how

> My identity is what I am and how I am recognized rather than what I choose, want or consent to. ... An identity is established

in relation to a series of differences that have become socially
recognized. These differences are essential to its being. If they
did not coexist as differences, it [my identity] would not exist
in its distinctiveness and solidity. ... Identity is ... a slippery,
insecure experience, dependent on its ability to define difference
and vulnerable to the tendency of entities it would so define
to counter, resist, overturn, or subvert definitions applied to
them.[66]

All too often, debates surrounding identity politics ignore these
points and instead function as a reaction against an impossible
desire to secure one's identity against ongoing encounters with
people who have ostensibly competing identity claims. Put
another way, we seek to secure ourselves at the expense of
others. This move is not necessarily a partisan one, although it
might often seem to be. Rather, this is precisely how arguments
against political correctness function: by pretending that such
encounters weaken one's own cultural and identity claims.
Instead, the point of political correctness is to reveal views that
society recognizes as abhorrent—and this changes over time.
Political correctness is a marker of norms. However, political
correctness has come to be felt by many as a form of political
silencing, and this view is encouraged by arguments that seek
to secure one's identity against being insulted.

However, what the pundits and, I would suggest, quite a
few political theorists have missed is that while identity politics
is clearly important in understanding the current political
climate, it is not because of multiculturalism. Fears about
immigration in Europe are largely devoid of any empirical
basis, as immigrants comprise relatively small numbers across
the continent (although there have been surges).[67] In the UK
referendum, some of the areas that most strongly voted to
leave and held anti-immigration views had hardly any local
immigrant populations, and London, the most heavily
immigrant-concentrated city in the UK, voted Remain. *The
Economist* has argued that it was not absolute numbers that
mattered here but proportional increase,[68] and while they may
have a point, it is also true that quite a few of the Leave voters
who held strongly antagonist views toward immigrants had

very little contact with any, and also tended to target immigrants from specific countries, or Muslims. Thus, as a white Canadian immigrant, I am considered okay, whereas if I was from Eastern Europe or a refugee from Syria, I would not be.

While Trump spoke about building a wall and banning Muslim immigrants, and UK politicians fixated on immigration, spurred on no doubt by the press, and as we witness immigration-related concerns spreading across Europe, it remains all too easy to argue that the issue is about national identity and diversity—of identity politics. Some might want to claim that the true story is that immigrants make for easy targets in an era of declining productivity and the economic consequences of globalization. However, I suggest that the issue is really one of narratives.

The danger of political correctness is in being vilified for saying something potentially offensive. In an age of identity politics, it is easy to think that the sources of offence are those insults that fall foul of political correctness because of identity-based discriminations. To be sure, there is something important in this, as people of different ethnicities, religions, genders, socio-economic class, and sexual orientation do not deserve to be discriminated against because of who they are. This, in fact, is consistent with both the multiculturalists and the universal egalitarian liberals, at least in a general sense. The United Nations Declaration of Human Rights states in Article one: "All human beings are born free and equal in dignity and rights." Similarly, the 1789 Declaration of the Rights of Man begins its Article one with a similar statement, although the language is gendered: "Men are born and remain free and equal in rights." People, because they are human beings, have a right not to be discriminated against. Since people have different identities, it follows that all of us need to respect each other's differences.

This is where, presumably, the multicultural politics of identity issue comes up. But to take this logical step is a mistake. The real issue is that when we make identity claims we do so on the basis of narratives. Our identities function according to the stories that we locate ourselves in, and that others identify us as belonging or contributing to. When we question our ability to interrogate each other's narratives—note the word interrogate and not insult—we do so on the basis that our narratives are meaningful and thus important. Fears of political correctness imply that some narratives are in fact not meaningful.

To see how this is the case we need to work out what the function of political correctness is. It is supposed to be about respecting diversity and it involves limiting our own speech in the process. This is reasonable. However, when political correctness becomes an obstacle to recognizing our self-constructed and self-driven narratives, it undermines our sense of self and thus of belonging. I will address this shortly, but when Thomas Frank explores the politics of Kansas and highlights the role of authenticity,[69] this is what he is getting at.

It is not the inability to respect different people that is the problem. It is that somehow we have made it hard to respect the narratives that we each come from, belong to, and engage with, as though some identity narratives matter more than others, so that my narrative claims become stronger than yours, and conversely, your narrative claims become offensive and thus need to be silenced. Barry is correct in pointing out that we need our public institutions to work for us, and that this can help in fostering social solidarity across the state. But he is wrong to argue against the politics of diversity. The problem here is not about identity, but about the state, and of the institutions within the state that support our negotiations of difference. There will always be self-imposed limits of respect that we owe to our fellow human beings, and being politically correct is not necessarily a problem until it is felt to prevent important debates from taking place in the public sphere. When this happens, political correctness serves to undermine our democratic legitimacy because it prevents a public discussion on important identity-related matters. Identity politics has come to be framed within zero-sums, so that one politically based identity claim is thought to override all others, and in the process political correctness becomes the proxy identifier of this zero-sum mentality. The danger is when we use political correctness to curtail our ability to tell our stories, when political correctness serves as a fig leaf to emphasize our own narratives and normative perspectives at the expense of others. To be clear, this is not about creating open spaces for racists or for those who want to engage in hate speech. Rather, it is about being able to carry on a conversation where the underlying narratives are identity-based but still allow for respect and responsibility. In such conversations, it becomes possible to acknowledge the role of how our multiple narratives function in our political lives. Having the conversation is what matters, and learning why the conversation is taking place and why it may be necessary is a part of its significance. However, in order for such discussions to happen, there needs to be a political space in which they can take place. Currently, this political space is lacking.

The failure of the state

Political theory, if it has been about anything at all, is about the state. In his book, *The Search for Political Space*, the urban political theorist Warren Magnusson writes that, "According to the conventional accounts, it was in the context of the creation of the modern state—in Europe, roughly from the sixteenth century onward—that politics came to be recognized (or recognized more clearly) as a distinct activity."[70] Magnusson quotes Frederick Watkins who, in the 1930s wrote that "Among contemporary social scientists it is a virtually unquestioned assumption that the state forms the basic concept of political science."[71] The state is, if nothing else, the basis upon which modern politics happens. "For us, the lucky ones," writes Magnusson, "the state is the domain of opportunity. It is a protected space where we can live out our lives, a source for services we need, and a place where we can be citizens in the fullest sense."[72] At least, that is the idea. Magnusson is critical of this view, arguing that there is something unsettling

about how this discourse of the modern state monopolizes
our political imagination so that "To be included in the state
and the market—as most people in the West and a substantial
number elsewhere evidently are—is evidently an important
privilege."[73]

How exactly we understand or interpret this privilege is an
important question, which is a large part of what Magnusson
is getting at. As he suggests, it may not be the type of privilege
that we might take it for. This was one of Karl Marx's important
insights, to highlight that the political, economic, and even
social choices we make may not actually be choices at all. While
the Marxist argument rests in part on the rather problematic
notion of false consciousness, Magnusson provides a different
take by arguing instead that,

> by participating in consumer sovereignty, people who are
> otherwise producers take part in their own subjugation to the
> tyranny of market demand. People have to produce themselves
> for the market in a form that the market requires, and this
> means abiding by rules of conduct that are in many ways stricter
> than the ones the state itself would care to enforce.[74]

Magnusson's important work directs the reader to exploring alternative understandings of political space (of where
politics happens) and thus of what we consider to be political.
Magnusson, building on Arendt, questions whether politics
has to be built on the idea of enclosure, and suggests that
there are different ways to understand political spaces in which
freedom is possible. Concerns about the normative possibilities
that the state enables or curtails are, of course, not new, but
they did take on a particular seriousness in the 1980s and
1990s as the forces of global capital seemed to break down
the economic enclosures of the state while maintaining the
idea of political enclosure.

It was this combination that, I would argue, provided the
foundations for today's crisis in politics. We can see this through
a brief overview of some of the critical literature of that time.
For example, Jean Bethke Elshtain writes in her 1993 book,
Democracy on Trial, how the linkage between the free-market

society and politics has led to a situation where the logic of consumer choice damages the integrity of democracy:

> The presumption behind this theory is that each and every one is a "preference maximizer." Aside from being a simplistic account of human motivation, preference theory lends itself to blurring important distinctions. According to preference maximizers, there is no such thing as a social good—there are only aggregates of private goods. ... Under the banner of more perfect democratic choice, we become complicit in eroding even further those elements of deliberation, reason, her incompetence and questionable judgment, and shared goodwill that alone makes genuine choice and democracy possible.[75]

Elshtain offers a laundry list of the challenges facing American democracy[76] at the time:

> The growth of cynicism and the atrophy of civil society; too much privatization, acquisitive individualism that translates "wants" into "rights"; an increase in disrespect, even contempt for, the rule-governed practices that make democracy work, from the franchise to due process' a politics of displacement that disdains any distinction between public and private and aims to open up all aspects of life to the harsh glare of publicity; a neglect of practical politics in favour of rageful proclamations of one's unassailable and unassimilable identity as a member of a group; impatience with democratic citizenship and growing enthusiasm for identities based on race, gender, or sexual preference over that of the citizen; a waning of our ability to transmit democratic dispositions and dreams to succeeding generations through education.[77]

From this list, it is hard to see that anything has changed, other than perhaps getting worse. Elshtain, however, relies on the idea of the social covenant as the means to break through the challenges of the day, and as can be gathered from the above discussion, her critique here of identity politics misses the mark considerably.

As part of the same series in which Elshtain's book was published, two years later John Ralston Saul, in *The Unconscious Civilization*, challenged the conventional wisdom that "democracy was born out of economics, in particular the Industrial

Revolution. And that democracy is based on individualism."[78]
Much of Saul's critique is directed at the overwhelming role
that economic thinking has had on our political system.
In this world of political economic dominance, citizens
become reduced to subjects. Saul is especially damning of
economics:

> Over the last quarter-century economics has raised itself to the
> level of a scientific profession and more or less foisted a Nobel
> prize in its own honour onto the Nobel committee via bank
> financing. Yet over the same 25 years, economics has been
> spectacularly unsuccessful in its attempts to apply its models
> and theories to the reality of our civilization. It's not that
> economists' advice hasn't been taken. It has, in great detail,
> with great reverence. And in general it has failed. ... If economists
> were doctors, they would today be mired in malpractice
> suits.[79]

His criticism of Tony Blair, who was then the leader of the
British Labour Party, follows from his dismal view of our
politicians' succumbing to the ostensible power of economic
thought:

> Tony Blair ... goes out of his way to fall into line. He tells *The
> Financial Times* of London: "The determining context of eco-
> nomic policy is the new global market. That market imposes
> huge limitations of a practical nature—quite apart from reasons
> of principle—on macroeconomic policies." These two sentences
> may sound familiar. They should. They have been uttered in
> varying forces by hundreds of public figures from the Right to
> the Left.
>   Globalization and the limits it imposes are the most fashionable
> miniature ideologies of our day. Mr Blair's statements means
> two things. One: "I am in fashion, so it's safe to vote for me."
> Two: "The ideology is in charge, so don't worry, I won't be
> able to do much."[80]

Saul's words would sound a bit hyperbolic were it not that he
is not alone in identifying how the logic of modern capitalism
has undermined many of our political possibilities and harmed
so many.

In his 1998 book, *False Dawn*, republished in 2009, the philosopher John Gray, writes how

> [a] single global market is the Enlightenment's project of a universal civilization in what is likely to be its final form. ... The Utopia of the global free market has not incurred a human cost in the way that communism did. Yet over time it may come to rival it in the suffering that it inflicts. Already it has resulted in over a hundred million peasants becoming migrant labourers in China, the exclusion from work and participation in society of tens of millions in the advanced societies, a condition of near-anarchy and rule by organized crime in parts of the post-communist world, and further devastation of the environment.[81]

What this literature shares in common is a profound concern about the relationship between politics and economics, and how economics has seemed to regularly outmanoeuvre our political interests. The classic work *No Logo*, by Naomi Klein, provides perhaps the seminal text that demonstrates the extent to which such forces have gone, with branding becoming the *sine qua non* of contemporary social and political spaces.[82] However, it is in the international dimension that the crux of the matter lies and where the forces of global capital appear to be weakening the role of the state, thereby removing any real accountability from our domestic political leaders who are expected to "fall in line," thus undermining our democratic political system.

The international political economist Susan Strange starts her 1996 book, *The Retreat of the State*, as follows:

> Today it seems that the heads of governments may be the last to recognize that they and their ministers have lost the authority over national societies and economies that they used to have. Their command over outcomes is not what is used to be. Politicians everywhere talk as though they have the answers to economic and social problems, as if they really are in charge of their country's destiny. People no longer believe them. Disillusion with national leaders brought down the leaders of the Soviet Union and the states of central Europe. But the dissolution is by no means confined to socialist systems. Popular contempt

for ministers and for the head of state has grown in most
countries—Italy, Britain, France and the United States are
leading examples. Nor is the lack of confidence confined to
those in office; opposition parties and their leaders are often
no better thought of than those they wish to replace.[83]

Strange's words remain incredibly accurate in 2017. What we
see in this literature from the 1990s is a repeated acknowledgement that the relationship between economics (capitalism really)
and modern politics is not working. The de-territorialization
of economics, described more generally as globalization, has
not accompanied an appropriate political response.

Whereas some, such as the Nobel prize-winning economist
Joseph Stiglitz, seek out a more just form of globalization,[84]
their argument, although important, misses the point that there
are those in the US, the UK, and elsewhere who, although
they are in industrialized democratic countries, are feeling
the pinch of a disillusioning and disenfranchising political
economic order. The state, which was crucial for protecting
and spreading the forces of modern capitalism, has been unable
to control the monster of individual narrow self-interest and
privatization that has accompanied if not partially defined the
neoliberal globalization agenda. The state, in short, appears
to be failing, and while some of the more popular texts on
this subject, such as those by Naomi Klein, John Gray, and
Joseph Stiglitz, focus on political economy, they struggle to
articulate an account of politics that can be understood as being
able to respond to the challenges of global capital while still
providing appealing economic conditions of opportunity. It is
not that they do not provide such answers, it is that the logic
in the answers remains largely within the same conditions of
politics that led to the problems in the first place, or they set
out false dichotomies between the global and the local. This
binary, however, no longer makes any sense (if it ever did).
However, it was precisely accepting this binary and prioritizing
a particular culture of capitalism instead of a democratic politics
of responsibility that led to Brexit and Trump.

As these authors and many others recognize, there is a lot
at stake in these debates. It is not simply the collapse of the

traditional working class (recall the increasing mortality of this constituency in the US), it is also the increasingly dire prospects for current and future generations.[85] Our current political order is failing too many people. The search for political space is failing because of the "shift away from states and towards markets."[86] Consequently, it is no surprise that so many voted for Brexit, so many voted for Trump, and so many stayed at home instead of voting for Clinton. At issue in all this, however, is not economics, it is politics. The issues might appear to be economic in nature, but the concern is about our ability to control the forces of capitalism, which much like the logic of warfare, tends toward the extreme: extremes in wealth inequality and in deregulation, extreme faith in the invisible hand of market forces, and so on.

The political theorist Wendy Brown highlights the range of critical arguments against this globalized neoliberal order, noting that across this literature:

> Intensified inequality, crass commodification and commerce, ever-growing corporate influence in government, economic havoc and instability—certainly all of these are consequences of neoliberal policy, and all are material for loathing or popular protest, as indeed, occupy Wall street, the Southern European protests against austerity policies, and, earlier, the "Antiglobaliza-tion" movement loathed and protested them.[87]

Her definition of neoliberalism is different in its Foucauldian focus on how neoliberalism is a normative order with its own form of rationality. Her normative argument is directed against the neoliberal challenge to democracy. "This book," she writes, "is a theoretical consideration of the ways that neoliberalism, a peculiar form of reason that configures all aspects of existence in economic terms, is quietly undoing basic elements of democracy."[88] Guiding Brown is the branding or the construction of ourselves as primarily economic agents, *homo economicus*, and of how this reduces citizens to "investors or consumers, not as members of a democratic polity who share power and certain common goods, spaces, and experiences."[89] In this regard, Brown also highlights how our political spaces, our political identities, and our political practices are failing us when they become treated or understood according to the economic logic of neoliberalism.

In a related sense, as politics becomes displaced by economics, the state loses its political identity. The consequence is that the state is failing in its ability to protect its inhabitants, but the answer is not to strengthen the state at the expense of economic interdependence. This is to fall back into the zero-sum logic of binaries and dichotomies. Rather, the challenge is to explore more fully what we expect politics to be about, and where to locate political practice. There is a paradox here. Economics requires politics, and our political systems have to enable and protect some kind of economic order, but the more politics is about economics, the harder it gets to actually engage in any politics. This is part of the context that enables the populist right, allows Trump to come off as a working-class hero, and allows Brexit to be viewed as being in the interests of the working class when those advocating Brexit were largely the Eton-educated privileged set, and there was, for one brief moment, a convergence of the financial sector with the manufacturing sector (if not the actual workers) about the economic benefits of the EU. Consequently, the question we should be asking is the one Thomas Frank asks: "So how does one go from criticizing privilege to fawning over a region's business leaders? How do you square your concern for the downtrodden with a drooling admiration for the very rich?"[90]

Answers to this question vary, but as Frank identifies in his analysis of the politics in the state of Kansas, and Arlie Hochschild does in her similar discussion of Louisiana, they have something to do with identifying who will pay in the long run, which comes down to providing a narrative in which people can locate their lives and their views as having authenticity while still finding a place in a political system that no longer works for them.

Frank's book explores the choices of residents who vote for cultural issues instead of economic ones, and what he reveals is a political system whereby both major parties are largely beholden to similar economic ideologies, but one of them has been able to construct a narrative that displaces the economic concerns with a faux-political narrative about identity. The paradox here is that voting becomes less about economic interests even though the political decisions end up affirming the very significance of economic interest. Lower-income voters end up voting for candidates who only worsen their economic futures. Hence the use of anti-intellectualism, and even racism to win elections. As Frank quotes one voter in Wichita: "I don't worry too much about who's in control because I think God's in Control. But I'd rather have a Christian in there."[91] The point Frank is ultimately getting at is that "What divides Americans is *authenticity*, not something hard and ugly like economics."[92] However, this has been possible precisely because politics has been unable to adequately respond to the challenges of economics, and so voters end up turning to topics that they feel make more sense to who they are. It is, ultimately, the narratives that appear to matter above all else.

Even Arlie Russell Hochschild, in *Strangers in Their Own Land*, comes to a similar conclusion despite a rather significant gulf between her interpretation and that of Frank. Frank's book, which inspired Hoschchild's,[93] can be read as contributing to the view that right-wing voters are being tricked into voting against their interests. Hochschild notes, when she explores how those who vote against social welfare programmes simultaneously make use of them and even go out of their way to do so, that there is some accuracy to this claim. Cutting to the chase, Nathaniel Rich wryly repackages Hochschild's conclusions when he writes in his review of her book: "The more conservative you are, the worse off you are likely to be and the sooner you are likely to die."[94] The paradox that both Frank and Hochschild are at great pains to understand is why people vote in ways that are so clearly against their interests. As Hochschild writes:

> Across the country, red states are poorer and have more teen mothers, more divorce, worse health, more obesity, more trauma-related deaths, more low-birth-weight babies, and lower school enrollment. On average, people in red states die five years earlier

than people in blue states. Indeed, the gap in life expectancy between Louisiana (75.7) and Connecticut (80.8) is the same as that between the United States and Nicaragua.[95]

Voters in Louisiana vote in ways that undermine environmental protection even when these same voters are the first in line to witness and then experience the destructive tendencies of the gas and oil industry. The stories are too horrible: workers getting cancer because of their work; birds dropping out of the sky because the fumes are so bad from toxic waste; turtles blinded and then starving to death because of chemical pollution; workers having their teeth rot because of fumes in the workplace; homes being destroyed because of unsafe drilling practices miles away.[96] Hochschild explains all this with the term the "great paradox," which is the opposition to federal assistance by those who most need it, the reasons they do so being ones of anger and of narratives, of how they feel let down by the state, or rather, by government.

The distinction here between the state and the government is not always clear. Note for example the words of one of Hochschild's interviewees:

> The state always seems to come down on the *little* guy. Take this bayou, if your motorboat leaks a little gas into the water, the warden'll write you up. But if *companies* leak thousands of gallons of it and kill all the life here? The state lets them go. If you shoot an endangered brown pelican, they'll put you in jail. But if a company kills the brown pelican by poisoning the fish he eats? They let it go. I think they *overregulate* the *bottom* because it's *harder* to regulate the *top*.[97]

What comes across in both Frank's and Hochschild's books is disillusionment with government, and of people looking for avenues in which their stories, their narratives, can find a place in politics. They have, in a sense, been disenfranchised and because there is no real contract for them (not even heuristically) to renegotiate or terminate, they vote on matters that make sense in their narratives and/or in ways to undermine a system that they see as discriminating against them—and they have the illnesses and the poor job prospects to show for it. That those they vote for end up making things worse[98] only further demonstrates the failure of politics.

This is demonstrated particularly in Hochschild's book, where there are two failures. The first is that which the author notes and pertains to the state's failure to regulate big business, protect the environment, maintain infrastructure, hold corporations accountable, and in general follow the premises of "good government."[99] The second is that of the Tea Party-types she encounters, where the government cannot be trusted, meddles in people's lives, makes a mess of things when it does get involved, and rewards others who are less deserving. Both Hochschild and the people she interviews in her book regularly appear to conflate the state with the government. The failures are both of the government and of the state. To be sure, there is a difference between the state and the government, but the failures run so deep that the distinction may not matter.

In a democracy, if our government is failing, it is possible to vote in a new government. But when successive governments fail, and do so in the same way, it might be that the issue is not just with those in office but with something much more serious.

In political theory, a failure in politics can be interpreted as a failure of the state. This interpretation is because if political theory is primarily concerned with the state and the political order and normative possibilities that the state enables, the inability of the state to function accordingly is tantamount to a failure of politics. This formulation also follows in the traditional logic of the contract, that the state exists as part of a grand bargain where we give up some freedoms in return for benefits that only the state can provide. As the forces of economic globalization weaken the state's ability to represent the needs and rights of its citizens, and instead protect global free trade and the ostensible rights of private capital, the arguments from both the populist right and the traditional left emphasize the need to strengthen the state, albeit in different ways and for different ends. Yet this convergence, clearly evident in Brexit and Trump's election, is a mistake. Yes, the state and our governments are failing, but not in the ways that either of these responses can react to.

In Magnusson's more recent book, *The Politics of Urbanism*, he responds to the challenging argument advanced by

James S. Scott in his *Seeing Like a State*. Scott's argument is
that when we "see" like a state, political and social questions
end up being treated as large-scale generalizable problems,
where local knowledge is a hindrance and where centralization
of knowledge and of power are solutions. The hubris that
accompanies this political imagination is dangerous. It can end
in millions of deaths, the product of American-planned large-
scale monoculture in the Soviet Union.[100] Without any local
knowledge or relevant experience, the planners were unable to
take into account the nuances of local weather, water tables,
river flows, environment, etc. and thus grossly miscalculated
the yields. Scott explores a similar pattern of rationalization in
architecture (Brasilia) and also in modern forestry, the methods
of which resulted in forests being prone to infection and thus
demanded that humans attempt to recreate the ecosystem they
had destroyed.[101] Magnusson argues that instead of seeing
like a state, when we "see like a city," politics becomes less
prone to the generalizable rationalities of a sovereign gaze,
and instead has to deal with local and diverse movements
of people and of social links that correspond more to a fluid
network than to the harsh calculating logic of a top-down
administrative system. There is, in short, politics outside of
sovereignty that exists within the state but is not conditioned
by the forces of sovereignty, and might even resist such
forces.

For example, Jonathan Havercroft advances an argument for
politics that is community-based as opposed to sovereignty-
based.[102] This kind of politics is understood to follow from
our need and abilities to communicate with others, and that
language changes. There is always the possibility of change, and
also recognition that although politics may be conflictual, it is
based on our ability to communicate amongst ourselves. Trying
to think up a new political order can be difficult, but it is not
as though within our existing multiplicity of political orders we
cannot find evidence of thinking and acting differently. Sometimes local, national, and international actors come together
to fight for specific rights against a neoliberal world. This
was the case in the environmental and First-Nations protests

against logging at Clayoquot Sound on Vancouver Island, in Canada.[103] The point is not that the state is unimportant. Rather the issue is that our politics is failing and that the combined forces of a sovereign political order and globalized capitalism have removed political responsibility from our politics.

Conclusion

At the time of writing, the signs of what Trump will do as President are not good: there has been the ban on immigrants from select Middle Eastern countries travelling into the US (even if they have a green card), his obsession over the size of the inaugural crowd, and the lack of any mention of Jews in the White House's Holocaust memorial statement (and that was all in the first week). In the UK, and even though no explicit UK government policy has yet been legislated, the government has repeatedly either encouraged or incited the view that "foreigners" are a danger to our society, to the NHS (which actually depends on immigrant nurses and doctors), to our expertise, and to our economy. The government at one point wanted employers to provide lists of all "foreign" workers, initially in order to "shame" the employers (and presumably the employees as well), although they have backtracked on the public shaming part of their proposal. More alarming was the request sent to parents requesting that they inform the school about what foreign languages the children are exposed to at home. In addition, the government at one point stated that "foreigners" are not allowed to advise government on Brexit negotiations, ostensibly using security as an excuse. That our political elites feel it appropriate to even make such a proposal is outrageous, and reveals the racist, hurtful, and ugly character of our current political climate and what is now deemed acceptable. Even if we take the security argument, it makes no tangible difference to the immoral and racist underpinnings of the demand. The focus simply reframes a racist argument into a security one by invoking, implicitly in this case, a concern about dual loyalty.

The same argument about security was made in the US prior to the Second World War in order to "justify" the internment of anybody of Japanese descent, and it was wielded to even worse effect by the Nazis, as Jews were treated as internal enemy aliens. In the late 1800s Jews were subject to exactly this accusation in France, after they went to the aid of their brethren in Damascus who were being attacked on the basis of a blood libel accusation. The infamous Dreyfus Affair, from 1894–1906, was similarly based on the idea that foreigners—in this case Jews—pose a security threat.

So far the government and government ministers feel that simply saying that they "are not racists" is sufficient to excuse them from their racist demands. However, as Hannah Arendt noted in her reporting of the Eichmann trial, Eichmann also didn't see anything wrong with what he did. The demand that employers provide lists or at least create new ones of all foreign workers reflects a tragic history whereby good people sit by and do nothing while government acts with impunity against those it deems alien. Foreign workers already need visas to work in the UK, and if they are from other European countries, they are here legally. To demand that such lists be created is the equivalent of a bureaucratic attempt to legitimize blatantly racist fears and create a tiered society based on ideological nativism. The government might as well tattoo a number on my forearm or ask me to wear a six-pointed star. Such extreme fears are not unwarranted. We know exactly where such administrative requirements for the listing of foreigners can lead us.

I do understand why people have issues with the EU (the Commission has a serious accountability problem) or want to shake things up in Washington (the US political system has not been serving the country very well for years). I get it. But what I, along with many others, am so shocked at is how people could side with what was being advanced and with the people advancing it.

Which brings us back to the socio-economic argument for why Clinton lost and Brexit won. This is in some ways the easy argument. There have been arguments for years about the dangers to our society and our politics of continuously following the path of neoliberal market ideology. It would be ironic if it was not so tragic, but even the International Monetary Fund—one of the main global forces that has pushed this ideology—has recently admitted as such. However, while the political economic argument is an important one, what it does not and indeed cannot account for is the possibility that our politics is based on a fundamental deception. The very ability of our political system to enable these outcomes is not just a fault of an ugly capitalism or a rural/urban divide. It is, rather, a consequence of how, for most of us, politics just does not seem to matter because it has become so removed from our lives. Instead of politics, our systems have come down to contract-management, and those who have no seat at the table the forces of management can simply ignore. This includes the vast majority of us—the middle class which is shrinking, and can no longer afford to send their children to university; the middle and working classes who struggle to get a mortgage or save enough to take a short holiday to recharge their batteries. The great tragedy is how the richest countries in the world appear incapable of providing for a decent system of social life, investing instead in protecting banks that are too big to fail but without thinking that perhaps spending on vocational colleges or university education could be even more important. What world do we live in where it makes sense that we don't view our social and cultural institutions with the same concern that we do our economic ones? Why is a bank too big to fail, but an education or health care system is not? Why is there money for nuclear weapons but not for health care?

However, it is a mistake to view these as primarily economic issues. They are political choices first, cultural and social ones second, and economic ones third. However, our political system treats these all as economic, which helps explain (1) why so many businessmen and corporate lawyers get into politics, and (2) the revolving door between government and business consultancy. Political choices have become subservient to economic ideology, and so social democracy and traditional socialism still focus on the important but incomplete Marxist argument that emphasizes the forces of production. We look to the opportunity to address the injustices of global capitalism as though our political structures and political system is up to the task. But what if we have been looking in the wrong place this whole time? What if we have failed to take seriously that we have lost sight of what politics is about? What if the failure of the left and the ascendancy of the populist right is because of a deception, one that protects the interests of the 1% and one that we have been unable to identify because we too have become co-opted into a political system that is devoid of actual politics, where politics becomes the handmaiden to economic interest. What kind of political responsibility exists in this world?

Notes

1 These numbers were taken from *The New York Times* election news website: The New York Times, "Presidential Election Results: Donald J. Trump Wins," www.nytimes.com/elections/results/president. Accessed September 25 2107.

2 Carl Bialik, "No, Voter Turnout Wasn't Way Down from 2012," FiveThirtyEight, http://fivethirtyeight.com/features/no-voter-turnout-wasnt-way-down-from-2012/. Accessed February 3 2017. See also Michael P. McDonald, "United States Election Project," www.electproject.org. Accessed September 25 2017.

3 Gregory Wallace, "Voter Turnout at 20-Year Low in 2016," CNN, November 30 2016.

4 UKIP: 26.77%; Labour: 24.74%; Conservatives: 23.31%. Data taken from: European Parliament, "Results of the 2014 European Elections," Europarl, www.europarl.europa.eu/elections2014-results/en/country-results-uk-2014.html#table01. Accessed February 3 2107.

5 The Electoral Commission, "EU Referendum Results," The Electoral Commission, www.electoralcommission.org.uk/find-information-by-subject/elections-and-referendums/past-elections-and-referendums/eu-referendum/electorate-and-count-information. Accessed February 7 2017.

6 James Warren, "The Press Blames Itself for Trump Win," *Vanity Fair*, November 10 2016.

7 Polls reported in the press in Switzerland represent more accurately that polls are probabilities by including the confidence interval and the standard error. I would like to thank Patrick Kuhn for this information.

8 Arendt, *On Violence*, 6–7.

9 Arnau Busquets Guàrdia, "How Brexit Vote Broke Down," Politico, www.politico.eu/article/graphics-how-the-uk-voted-eu-referendum-brexit-demographics-age-education-party-london-final-results/. Accessed February 3 2017.

10 Caelainn Barr, "The Areas and Demographics Where the Brexit Vote Was Won," *The Guardian*, June 24 2016.

11 The Electoral Commission, "EU Referendum Results".

12 '2016 Election Exit Polls,' *The Washington Post*, November 29 2016, https://www.washingtonpost.com/graphics/politics/2016-election/exit-polls/. Accessed September 21 2017.

13 Jon Huang et al., "Election 2016: Exit Polls," *The New York Times*, November 8 2016.

14 Ted Barrett, "Pol: Trump Defended Articles of the Constitution That Don't Exist," http://edition.cnn.com/2016/07/08/politics/sanford-questions-trump-constitution-gaffe/. Accessed February 3 2017; Evan McMullin, "Trump's Threat to the Constitution," *The New York Times*, December 5 2016.

15 Radhika Sanghani, "Inside Britain's 'Worst' Immigration Removal Centre at Christmas," *The Telegraph*, December 24 2014.

16 Jonathan Foreman, "Theresa May's Record as Home Secretary is Alarming, Not Reassuring," *The Spectator*, July 15 2016.

17 Ibid.

18 Alan Travis, "What Does Theresa May's Record as Home Secretary Tell Us?," *The Guardian*, July 18 2016.

19 Ibid. See also Jessica Elgot, " 'Absurd' Visa Rules on Income Force UK Citizens into Exile, Court Told," *The Guardian*, February 22 2016.

20 Travis, "What Does Theresa May's Record as Home Secretary Tell Us?"

21 Patrick Wintour, "UK Lacks Expertise for Trade Talks with Europe, Says Top Civil Servant," *The Guardian*, June 28 2016. Peter Spence, "Government Faces Worldwide Hunt for Trade Negotiators, Experts Warn," *The Telegraph*, July 3 2016.

22 The original report by Moore can be found here: Michael Moore, "Is Trump Purposely Sabotaging His Campaign?," http://michaelmoore.com/TrumpSabotage/. Accessed February 3 2107.

23 The Editors, "Against Donald Trump," *The Atlantic*, November 2016, www.theatlantic.com/magazine/archive/2016/11/the-case-for-hillary-clinton-and-against-donald-trump/501161/. Accessed September 21 2017.

24 Chris Moody, "Trump in '04: 'I Probably Identity More as Democrat'," CNN, 2015.

25 Moore, "5 Reasons Why Trump Will Win".

26 Ibid.

27 Ibid. Emphasis in original.

28 Ibid.

29 Ibid.

30 Ibid.

31 Welch, *Hyperdemocracy*, xi, 3.

32 Ibid., 26.

33 Alexis de Tocqueville, *Democracy in America*, trans. Harvey C. Mansfield and Delba Winthrop (Chicago: Chicago University Press, 2000), 243.

34 Ibid., 239. This quote is the title of one of the sub-sections of chapter 7, volume 1, part 2.

35 Ibid., 241.

36 Ibid., 243.

37 Ibid., 244.

38 Fareed Zakaria, "The Rise of Illiberal Democracy," *Foreign Affairs* 76, no. 6 (1997).

39 See, Arendt, "Thinking and Moral Considerations: A Lecture."; *The Origins of Totalitarianism*.

40 de Tocqueville, *Democracy in America*, 583.

41 Peter Mandelson, "Why is the Brexit Camp so Obsessed with Immigration? Because That's All They Have," *The Guardian*, May 3 2016. See also Watt, "EU Referendum."

42 Owen Bennett, *The Brexit Club* (London: Biteback Publishing, 2016), chapter 28.

43 Alia Wong and Adrienne Green, "Campus Politics: A Cheat Sheet," *The Atlantic*, April 4 2016. Ellen Brait, "Princeton Students Demand Removal of Woodrow Wilson's Name from Buildings," *The Guardian*, November 23 2015. See also Anemona Hartocollis and Jess Bidgood, "Racial Discimination Protests Ignite at Colleges Across the U.S.," *The New York Times*, November 11 2015.

44 Rupert Cornwell, "Campus Protests: Students Fighting for Free Speech and the Eradication of Racism Should Be Working

Together—Not against Each Other," *Independent*, November 14 2015.

45 Mark Lilla, "The End of Identity Liberalism," *The New York Times*, November 18 2016.

46 Ibid.

47 Malik Kenan, "The Failure of Multiculturalism "*Foreign Affairs* 94, no. 2 (2015).

48 Brian Barry, *Culture & Equality* (Cambridge: Polity, 2001), 5.

49 Ibid., 11–12.

50 He takes this example from: James Tully, *Strange Multiplicity: Constitutionalism in an Age of Diversity* (Cambridge: Cambridge University Press, 1995). See, Barry, *Culture & Equality*, 255–58.

51 Barry, *Culture & Equality*, 300.

52 Ibid., 79.

53 Ibid., 266. Emphasis in original.

54 Ibid., 67.

55 James Clifford and George E. Marcus, *Writing Culture: The Poetics and Politics of Ethnography*, 25th anniversary ed. with a new foreword by Kim Fortun (Berkeley: University of California Press, 2010).

56 See, for example, Benhabib, *The Rights of Others*.

57 Ilan Zvi Baron, "The Problem of Dual Loyalty," *Canadian Journal of Political Science* 42, no. 4 (2009).

58 Robin Cohen, "Diasporas and the Nation-State: From Victims to Challengers," *International Affairs* 72, no. 3 (1996). See also Jonathan Frankel, *The Damascus Affair: "Ritual Murder," Politics, and the Jews in 1840* (Cambridge: Cambridge University Press, 1997).

59 William Connolly, *Identity/Difference: Democratic Negotiations of Political Paradox*, expanded ed. (Minneapolis: University of Minnesota Press, 1991), xiii.

60 Charles Taylor, "The Politics of Recognition," in *Multiculturalism*, ed. Amy Gutmann (Princeton: Princeton University Press, 1994), 39.

61 Connolly, *Identity/Difference*, xv.

62 Ibid., xix.

63 Ibid., xv.

64 Influenced by Connolly, I am making a subtle distinction here between identity politics, which is concerned with public political arguments that are based on or in identity claims, and the politics of identity, which is about how identity is political and/or is

related to political/normative concerns. The politics of identity provides a basis for identity politics.

65 We find this argument also advanced by the philosopher Emmanuel Lévinas. See Emmanuel Lévinas, *Totality and Infinity: An Essay on Exteriority*, trans. Alphonso Lingis (Pittsburgh: Duquesne University Press, 1969); *The Levinas Reader* (Oxford: Blackwell, 1989); *God, Death, and Time*, trans. Bettina Bergo (Stanford: Stanford University Press, 1993); *Otherwise Than Being: Or Beyond Essence*, trans. Alphonso Lingis (Pittsburgh: Duquesne University Press, 1993); *Is It Righteous to Be?*, trans. Jill Robbins (Stanford: Stanford University Press, 2001).

66 Connolly, *Identity/Difference*, 64.

67 Kenan, "The Failure of Multiculturalism."

68 "Britain's Immigration Paradox," *The Economist*, July 8 2016.

69 Frank, *What's the Matter with Kansas?*

70 Magnusson, *The Search for Political Space*, 36–37.

71 Ibid., 32.

72 Ibid., 37.

73 Ibid., 58.

74 Ibid.

75 Jean Bethke Elshtain, *Democracy on Trial*, CBC Massey Lecture Series (Concord, Ontario: Anansi, 1993), 29.

76 Although the book was actually part of the Canadian Broadcasting Corporation Massey Lecture Series.

77 Elshtain, *Democracy on Trial*, 120.

78 John Ralston Saul, *The Unconscious Civilization*, CBC Massey Lecture Series (Concord, Ontario: Anansi, 1995), 3.

79 Ibid., 4.

80 Ibid., 19–20.

81 John Gray, *False Dawn: The Delusions of Global Capitalism* (London: Granta, 2009 (1998)), 3.

82 Naomi Klein, *No Logo*. 10th anniversary ed. (New York: Picador, 2009). In an interesting coincidence, both Klein and Hochschild are concerned with the politics of walls or fences (although Hochschild's concern is more abstract with "empathy walls"). Naomi Klein, *Fences and Windows: Dispatches from the Front Lines of the Globalization Debate* (London: Flamingo, 2002); Hochschild, *Strangers in Their Own Land*.

83 Susan Strange, *The Retreat of the State: The Diffusion of Power in the World Economy* (Cambridge: Cambridge University Press, 1996), 3.

84 Joseph Stiglitz, *Globalization and Its Discontents* (London: Penguin, 2002); *Making Globalizaiton Work: The Next Steps to Global Justice* (London: Penguin, 2006).

85 BBC, "Young 'to Be Poorer Than Parents at Every Stage of Life'," BBC News, www.bbc.co.uk/news/business-34858997. Accessed February 5 2017; Daniel Boffey, "Middle-Class Young 'Will Fare Worse Than Their Parents'," *The Guardian*, October 12 2013. Equality and Human Rights Commission, "Is Britain Fairer? The State of Equality and Human Rights 2015" (Manchester, 2015). Resolution Foundation, "Millennials Facing 'Generational Pay Penalty' as Their Earnings Fall £8,000 Behind During Their 20s," news release, July 18 2016, www.resolutionfoundation.org/media/press-releases/millennials-facing-generational-pay-penalty-as-their-earnings-fall-8000-behind-during-their-20s/. Accessed September 25 2017; Jonathan Cribb, Andrew Hood, and Robert Joyce, "The Economic Circumstances of Different Generations: The Latest Picture" (London: The Institute for Fiscal Studies, 2016).

86 Strange, *The Retreat of the State*, 43.

87 Brown, *Undoing the Demos*, 30.

88 Ibid., 17.

89 Ibid., 176.

90 Frank, *What's the Matter with Kansas?*, 162.

91 Ibid., 190.

92 Ibid., 27

93 Hochschild, *Strangers in Their Own Land*, 8.

94 Nathaniel Rich, "Inside the Sacrifice Zone," *The New York Review of Books*, November 10 2016.

95 Hochschild, *Strangers in Their Own Land*, 8.

96 Charles J. Sykes, "Charlie Sykes on Where the Right Went Wrong," *The New York Times*, December 15 2015; Hochschild, *Strangers in Their Own Land*.

97 Hochschild, *Strangers in Their Own Land*, 52. Emphasis in original.

98 Writing about Louisiana's Republican governor, in his review of Hochschild's book ("Inside the Sacrifice Zone"), Nathanial Rich reports:

> Louisiana's governor is among the most powerful chief executives in the nation, a legacy that dates back to Huey Long's administration, and under Governor Bobby Jindal's

dictatorship, between 2008 and 2016, the state's prospects declined with unprecedented severity. After he reduced corporate income taxes and expanded the exemptions granted to oil and gas companies, the state's revenue tumbled roughly $3 billion. He transferred $1.6 billion from public schools and hospitals to oil companies in the form of new tax incentives, under the theory that the presence of oil and a robust petrochemical infrastructure were not incentives enough. (The Louisiana Legislature is not only soaked with oil and gas lobbyists—during a recent session there were seventy for 144 legislators—but many lawmakers themselves hold industry jobs while serving in office.) Jindal fired 30,000 state employees, furloughed many others, cut education funding by nearly half, and sold off as many state-owned parking lots, farms, and hospitals as he could.

Despite these punishing cuts, he managed over the course of his administration to turn a $900 million budget surplus into a $1.6 billion deficit. National agencies downgraded the state's credit rating. The damage was so great that it helped to bring about one of the most unlikely election results in recent American history. Jindal's successor is John Bel Edwards, a Democrat—the only one to hold statewide office. Edwards is vehemently pro-life and agnostic about climate change, but he is determined to hold the oil and gas industry responsible for funding their share of coastal restoration. He currently enjoys a 62.5% approval rating. Almost a year into his first term, however, despite several emergency measures, the state remains in arrears.

 99 Hochschild, *Strangers in Their Own Land*, 99–115 (chapter 7), esp. 12.
100 James C. Scott, *Seeing Like a State* (New Haven: Yale University Press, 1998), 193–222, esp. 200–02.
101 The forestry discussion can be found at: ibid., 11–22.
102 Havercroft, *Captives of Sovereignty*.
103 Warren Magnusson and Karena Shaw, eds, *A Political Space: Reading the Global Through Clayoquot Sound* (Minneapolis: University of Minnesota Press, 2001).

4
Saving politics

Introduction

If I were a Marxist, I would be very tempted to argue that the ascendancy of Trump and the Brexit result are signs that the internal contradictions within capitalism are finally starting to work out as expected. The revolution is near! It all seems ripe for a Marxist revolution, and indeed the rise of Momentum in the UK suggests something similar. However, history in this Hegelian sense is unlikely to return, and Momentum (the grassroots left-wing movement that supports Jeremy Corbyn), while popular, remains a minority. Nevertheless, there are good reasons to think that something is going on: the convergence of right-wing populism with the traditional working-class left, the rising dissatisfaction with our political institutions combined with increasing inequalities in our societies all bear striking similarities to the conditions that gave rise to fascism and a World War. It would be foolish to ignore such concerns. It is, as such, of some concern that as populism gathers steam Jeremy Corbyn, the current leader of the British Labour Party, wants to rebrand himself as a left-wing populist.[1]

In the late 1990s, around the time of the Battle in Seattle, it seemed odd to me that both the right and the left appeared to be making very similar arguments in response to the neoliberal forces of globalization. It seemed to me then, and still does now, that the left ended up adopting the same structural solution as the right: increase the power of the state. For the left, the argument was for government to protect workers' rights, local jobs, and an economy based on the production of goods (although we should add services) other than financial products. For the right, the argument was about the state (although not necessarily government) focusing inward, protecting its borders, limiting engagement with international institutions, and (barring the neoconservative movement) staying out of foreign wars or international military interventions.

In the UK, when Theresa May became Prime Minister she spoke about not letting the workers of Britain down. While her words were most likely empty catch-phrases, designed to wean over to the Conservatives those Labour voters who voted Leave, there was something surreal about a Conservative Prime Minister—one whom you would expect to advocate deregulation, low rates of corporate taxation that might as well be corporate welfare, and further integration into the global economy at the expense of local business—speaking as though the opposite was the case. It is as if we are in a parallel universe; whereas Tony Blair co-opted a red Tory approach to political economy, it is now the Conservatives co-opting the Labour Party's position in support of working-class rights. We would be foolish to accept any of it, but it is interesting nonetheless, and it provides a further indication of how our traditional social and political cleavages are making increasingly less sense.

Two contradictory consequences of this blurring of right/left-wing rhetoric and economic policy have been a retrenchment into traditional ideological divides (see Momentum in the UK, Bernie Sanders and the increasingly robust partisan divisions in the USA) and not knowing where to turn for answers. In some cases, these forces coincide, which explains why people vote for parties that do not reflect their economic and political interests but claim to reflect their values.[2] The political success of Donald Trump and of the Leave campaign are also further signs that, in political economic terms at least, many of the answers have come to sound remarkably similar, thus encouraging a desire for anything that appears different. The similarities revolve around the promise of capitalist expansion to provide for rising GDPs and living standards.

The Bretton Woods system, established in 1944 with the creation of the International Monetary Fund and the World Bank, is sometimes used as a blanket term to refer to the neoliberal economic order of laissez-faire capitalism. This particular brand of unfettered capitalism became increasingly influential after President Nixon severed the remaining ties that the US economy had with the Gold Standard in 1971. This decision to allow a free-floating currency was the end of the Bretton Woods system, as central to Bretton Woods was maintaining pegged exchange rates. In any case, the search for answers to declining living standards, worse job prospects and an increasing concentration of wealth tend to fall back on the economic success experienced by the Baby Boomer generation (provided they were lucky enough to have been born in the right country). However, their choices are starting to come back to haunt them and their children.[3]

We live in a time when children are likely to be worse off than their parents. I cannot even imagine what it must be like to want to study at university when doing so runs the risk of bankruptcy and where the jobs available will barely cover the loan payments. If you can even get a good job. Saving up for the future? Forget about it. Looking forward to a possible retirement and good pension? Sorry, out of luck. But it is not just education, or job prospects, it is the destruction of entire social communities because of a political economy that has protected the interests of the rich at the expense of pretty much everyone else.

In the north-east of England, every year in Durham there is a large public celebration in July. On July 9 2016, it was the 132nd of these Miners' Galas. The event is massive. A huge local celebration of mining culture. Jeremy Corbyn came to speak in 2016. But the entire event is decidedly bizarre. The mines have not been open in Durham for years. The entire industry is gone. There are no miners left, at least no active ones because there are no mines left. Yet they have children dress up in miners' gear, as part of some kind of nostalgic romanticization of a time long since past and of very gruelling jobs. Nevertheless, there remains in the area a very strong association with this past, one that continues to speak to people's sense of identification. They locate themselves in a time that no longer exists, in professions that will not return.

I have to ask, how is this healthy? It is not, because the entire narrative is completely backwards looking, searching for a seemingly simpler time (regardless of whether or not the memories of this time are accurate reflections). However, the left, as evident with Jeremy Corbyn, seem to think that the only way to confront a neoliberal political economy is to think as though we are back in the 1930s, as if back then the state could stand up against big business in protection of the workers. In a sense, it did under the hallmark of National Socialism. It was also this decade that gave us the infamous Ford Hunger March, which resulted in the Ford Motor Corporation hiring armed guards who ended up shooting unemployed protestors. The event was important in the unionization of the American automobile industry, but people died. The ascent of National Socialism to power, which occurred on January 30 1933, and the Ford Hunger March of March 7 1932 were separated by less than a year.

The point I am trying to make here is that it is not clear what kind of politics can help us in this Brexit-Trump-post-truth world. The adjective "post-truth" was proclaimed by Oxford Dictionaries as the word of the year in 2016. Their definition of post-truth is:

> Relating to or denoting circumstances in which objective facts are less influential in shaping public opinion than appeals to emotion and personal belief:
> "In this era of post-truth politics, it's easy to cherry-pick data and come to whatever conclusion you desire."
> "Some commentators have observed that we are living in a post-truth age".[4]

This post-truth turn has since become the foundation upon which right-wing populist movements have flourished (including the alt-right, one of the shortlisted Oxford Dictionaries words of the year in 2016), in which fake news is accepted unproblematically, and where news stories are treated as ideological talking points instead of sound reporting.

Especially disturbing is that some of those who enabled precisely this post-truth phenomenon to take hold are now bemoaning the results. Note for example Glen Beck's *mea culpa* in *The Atlantic*[5] and a related former right-wing radio talk show host, Charles Sykes, who wrote in an op-ed in the *New York Times*:

> For years, we ignored the birthers, the racists, the truthers and other conspiracy theorists who indulged fantasies of Mr. Obama's secret Muslim plot to subvert Christendom, or who peddled baseless tales of Mrs. Clinton's murder victims. Rather than confront the purveyors of such disinformation, we changed the channel because, after all, they were our allies, whose quirks could be allowed or at least ignored.
>
> We destroyed our own immunity to fake news, while empowering the worst and most reckless voices on the right.
>
> This was not mere naïveté. It was also a moral failure, one that now lies at the heart of the conservative movement even in its moment of apparent electoral triumph. Now that the election is over, don't expect any profiles in courage from the Republican Party pushing back against those trends; the gravitational pull of our binary politics is too strong.
>
> I'm only glad I'm not going to be a part of it anymore.[6]

Especially interesting is Sykes's coming to the conclusion of the dangers of the dichotomous world that American politics inhabits.

> What they *did* buy into was the argument that this was a "binary choice."
>
> In this binary tribal world, where everything is at stake, everything is in play, there is no room for quibbles about character, or truth, or principles. If everything—the Supreme Court, the fate of Western civilization, the survival of the planet—depends on tribal victory, then neither individuals nor ideas can be determinative. I watched this play out in real time, as conservatives who fully understood the threat that Mr. Trump posed succumbed to the argument about the Supreme Court. As even Mr. Ryan discovered, neutrality was not acceptable; if you were not for Mr. Trump, then you were for Mrs. Clinton.[7]

This binary condition of and for politics, the dangers of which I have highlighted in previous chapters, is very unhealthy when it becomes the condition in which all political decisions end up being made. In such a condition, politics becomes a zero-sum game where there can be no compromise. Compromise is not part of politics in this worldview, it is the equivalent of losing.

Most of the public discussions on this point seem to focus—at least as far as I can tell—on the problem of being unable to discern "real" from "fake" news. Even Sykes gets in on this problem. But this focus is to miss the point that in the current state there is no way to overcome this problem unless we can foster greater responsibility on the part of our politicians and the media not to peddle falsehoods. However, the professional gains for those who rely on "truthiness" are too great to ignore—it brought them into the White House. Moreover, what such a critique fails to take seriously is that, as Welch points out,[8] it makes no difference because the facts simply no longer matter, as facts are understood as inherently corruptible. What we need is a different form of providing and producing knowledge about politics in which we are able to make sense out of empirical phenomena, but which has a greater methodological arsenal by which to fight against those who refuse to accept the significance of recognizable forms of knowledge production (i.e. knowledge that counts as knowledge and not opinion or superstition).

The great irony here is that while Sokal may have had the point right in his critique, he got the target wrong. It is in fact within the post-structural or post-modern turn that we can find precisely such a methodological approach. I would rather describe this turn as interpretive or post-Heideggerian, but in any case, underlying much work in so-called post-modern or post-structural social and political thought is precisely the significance of ethics, and of the relationship between the human condition and normative value. The meanings that people give to the world are incredibly important. However, meaning cannot be divorced from ethics. The assumption that a focus on human-driven meaning leads to moral relativism is misguided.

There are two errors in this assumption. The first is that it ignores the reflexive paradox. This is what Welch describes as when "out of the development of a condition emerges its contrary."[9] In one sense this is a recasting of Marx's critique that within capitalism rest the seeds of its own destruction, but the crucial difference is that whereas with Marx the change is a radical break from the past, in Welch's account the change remains part of the existing system. The paradox is that the contrary emerges within the system and does not overthrow it. There is no paradigm shift, no revolution.

The political theorist and student of Martin Heidegger, Hans Jonas, a German Jew who lived through some of the most traumatic events of the twentieth century, made a similar observation with regard to the dangers of modern nihilism. As Richard Wolin writes about Jonas's political thought:

> In direct response to the agonizing historical catastrophes that Jonas had witnessed firsthand—the rise of Nazism, two world wars, and the Holocaust—he set himself an enormous intellectual task: to uncover the philosophical origins of the crisis of Western civilization, and thereby to suggest, however tentatively, a new, positive orientation for humanity.[10]

Jonas's account of political responsibility, which I will return to shortly, can be read as one part of his response to this challenge. But another point of interest is in his diagnosis of nihilism, which bears a striking resemblance to the methodological conditions out of which contemporary "truthiness" emerges. As Wolin explains, for Jonas, "Modern nihilism was preponderantly an outgrowth of modern science. Science had been so successful in challenging and unmasking every variety of superstitions and ungrounded belief that, in the end, it left men and women with nothing left in which to believe."[11] This same logical paradox provides the foundation for the unmitigated and relentless questioning of evidence on the part of the populist right so that evidence no longer matters. Since the method of science is about constant questioning or challenging of pre-existing knowledge, it follows that all knowledge is subject to doubt and no knowledge is unassailable.

All one has to do is wait for another scientist to come around to question the existing knowledge. This kind of scepticism misunderstands how the scientific method functions, confusing the testing of hypothesis with what is gained from the conducting of experiments—a distinction clearly elaborated on in Robert M. Pirsig's 1974 classic, *Zen and the Art of Motorcycle Maintenance.*[12] In this text, Pirsig also notes how science undermines itself almost necessarily:

> The more you look, the more you see. Instead of selecting one truth from a multitude you are *increasing the multitude.* What this means logically is that as you try to move toward unchanging truth through the application of scientific method, you actually do not move toward it at all. You move *away* from it.[13]

As science seeks to improve our knowledge of the world, constantly edging us closer to truth although never arriving there, it produces new knowledge, undermining old forms in the process. The speed of this change increases in proportion to scientific activity. The more research there is, the shorter the lifespan of scientific discovery. The culmination of this process is the implication of science's inability to move closer to the truths that it seeks. The concern expressed here is remarkably similar to that of Jonas's where, in his work on political responsibility, he confronts directly the ethical challenge of what happens when scientific knowledge outstrips its ability to manage such knowledge, of when through scientific achievement we develop the tools to destroy human life. The more knowledge of the world science provides, the greater our abilities to undermine and destroy this same world.

The combination of induction and deduction in science and of the many different ways through which knowledge is produced in the scientific method, all of which led to Feyerabend's controversial conclusion that within science "anything goes,"[14] does not mean that there can be no knowledge claims. However, that the logic of science is unable to prevent the inference that ongoing questioning of its conclusions can undermine scientific knowledge, and that science is not always able to provide the guidance necessary to deal with the knowledge it produces are, as Jonas correctly notes, dangerous problems. There is, admittedly, nothing here that is new. This kind of epistemological concern is as old as philosophy itself, made most famous in the post-Cartesian philosophical project of trying to identify secure knowledge that cannot be undermined: *cogito ergo sum* (I think, therefore, I am). Yet what Jonas is getting at, which may be just as important now as it was then, is that it is a mistake to presume that within science we can resolve this problem. Science cannot do everything, and the more we try to emphasize the merits of scientific knowledge, the more we undermine such claims. The solution is not there to be found. In this sense, the lesson from the philosopher of science, Paul Feyerabend, is not that there is no such thing as a single unifying scientific method, it is that because there can be no single method that defines science, it is hubris to presume that science is able to defend itself.

The second error is that if we judge morality as though there exist clear rules for what is right or wrong, just or unjust, then anything that does not stack up to these rules is morally problematic. We can argue that morality is not grounded in universal rules but in culture. But if morality is culturally distinct, how are we to judge when cultures act in immoral ways? How can we argue against slavery, or for that matter genocide? The actions of any cultural group need to be judged by the norms of that culture, and thus whatever they do is necessarily ethical since they are doing it. If ethics is culturally determined, it is relative. At least, that is the argument that Sokal and many others assume (or something like it).

However, there is another argument which is that ethics rarely follow universal rules, that the search for a universal law of morality is a legacy of theologically driven arguments for how societies are to be governed and how people ought to govern themselves. Instead, ethics are bound up in how we act on the meanings that shape our understanding of the world, and because we cannot avoid contact with other people and other ideas, our morals need to take into account that there are alternatives to our own preconceived ideas. Ethics, as such, needs to be concerned not only with extreme events like war or genocide, but also with the everyday encounters of life. These encounters involve negotiations with different or competing meanings.

In this sense the idea of relative versus objective standards for ethics is misleading. There are, or there can be, certain types of moral rules that are close to universal, such as moral arguments against killing, but even these can be found to be mitigated in cases of self-defence. Rather, the real question for ethics is about our ability to engage in negotiations with others according to a shared ability to encounter and communicate the world. It is not, however, that communication necessarily drives our ethical possibilities (this is Habermas's argument), but rather that we are able to encounter the world, a world made up of other people. This encountering involves our giving meaning to these encounters, our ability to interpret how others understand these same encounters and may have their own meanings or interpretations, and our constant ability to interpret each other's interpretations. This circularity of communication and meaning is what is often called the hermeneutic circle, and it is an important part of what characterizes our identity as human beings. It is also very important if we are to identify a form of politics that can respond to a post-truth world.

In this final chapter I build on the previous discussions about methodology and politics and suggest that there are ways to locate politics when we focus less on facts and more on interpretation and narrative, and on how we think about power and politics. The point here is not to dismiss empirical research as irrelevant for politics. To be sure, it remains important to identify levels of inequality, for example, and this is clearly an empirical question. But the following is sceptical of the methodological idea that we can take the methods of descriptive empirical analysis and use them to explain causal relations. Once we do this, regardless of whether there are relations between variables, we dismiss the seriousness of our narratives, and instead treat humans as empty vessels to be coded, and meaning as variables to be controlled. There is a very fundamental difference between being able to study the laws of nature and the socially constructed and continuously interpreted rules or norms of social and political conduct. If we are to respond to a politics where facts appear not to matter we need to: (1) reduce the extent to which we keep falling back on facts and thus slow down the drive for constantly discovering new facts as though only with a specific kind of evidence can we develop policy; and (2) start to seriously listen to the philosophy from precisely those who were on the "other side" of the science wars, those who are concerned with context, meaning, interpretation, and intersubjectivity. In philosophy this turn has its modern start in hermeneutic phenomenology, and that is where we need to begin. The chapter ends by arguing for the importance of political responsibility and of how by recasting and re-emphasising the politics of responsibility in an intersubjective world it becomes possible to address the current failures of our political leaders and political systems.

Interpretation and responsibility

There are some good reasons why hermeneutics and phenomenology have not found a clear path into political theory, but the main one is no doubt Martin Heidegger, one of the most controversial philosophers of the twentieth century. The case of Heidegger is a very long and contentious topic which largely revolves around his affiliation with the Nazis, and the relationship between his philosophy and National Socialism,[15] combined with his significant philosophical impact. Heidegger's influence is evident in the works of both Charles Taylor and Sheldon Wolin. More generally, Heidegger's influence is hard to underestimate, cutting across Sociology (Anthony Giddens), Anthropology (Clifford Geertz), and Cultural Studies (Fredric Jameson). In the continental tradition, Heidegger is especially important for the work of Jacques Derrida, Michel Foucault, Pierre Bourdieu, Jürgen Habermas, Hans-Georg Gadamer, and Maurice Merleau-Ponty, and in the case of Emmanuel Levinas we find an approach to philosophy directly opposed to Heidegger. William Blattner writes that "*Being and Time* was published in 1927 and rapidly became one of the most

significant and controversial philosophical texts of the twen-
tieth century."[16] Charles B. Guignon similarly writes how,
"As the twenty-first century begins, it is clear that Heidegger
will stand out as one of the greatest philosophers of our
times. His writings have had an immense impact not only in
Europe and the English-speaking world but in Asia as well."[17]
Intriguingly, due to his mention of management consultants,
Hubert Dreyfus notes how, "At an international conference
in Berkeley commemorating the hundredth anniversary of
Heidegger's birth, not only philosophers but also doctors,
nurses, psychotherapist, theologians, management consultants,
educators, lawyers, and computer scientists took part in a
discussion of the way Heidegger's thought had affected their
work."[18] It is not sensible to imagine contemporary philosophy
without the influence of Heidegger.

Heidegger was not the first to write about phenomenology,
but unsurprisingly, since much of *Being and Time* is a dramatic
critique of Western philosophy and involves him providing new
definitions for multiple terms, he offers his own definition of it.
Phenomenology is not about explaining people's experiences
of the world. It is about uncovering the structures through
which we experience and inhabit the world. In addition, as he
writes, "The expression 'phenomenology' signifies primarily a
methodological conception. This expression does not characterize
the what of the objects of philosophical research as subject-
matter, but rather the *how* of that research."[19] For Heidegger,
what phenomenology does is provide a methodology for being
able to uncover not just things themselves, but phenomena
that are hidden yet are fundamental to our being:

> Manifestly, [phenomenon] is something that proximally and for
> the most part does *not* show itself at all: it is something that
> lies *hidden*, in contrast to that which proximally and for the
> most part does show itself; but at the same time it is something
> that belongs to what thus shows itself, and it belongs to it so
> essentially as to constitute its meaning and its ground.[20]

Phenomenology is thus concerned with ontology. However,
as explained in an introductory overview of *Being and Time*,

"Traditional ontology ... has misconstrued our being as human beings by assuming that we share the same *mode of being* as other entities we encounter within the world, such as tables, rocks, dogs, atoms, or numbers."[21] Why this matters is because, as Dreyfus writes, "In Heidegger's hands, phenomenology becomes a way of letting something shared that can never be totally articulated and for which there can be no indubitable evidence show itself."[22] In short, the ontology of humans is fundamentally different from that of other things. Humans are not a substance with minds, and there can be no external category of being human in which this being is independent of the world in which it exists. For Heidegger, we share in the world and are always a part of that world. However, central to our being-in-the-world is hiddenness. "The subject of phenomenology," Dreyfus writes, "must be something that does not show itself but can be made to show itself."[23]

The main, indeed the essential and necessary, example of this something is *being*, *Dasein*, the "*Being* of entities" which, "is something that belongs to what thus shows itself, and it belongs to it so essentially as to constitute its meaning and its ground."[24] Consequently, "phenomenology is the science of the being of entities—ontology."[25] This science is interpretive and, consequently, is hermeneutical. The reason is because at issue is not the existence of being, but rather the meaning of being: "The phenomenology of Dasein is a *hermeneutic*."[26] As Dreyfus writes, "For Heidegger, hermeneutics begins at home in an interpretation of the structure of everydayness in which Dasein dwells."[27] These structures are represented in the various for-the-sake-of-which, in-order-to, and towards-which that characterize our being-in-the-world. Heidegger's hermeneutic phenomenology is about revealing the daily structures of the world that we inevitably and necessarily engage with, but rarely think about. What concerns phenomenology is "on the basis of which entities are already understood."[28]

There is, consequently, an unavoidable circularity to this kind of analysis, which Dreyfus describes as a "hermeneutics of everydayness."[29] This circularity follows the inevitability of the hermeneutic circle, but Heidegger provides a more

fundamental definition of this circle than the one we have
already provided. As I have explained previously, with Taylor
the circle is about how any interpretation in turn relies on its
ability to be communicated and for this communication there
needs to exist a shared language. Anthony Giddens similarly
describes this circle as the interpretation of interpretations.
Heidegger, however, makes a more fundamental claim by
arguing that we can only interpret that which we are already
a part of. What this ultimately means is that there is a potentially
never-ending series of contexts in which any interpretation
can take place: identity, geography, gender, age, profession,
task, etc. Moreover, this kind of phenomenology assigns
great significance to the everyday knowledge of coping or of
managing/being able to get by in the world. This is the kind of
practical knowledge that is rarely taught, but which we need
to have. One of the examples that Dreyfus uses of this type of
knowledge is the spatial proximity that people are comfortable
with when speaking with someone else.[30] It is not as if we are
taught to stand a particular distance from another person, we
just pick it up—or at least, most of us do—and this distance
can vary between cultures. There are, consequently, contexts
within contexts, and a type of knowledge that is not formally
learned.

It is tempting to see this circularity of never-ending contexts
as inherently inconclusive if not relativist to the point of
meaninglessness. However, as Blattner points out:

> Circularity is not necessarily a problem, because ontology
> proceeds hermeneutically and hermeneutics is essentially circular
> in method. ... Just as in reading a book we move back and
> forth between an understanding of the part of the book we
> are reading and our understanding of the whole book, so in
> doing ontology we move back and forth between articulating
> some specific mode of being and our vision of the whole field
> of being.[31]

Heidegger is not concerned about the circularity, but rather
that we approach it correctly: "What is decisive is not to get
out of the circle but to come at it in the right way. This circle

of understanding is not an orbit in which any random kind of knowledge may move; it is the expression of the existential *fore-structure* of Dasein itself."[32]

For Heidegger, the basic verb of human being is understanding—this is the basic thing that we do—and understanding is to see something as referring to something else and this is how meaning is produced. We are never faced with objects that are empty or bare of meaning, that are inherently meaningless, and this means that we do not encounter empty vessels and then fill them with meaning. We encounter the meaning. The hermeneutic circle is an expression that refers to how, in order to understand anything, we already have to have some kind of understanding. Understanding, in this sense, is circular. The question, consequently, is not about the existence of the circle but how we enter into the circle. Entering into the hermeneutic circle is how we encounter meaning. The basic mechanism that is the basis for the entire system of meaning is that we are self-referential. We do not just exist, existence is already being concerned with our being. We care about our being and because we are busy caring about our being we generate a world in which our being makes sense, which gets us back to our encounter with meaning.[33]

Accepting the circle is important because it is part of what differentiates this methodology from any methodology where there have to be clear entry and exit points that determine what is studied from the contexts in which it is studied, or which provide stationary reference points. Hence Heidegger's insistence that "Any interpretation which is to contribute understanding, must already have understood what is to be interpreted."[34] It is in this discussion that Heidegger gives the natural sciences their own place, and acknowledges their contributions to knowledge. This does not mean that the natural sciences are "more rigorous"[35] but instead that the science of interpretation is inherently of a different type. In short, they have their own methodologies, their own questions and the methodology of hermeneutic phenomenology is fundamentally of a different order.[36] This difference is, in part, defined by the hermeneutic circle.

The hermeneutic circle, however, can be difficult to grasp in normative terms, especially when we consider Heidegger's own politics. The potential relativism, if not outright ugliness, of his own political choices makes it inherently difficult to take his methodology and claim it has normative potential in a good way. This rejection of Heidegger can be quite persuasive when we take into account his Nazi past. In this regard Habermas's concern with Heidegger is with the potential absence of any moral perspective within his ontology, arguing that such absence is fatal.[37] That fatality is because Heidegger's own politics suggest a moral vacuum that is ostensibly consistent with Heidegger's philosophy. In this regard, there have been attempts to isolate Heidegger's own politics from his philosophy. Yet this is hard to do when Heidegger provides evidence of his own inhumanity.[38] Even philosophers heavily engaged with Heidegger—indeed, indebted to him—like Hubert Dreyfus are damning critics of his political thought. Instead of a potential relativism or nihilism, Dreyfus argues that the danger in Heidegger is fundamentally different and potentially even worse:

> Heidegger's *philosophy* ... is dangerous because it seeks to convince us that only a god—a charismatic figure or some other culturally renewing event—can save us from falling into contented nihilism. It exposes us to the risk of committing ourselves to some demonic event or movement that promises renewal.[39]

However, Dreyfus makes the important point that even within Heidegger we find the warning that "any guidelines must always be interpreted."[40] This is an important point because although it does not excuse Heidegger, it does provide a point in defence of his methodology of interpretation. There is always another interpretation.

However, just because there is always the possibility of another interpretation does not mean that all knowledge is either relative or universally fixed. This choice only works if we accept these as the only options that exist, and they do rely on each other. Taking one option necessarily requires rejecting the other. It is not that one choice is better, it is that the other one is worse. Thus, the idea that only a fixed moral argument can provide normative guidance is just as problematic as Heidegger's philosophy may be to politics. The connection between Enlightenment rationality and the Holocaust should, if nothing else, give us pause before we decide to celebrate the Enlightenment ideal of universal rationality as underlying morality.[41] It is, for example, worth recalling John Stuart Mill's writings about international relations, when he, one of the foremost philosophers of liberty, writes that

> There is a great difference (for example) between the case in which the nations concerned are of the same, or something like the same, degree of civilization, and that in which one of the parties to the situation is of a high, and the other of a very low, grade of social improvement. To suppose that the same rules of international morality can obtain between one civilized nation and another, and between civilized nations and barbarians, is a grave error .... [The] rules of ordinary international morality imply reciprocity. But barbarians will not reciprocate. They cannot be depended on for observing any rules. Their minds are not capable of so great an effort, nor their will sufficiently under the influence of distant motives.[42]

Mill, who is otherwise known for his writings on liberty and women's rights, nevertheless still found it within his enlightenment rationality to include such discrimination. There is a bit of irony in the liberal philosophers arguing against post-Heideggerian thought because of its normative problems, when the Enlightenment liberal tradition is by no means innocent.

The idea of universal morality is, however, appealing because it ostensibly avoids the problems of moral relativism (Mill, in this sense, can be accused of not following through his own logical assumptions, although this raises the question of how strong the idea of universal reason is in the first place). Universal rational moral principles can be useful to moral philosophers, and of course they can inform our legal systems, but they are rarely practically applied in our daily lives. They imagine a world in which our interpretations about normative issues can be framed in the certainty of principles. Even our legal discourses are subject to interpretation, so, for example, in international law deliberation is required in order to decide if a military response is proportionate or discriminate. The idea that a moral rule can provide the solution to Heidegger is easily questioned when, in the case of Eichmann, we have a human being of clear intelligence who understood Kant's categorical imperative (in a general way) and yet still saw nothing wrong with his actions.[43] This situation is not so much about cognitive dissonance, it is that people can and do interpret rules, norms, and situations in a variety of ways. In other words, Heidegger may not provide us with a moral or political philosophy,[44] but he does provide an ontological argument that is clearly relevant to people's experiences of being, and in this regard his hermeneutic phenomenology is relevant to politics.

The argument against post-Heideggerian political thought is that it is somehow nihilist or worse. Yet, even if we claim that only with a clear foundational moral rule can we be sure of avoiding the dangers that Heidegger himself succumbed to in his Nazism, we still risk the potential dangers of relativism. Enlightenment morality has not been without its own dangers that seem relativist. For example, Locke's political thought was fundamental to the worldview that led to the genocide of First Nations in North America, thus placing two different value systems in conflict. The internal logic of the way in which the First Nations were treated worked against them and imposed a relativist programme by way of a legal discourse of sovereignty that forced the indigenous population to play by the rules of a game that they could not win.[45] Even *the* philosopher of the Enlightenment, Immanuel Kant, held racist views,[46] contrary to what one might think from his categorical imperative. The idea that we have a choice between a rule-bound moral code or relativism is a false dichotomy.

Humans regularly contest unjust rules and vary their moral behaviour in different circumstances. Sometimes we get it right, sometimes not. But the errors cannot be attributed to moral relativism. One of Heidegger's most famous students, Hannah

Arendt, was on to something very important when she wrote that the only convincing argument against murder is that "I would not want to live in the presence of a murderer."[47] It is how we live with our moral acts that matters just as much as anything else, if not more so. Our condition is interpretive, and since we cannot escape from this condition, and our condition also involves a life among others in political communities, it seems perfectly sensible to embrace it in how we think about politics.

To understand how we can develop this normative methodology we need to appreciate more fully what exactly *das Man* refers to and why it is possible to view this from a normative perspective. Hubert Dreyfus provides such an overview in his explanation of why there can exist a value statement within an (existential) analysis of *das Man*, which Dreyfus translates as "The One" and which refers generally to the contexts in our world that require our conformity in order to function. As he writes:

> According to Heidegger, our trouble begins with Socrates' and Plato's claim that true moral knowledge, like scientific knowledge, must be explicit and disinterested. Heidegger questions both the possibility and the desirability of making our everyday understanding totally explicit. He introduces the idea that the shared everyday skills, concerns, and practices into which we are socialised provide the conditions necessary for people to make sense of the world and of their lives. All intelligibility presupposes something that cannot be fully articulated—a kind of knowing-how rather than a knowing-that. At the deepest level such knowing is embodied in our social skills rather than our concepts, beliefs, and values. Heidegger argues that our cultural practices can direct our activities and make our lives meaningful only insofar as they are and stay unarticulated, that, as long as they stay the soil out of which we live.[48]

Heidegger then argues that the shared practices "into which we are socialised ... provide a background understanding of what matters and what it makes sense to do, on the basis of which we can direct our actions."[49] This condition of being is described by Heidegger as "the clearing."[50] The claim is that we learn what matters to/for us within the cultural and social world in which we live.

Heidegger, of course, does not say what specifically should matter for us. However, I am not as interested in what Heidegger himself thought as I am in how this argument clearly suggests that our sociability is itself a normative condition. To take an extreme but important example, we do not need an objective moral argument to be able to argue why the Holocaust was wrong. Indeed, if we require a rule of some kind to tell us why genocide is wrong, I would say as human beings we are unable to interpret our world in any coherent normative way.

Such extreme examples, however, are of limited used. As Peter Novick writes, "Lessons for dealing with the sorts of issues that confront us in ordinary life, public or private, are not likely to be found in this [the Holocaust] most extraordinary of events."[51] Normative arguments need to make sense with regard to day-to-day issues, to our daily being-in-the-world. The search for a normative principle of universal validity would need to be so broad as to be potentially vacuous, or so narrow as to be effectively useless. The philosophical attempt to provide the answer in the universal logic of rationality runs up against the same problems. It might provide a philosophical foundation for moral thinking, but it is not especially helpful in having to make sense of our day-to-day moral and political choices. Moreover, the empty content of rationality does nothing to insulate it from violence against others who might not share in the same epistemological worldview (recall Mill's racism and the treatment of the First Nations peoples in North America).

When we find ourselves faced with an injustice, as human beings we are able to respond to such situations as moral creatures because of our abilities for interpretation. In this sense, moral interpretations form part of our being. Our moral norms can and do change, and these changes can be reflected in our laws. However, our laws can change in normative ways for reasons that are not based on morality but on ontology. This is one of Michel Foucault's great insights as he demonstrates how the way we punish criminals is not so much a consequence of moral progress but rather of a different way of understanding human beings so that certain forms of punishment do not make sense any more.[52]

We can find the same process in regard to ancient China and the use of technology in war. The strategic studies scholar Christopher Coker makes this point in his discussion about the ways that technological developments impact how we fight wars. The discovery of gunpowder completely changed how the West fought its wars, abandoning the previous projectile weapons in favour of firearms because it was easier, faster, and less expensive to produce a fighting force using firearms than one relying on the longbow.[53] Instrumental reason was the cause of change, and not necessarily the efficiency or effectiveness of the new technology. Yet "The invention of gunpowder did not lead to any revaluation of the Chinese way of war, even though by the mid-ninth century C.E. Taoist alchemical philosophers were the only ones in the world to have discovered the recipe for gunpowder."[54] The point to take away from this is that there can be a variety of reasons why we change how we do things, which can have long-term political and normative consequences but which may not start with anything explicitly normative in the first place. It is a mistake to view the changes we make socially or politically as though they necessarily contribute to some form of moral progress. Rather, our social and political decisions are largely the product of our ability to interpret the meanings of that which we come into contact with. It is, in this sense, interpretation that provides the starting point for subsequent normative enquiry. Or, to put this another way, the process of interpretation is itself necessarily normative.

What remains unclear is that if everything comes down to interpretation, in what way can we deploy normative arguments? The answer has to do with how we enter into the hermeneutic circle.

Deciphering which entry to use is, in some ways, easier said than done. What does it mean to enter into an interpretive understanding? "Understanding is," as Mark Wrathall writes, "to be in the world in such a way that everything is projected upon, that is, makes sense in terms of particular possibilities. Projecting is not necessarily a cognitive act but a stance or orientation to things around us."[55] What this means is that understanding (or thinking in Arendtian terms) is not "a discrete type of activity" but is instead "a structure present in all meaningful activity."[56] Philosophy has traditionally treated thinking as a discrete activity, whereas in Heidegger's hermeneutic phenomenology it is not something separate to our being, but part of the structure of being itself. This means that we are already within the hermeneutic circle. Searching for the entry point only makes sense if we presume that we are outside, looking to get in. In Wrathall's pragmatist interpretation of Heidegger, understanding is "the structure that makes all human activities *activities* as opposed to mere movements or events."[57] Wrathall's argument is a response to Dreyfus's classification of different types of understanding in *Being and Time*.[58] Learning from Taylor, Wrathall, and Dreyfus, we can now provide an example of how to employ hermeneutic phenomenology for political theory.

I will use an example borrowed from Wrathall, where he turns to baseball to explain the structure of projection. Baseball provides a situation in which there are norms and rules which have been created by people and which constitute the structure of the game. These rules and norms enable us to understand—to project—what a baseball bat is for, how it is intended to be used (and not used). Our projection of the bat also involves (indeed, requires) other projections that go along with the bat, which pertain to bases, pitcher, different types of pitches, swings, etc.[59] Along with these projections, the rules and norms of the game involve behaviours (not all of which are pleasant, such as tobacco chewing and spitting) and provide the basis for what is acceptable (behaviour) and what is possible (why a foul ball hit out of bounds is not a home run). Baseball players have to conform to these norms and rules in order to play, but they can also improvise.

Accepting that there are certain rules in the game is a consequence of also accepting that there is an authority that has provided these rules. Havercroft makes this point, and goes on to ask, "If the idea of a ball player disputing a call on the grounds that there is no such thing as a strike zone seems absurd to you, you are right. Why does a sceptical challenge make no sense in this context, yet seem so threatening when raised by a modern epistemologist such as Descartes or Hume?"[60] Havercroft answers: "If, as a baseball player, I reject the authority of Major League Baseball to create something called a strike zone, all that I have rejected is the ability to play baseball. But philosophical cases of challenging criteria appear so threatening because they challenge (epistemic, ethical, and religious) knowledge as such."[61] The relevance of this critique is that Havercroft is pointing out that in the tradition of modern Western philosophy, there has been a concerted effort to find external rules or criteria upon which to base our knowledge, but that this search is based on a profound misunderstanding. "The reason the skeptical argument appears to be so powerful and as such appears to require refuting is that it tricks us into believing that our language is founded upon reference to external objects."[62] The thing is that debating whether or not there is an external world or whether or not there is knowledge is precisely the kind of sceptical philosophy that adopts the conditions in which truthiness becomes possible, because there can always be doubt.

Doubt is baked into the very epistemological basis of most Western thought and, as Havercroft argues, provides the argument for why sovereignty is needed (it provides the solution, or rather, the resolution to doubt in its role as supreme authority as a guarantor of certainty).[63] Instead, it makes more sense to look at context, hence the importance of our ability to improvise, because we are thrown into a situation, learn the rules but are also able to interpret them and thus modify or manipulate them, provided that the general idea of the rule is not broken. In baseball, although there is an authority and there are rules, our knowledge of how to play the game (or even the ability to play) does not depend on this authority. We are able to interpret the rules for ourselves, while already being within the world of these rules. The rules limit the number of players on a team and on the diamond at any given time. However, in principle anybody can play baseball. All they need is some gear, some people to play with, and a place to play. We know that there are strike zones, but we can push them, and the zone is more flexible than the rules suggest. We can steal a base, and players can modify the location of their field positions quite extensively.

Moreover, even when there are rules that govern a set activity, there are also other contexts outside of these rules that can then have an impact on the world in which these rules pertain, such as social norms. This type of thinking is what characterizes political theory—the normative interpretation in which different worlds collide. There are normative features within baseball but there are also normative features outside of baseball that have influenced it, like segregation did. Political theory focuses on precisely these moments, when our normative values and our understandings come into conflict with other values and understandings, and it is the role of political theory to provide normative guidance for how to interpret such situations and then function within them as social or political critics. "Hermeneutic-interpretation ... is committed to a kind of holism ... that recognizes that the explanation of behaviour, ideas, beliefs, and so on requires reference to the larger complex of background practices, historical situation, and linguistic community that helps constitute and define the behaviour in question."[64] The strength of the argument will depend on its ability to be understood and to reveal normative features that otherwise lie unseen.

One of the fundamental insights in hermeneutic phenomenology is that, methodologically, it is easy to take a lot for granted. In particular, "what is taken for granted is the being of things as we first see them and the way in which we see them, such that they can be available for classification."[65] Furthermore, "When we stop using things and start to consider them as objects for analysis, and when we consider ourselves as objective analysers, we forget the worlds we take for granted, and therefore we forget our own standing in them."[66] Heidegger's *Being and Time* is largely about providing a philosophical language in which to bring forward what is forgotten and taken for granted. In this sense, Heidegger's philosophy is a radical methodological critique that constantly reminds us of just how much we have to take for granted.

As political theorists, our primary methodological currency is necessarily interpretation, but what exactly this means is easily forgotten, perhaps because it seems so obvious. Yet each of us has different ways of assessing interpretations, and judging what types of arguments are more persuasive or more insightful. The standards by which we make such judgements are methodological, but if interpretations can only take place within the context of other interpretations, then our methodological foundation is within the hermeneutic circle. It is within this circle that political theory methodology rests, and as such, we need to understand and consider our own methodological positions from within this circle. As Michael Gibbons notes:

> Typically, we compare competing claims to knowledge or competing interpretations with each other. That being the case, one test of the truth of an interpretation in human affairs is the extent to which it helps us understand or articulate the background pre-understanding that is the condition of our coping with or negotiating the world.[67]

Such interpretation is necessarily normative because "it often ends up taking a form of knowledge that is directed toward offering new understandings that also offer new ways to engage in the political life it seeks to explain."[68] Interpretation is necessarily normative, and because interpretation is central to our being, our positionality and thus reflexive awareness is also necessarily a part of our interpretive abilities. As political theorists engaged in normative critique, interpretation and the hermeneutic circle are central to the vocation. However, so too are judgements about positionality and the extent to which reflexivity is methodologically important (if who we are and what we think about who we are matters). Empirical claims, including a causal dynamic that links ideas to practice or values to judgement, also lie somewhere in the political theorist's toolbox. All of these are addressed in some fashion in hermeneutic phenomenology.

Hermeneutic phenomenology cannot tell us what to think, in the sense that it does not provide us with clear normative rules or syllogisms by which to develop moral position. However, it does not suggest that the absence of such heuristic tools necessarily requires that we treat everything as relative. Far from it. However, the path from hermeneutic phenomenology to political theory is not as clear as one might like. Indeed, it is noteworthy that Arendt does not use Heideggerian terminology in her political theory, even though it is hard to dismiss his influence. Similarly, Hans Jonas in his most political text, *The Imperative of Responsibility*, does not mention Heidegger—which is curious, considering that the text can be read as a rebuke of Heidegger insofar as Jonas appears to take our existence as beings, and transform this into an ought for our responsibility for our future being. Be that as it may, once we start to appreciate the significance that meaning and interpretation play in our encounter with the world, it follows that our understanding of politics itself has to change to take into account the intersubjective character of this world. In this sense, much could be said, but what I will focus on is how power and responsibility feature as core elements of politics.

Finding politics

So far I have tried to frame the Brexit and Trump results as a consequence of a series of failures. These have been a failure of politics in multiple senses: the failure of understanding the grounds and thus legitimacy of modern politics; the failure of political practice in its being overwhelmed by the logic of global capital; the inability of the state and its political institutions to manage the forces of global capital for the benefit of the majority of society, thus encouraging a further distancing and alienation from politics; and the failure of acknowledging a close relationship between methodology and politics. These various failures have demonstrated themselves not just in the narrow electoral success of the Leave vote in the UK and the

electoral college majority of Trump, but also in the ways that
the politics of identity have come to frame both these electoral
victories and the responses to them. I have also pointed out
mistakes that political theory makes in regard to its framing of
some of the core philosophical matters of relevance to these
two political events, including how we imagine the foundational
conditions for politics, debate about method and methodology,
and their significance for politics and identity politics. It may
seem that this argument is, consequently, inherently negative
without offering a positive account of where to find politics.
It is to this that I now turn.

I remember attending a Board of Education meeting when I
was a teenager. I cannot remember exactly why I was there but
there was some specific reason why a friend and I had gone.
But when this reason presented itself, we did not speak up. I
was under the impression that just being there was enough.
We were mistaken. From this vague memory all I recall is
that I should have followed my instinct to speak. But my
friend, who had much more political experience than I did
persuaded me not to. He was very good at political persuasion,
always able to wield some fact or statistic or story to provide
evidence on which to accept his interpretation of events or
his strategic choices. He was (and no doubt remains) a very
smart individual with an excellent grasp of politics. I learned
from him that there was great political power in being able to
wield facts and knowledge for political gain: if you have the
evidence, the argument is hard to challenge, because to do so
requires either having more knowledge of the same evidence
or knowledge of other superior evidence.

This was not a technique, however, that I agreed with, and
not because in the age before Google and the Internet it was
harder to find the much-needed evidence. The problem was that
it always seemed to me suspicious to rely on evidence as though
the evidence itself was enough, was robust and, conversely,
that the only way to argue was to contest with other evidence.
What about the normative argument for why we should hold
a particular position in the first place? The rhetorical device
of hammering away using example after example without

due methodological care, theoretical rigour, and normative reflection is a poor method.[69] There was something about this approach of relying always on data that did not sit well with me. At the time, my solution was to turn to political theory instead of more empirical political science studies. Theory, I felt (and still do) could always overwhelm facts because in using philosophy it is possible to understand why the facts themselves can be treated as containing some kind of political power. Admittedly, such philosophical knowledge does not work very well in political debates, but it did and does help me to make sense of the ways that political claims can be made, and of how knowledge itself is never value-neutral. Understanding the role of knowledge production remains, in my view, the most important part of understanding how politics functions, because without the ability to produce knowledge that has political purchase, there can be no politics.

When Arendt argues that power cannot be stored up and saved for later, like facts or statistics can, she was responding in part to this problem of approaching politics as though the accumulation of data provides a source of political power. It does not. However, the relationship between knowledge and power is better associated with Michel Foucault than with Arendt. It is to these two thinkers, both of whom challenged at around the same time the intellectual conditions of modern politics, that I will now turn, before expanding on the role of political responsibility. There are, I will suggest, three elements in finding politics. They function as a kind of continuum, mirroring the hermeneutic circle of how we, as self-interpretive beings, engage in making sense of the world. To find politics is to enter into this hermeneutic circle, but to do so in a particular way.

The relationship between knowledge and power functions in multiple ways, but across all of them is the linkage between how interpretation functions as a condition of possibility for action and interpretation. In the process of interpreting and thinking, we produce the conditions in which to engage with others on matters of mutual significance. In so doing, knowledge serves as the currency by which we evaluate each other's positions. The more knowledge we have, in a sense, the better equipped we are to engage in politics. But knowledge in this sense is not the accumulation of facts, it is the ability to think (recall Arendt's distinction between thinking and knowing) and to share the conclusions of the thinking process with others. The public manifestation of this process is in political responsibility, and we are able to make our normative judgements in this regard through our engagement with the narratives that underpin our interpretations. The three elements here are the relationship between knowledge and power, with a particular emphasis on the role of interpretation; political responsibility or the politics of responsibility; and the significance of narratives or meaning (hermeneutics).

The relationship between knowledge and power is, in one sense, fairly straightforward and can be easily grasped by anyone who has ever had to work with Robert's Rules of Order. Robert's Rules of Order may be the most infuriating procedural process ever conceived. At least, that is how it can appear to someone stuck in a meeting that follows the Rules of Order without having a close knowledge of them. Those that do are able to control the meeting to their advantage. The Rules are not brief. The 11th Edition of Robert's Rules of Order contains over 600 pages of rules.[70] They are largely for parliamentary procedure, and the significance of them is that they set out the basis upon which a parliamentary or other associated body runs its meetings and assemblies. Close knowledge of the Rules is thus incredibly powerful as it enables the use of procedures to direct, structure, and manage a discussion. Knowledge of the rules is power, and this example clearly demonstrates how knowledge itself can work as a form of power.

We can see similar examples in professional expertise, when certain types of knowledge grant specific individuals authority over others because of this knowledge, and that authority ends up being interpreted as a form of power, usually evident in the power to decide on a particular course of action. Foucault, however, adds the important facet of internal power, something that he refers to in his lecture on governmentality and in his discussion of the modern disciplinary society. In this example, the power is of self-governance, so that individuals internalize modes of conduct without having been told.[71] Power, in Foucault's work, is more complicated than that,[72] but the guiding point of immediate significance is that knowledge can function in a disciplining way, both enabling and inhibiting action.

This form of power as knowledge is, with Foucault, closely linked with politics. In *Discipline and Punish*, Foucault argues that by creating subjects who govern themselves in particular ways, individuals end up producing their subjectivity for the political system. Knowledge of the self thus serves a political role as people govern themselves in order to be governed.[73] Foucault is arguing that when we think of power as an external force that compels another agent, we are ignoring that there has to be something already present that enables such compulsion in the first place. We are not concerned here with power as a physical force, but rather with how human subjectivity and our sense of self cannot function without power. Foucault's great insight here is that power is not external to the human subject but constituent of it. It is this insight that underpins Foucault's multiple discussions of power.

With Arendt, however, power is decidedly different, as she locates power in the public sphere, famously writing that "Power corresponds to the human ability not just to act but to act in concert."[74] However, with Foucault, she is also careful in distancing political power as a practice enabled by sovereign politics, instead locating power in people. In the process, both thinkers encourage us to think about politics differently from the tradition in which politics is all about power.[75] Arendt is careful to note that power cannot be stored up and saved for later. It cannot, like bits of factual evidence, be collected and reserved to be brought out at the right time. In this sense, the type of political practices that rely on the ability to introduce the right bit of evidence at the right time might appear to be a form of power, but they are not. They are, in fact, the opposite.

The reason is that such forms of advocacy or persuasion do not rely on thinking. They rely on data dissemination and comparison of evidence. Evidence is of course very important in politics, but it needs to be understood not as politics but rather as a subsidiary of decision-making. Evidence helps us to decide what to do, but it cannot tell us why. There are other pieces of knowledge that tell us how to interpret the evidence into a normative position—this relates to what Arendt refers to as thinking, due to its necessarily abstract character. The challenge in this account of political deliberation is in identifying how this kind of politics is, in practical terms, different from the types of politics we are used to.

For starters, when we understand politics as flowing from an Arendtian account of power, there are a few important consequences. Two of them are the importance of plurality and the significance of inaction.

In the previous discussion about identity politics I suggested, in contrast to Brian Barry, that there is nothing to worry about from identity politics. However, I did not in that discussion advocate a multicultural position, although I did quote Taylor favourably at one point. The reason for this is that multiculturalism is not the direction I want to take, since it leads into the kind of debate that Barry and other critics of multiculturalism get us into. Instead, the point is to understand the significance of identity and also of politics differently.

Arendt helps us do this in a few ways. The first is her critique of the conditions in which we understand politics to function: sovereignty. Writing in her essay, "What is Freedom?," Arendt says that "if men wish to be free, it is precisely sovereignty they must overcome."[76] The political theorist Jonathan Havercroft argues, in his important book on sovereignty, that Arendt's concern with sovereignty is linked to her understanding of thinking and of human freedom. The problem, as she sees it, is that it is dangerous to identify sovereignty with freedom, which is largely what we do in modern liberal democracies. Havercroft writes that for Arendt, this association is dangerous "because it leads to only two possibilities: either the denial of political freedom, because it is impossible for each individual to be an absolute sovereignty over just themselves, or the belief that the freedom of the rulers is only possible at the expense of everyone else's freedom."[77] Arendt's critique here is partly targeted at political theorists or philosophers who, due to their cerebral occupation, ignore the public context of politics, and the fact that politics happens out in the world and not in the mind. Havercroft expresses this concern well: "Because political philosophers tend to prefer solitude and contemplation, they tend to understand freedom and power as modes of action exercised in isolation by individuals."[78] Arendt, however, "fears that this association of freedom with absolute self-sufficiency is inimical to plurality, which she argues is the very condition that makes politics possible."[79] Arendt's concerns here are multiple. First, she is deeply dissatisfied with the tradition of political thought that locates sovereignty as the condition in which politics and freedom is possible. Second, she finds the association of power with a sovereignty-based model of politics equally problematic. Third, both of these concerns find their origin in her own understanding of politics, which is tied not to the conditions of and for sovereignty, but rather in a key feature of the human condition itself: plurality. She writes, "men, not Man, live on the earth and inhabit the world."[80] This important quote is one of her most famous expressions of how the human condition on earth is one of diversity or plurality. There is simply no getting away from this, so we might as well accept it. Resistance is, one might say, futile. This acceptance, however, also means coming to terms with a very different way of thinking about politics than one rooted in sovereignty and which, in case we forget, is largely what the social contract tradition tells us: that sovereignty is the condition in which politics is possible, as outside of a sovereign order there is chaos.

Working with Arendt, however, does not mean accepting every political argument just because of the plurality of human-kind. Rather it means having to take seriously the inherent contingency of politics. When we recognize that there can be no homogeneous or uniform ontological character to the human condition, it then becomes incumbent upon us to appreciate that, as there will necessarily be a potentially infinite amount of diversity on this planet, our politics needs to correspond to this condition. Whereas the Hobbesian response to this condition is to presume that because of our universal equality this condition is necessarily violent and insecure—"solitary, poor, nasty, brutish and short"[81]—an alternative conception is to accept that with diversity come differences, and with differences come disagreement due to varying views and interpretations, but not violence. The move from disagreement to violence is a very significant leap that underpins the Hobbesian contract, and there is little reason to accept it. Instead, what is required is the acceptance that we will not always get our way, but that living in a society carries with it a range of goods that make compromises worthwhile. Politics is then best described as agonistic in the sense that it is necessarily conflictual.[82] However, of crucial importance is that we do not conflate this agonistic character of politics with violence or assume that because it is conflictual the choice open to us is all or nothing (one more reason why referendums are a bad idea). Instead, what it requires is a much clearer understanding of the character of politics, which can be understood according to the idea of political responsibility.

It is for this reason that the "Love Trumps Hate" slogan is politically ineffectual. While the slogan is clever and is helpful in bringing together a collective of protestors who find this way of defining themselves important, it ignores the fact that the people who supported Trump did not all do so because they cannot love and because they hate. To be sure, some probably do hate other people, but that misses the point. The point is in the need to change the terms of debate so that people are able to feel comfortable with their identity claims and related narratives in such a way that they become able to understand how their actions become implicated in how others experience the world. This is part of the condition of plurality: our public choices do have consequences that we are unable to witness directly. What we need is a mechanism by which it is possible to understand the role of such narratives in our political lives. It is in this regard that the matter of political responsibility becomes relevant.

There is another reason why it is a politically problematic slogan, which is that love is something that exists between individuals. It is not entirely clear how this emotion then translates into collective action. After the publication of her reporting of the Eichmann trial, which became the book *Eichmann in Jerusalem*, the philosopher and scholar of Jewish mysticism Gershom Scholem accused Arendt of being heartless and of having no love of the Jewish people. As he wrote, "In the Jewish tradition there is a concept, hard to define and yet concrete enough, which we know as *Ahabath Israel*: 'Love of the Jewish People ...' In you, dear Hannah, as in so many intellectuals who came from the German Left, I find little trace of this."[83] Arendt replied by saying that she did not understand what it means to love a people; we love persons.[84] The idea that love can function as a way to mobilize people who do not already agree with you in a political context is, alas, unlikely as it is very hard to make sense out of what love means politically. A big part of the reason for this is that politics necessarily involves a diversity of people, most of whom we do not and cannot be expected to love. This emotion is not a political one, and moreover it cannot be, because in politics we necessarily have to work with people who we not only do not love, but may not even like—and this provides one more reason why it is not love but responsibility that provides the normative undermining for politics.

This is not to say that there is no room in politics for emotions. Far from it. Martha Nussbaum offers a detailed and lengthy defence of the importance of emotion, starting by pointing out that "All societies are full of emotions."[85] Not only that; in contrast to Arendt, Nussbaum explicitly states that "love matters for justice."[86] Love, in other words, is an important emotion in and for politics, and the love that individuals feel can be aggregated into a shared public sentiment. Nussbaum acknowledges that there are different ways in which love is felt (for children or a beloved sports team, for example)[87] but this generalization confirms Arendt's point. It is not love that is important because patriotic love cannot be the same as love between two people (a state or nation cannot love one back, for example). Rather, it is how emotions function in our ability to interpret narratives that have or carry political significance. As Nussbaum acknowledges, "Compassion strongly motivates altruism, but it is also rooted in concrete narratives and images."[88] For emotions to have "motivational power" they need to connect themselves "to the concrete" as opposed to the ideal.[89] Indeed, emotions play an important part in how we engage with and make sense out of the (political) narratives that we encounter in our lives. As Michael Walzer writes, "There is a hidden issue at the heart of contemporary debates about nationalism, identity politics, and religious fundamentalism. The issue is passion."[90] Emotion is important in politics, and I do not take Arendt to be saying that emotion is not relevant, but rather that the emotion of love cannot be political, and once it becomes political it changes into something else. Politically, emotions matter when they feature in our abilities to navigate our normative commitments for the simple reason that political responsibility has to be felt just as much as it can be reasoned. But what this means is that responsibility is not necessarily always a causal. For example, I can feel responsible but that does not mean I am accountable for the consequences of another's actions, including the actions of our government.

When we think of responsibility, the tendency is to understand responsibility according to a causal framework: I am responsible for a particular outcome. This is most easily grasped in our legal understanding of responsibility as liability. This model of responsibility operates on the assumption that our decisions and actions make us accountable for their consequences. There can be a range of different ways of interpreting this relationship between deed and action[91] but what they share is that responsibility functions in a causal way, so the process of acting requires that the consequences of one's actions can be traced back to the agent who did the deed. This is an important part of responsibility, and it must play an important part in politics. Our political leaders and our political activists do have to be held to account for their actions and deeds.

However, what happens when, in spite of this, a candidate nevertheless still finds political success (e.g. Trump) and the system itself operates in contrast to the norms needed for it to function? What happens when political actors appear to be able to get away with violating all sorts of norms that underpin the political process? In a recent op-ed in *The New York Times*, two professors of government, Steven Levitsky and Daniel Ziblatt, wrote:

> Mr. Trump is a serial norm-breaker. There are signs that Mr. Trump seeks to diminish the news media's traditional role by using Twitter, video messages and public rallies to circumvent the White House press corps and communicate directly with voters—taking a page out of the playbook of populist leaders like Silvio Berlusconi in Italy, Hugo Chávez in Venezuela and Recep Tayyip Erdogan in Turkey.
>
> An even more basic norm under threat today is the idea of legitimate opposition. In a democracy, partisan rivals must fully accept one another's right to exist, to compete and to govern. Democrats and Republicans may disagree intensely, but they must view one another as loyal Americans and accept that the other side will occasionally win elections and lead the country. Without such mutual acceptance, democracy is imperiled. Governments throughout history have used the claim that their opponents are disloyal or criminal or a threat to the nation's way of life to justify acts of authoritarianism.[92]

In such a situation, responsibility is broken as the behaviour undermines the norms of the society. This kind of conduct needs to be held accountable, but when the system itself appears unable to stop such abuses it comes down to the people, the majority that de Tocqueville warned us about, to step up and demand accountability.

Writing about international relations, the scholar Hedley Bull noted that there exists in international relations a society, and part of the evidence of this society is that there are practices that establish norms, the prime one being to ensure the survival of the society.[93] Bull's argument is influenced by the legal philosophy of H.L.A. Hart, and his classification of primary and secondary rules (primary rules being those rules that

enable secondary ones). The role of rules is also addressed by
Wittgenstein. Wittgenstein points out that we could be following
rules without knowing it, without being taught the rule (this is
very similar to Heidegger's insight about unlearned informal
knowledge that is necessary for functioning in society).[94] For
every rule, however, there has to be another rule that tells you
the condition in which that rule is to apply, and this in turn
leads to an infinite regress.[95] Why this matters is that while
there are clearly rules pertaining to the conduct of individuals,
institutions, and even our societies, because of this infinite
regress there comes a point where we have to decide how to
act and why. This moment of decision can be understood as
the point where political responsibility presents itself.

Here, however, we encounter an entirely different and
altogether more complicated form of political responsibility.
There remains the liability model of responsibility, but there is
another form of responsibility, one that Hans Jonas describes as
a responsibility for the future of the human race,[96] and which
can be inferred also to refer to the survival of our societies—that
we have a responsibility to each other as members of the society
to preserve the conditions for our future, and this necessarily
requires upholding certain rules that enable our societies to
function. Levitsky and Ziblatt are referring in their own way
to a similar kind of responsibility. There is, however, a third
account of responsibility. In this understanding, we have to
take seriously the responsibility of inaction. How is it possible
to hold someone or a group, for that matter, responsible for
not acting? This was precisely Arendt's concern.[97] Reflecting on the Holocaust, she came to the conclusion that one
feature in its condition of possibility was that good people
did not speak out or stand up when they had the chance to.
Later writers, notably Iris Marion Young[98] and more recently
Jade Schiff,[99] have taken up this argument by exploring how
to foster an account of responsibility that does not require
liability.

For Schiff, political responsibility is about how to respond
to situations where we are implicated in the suffering of others,
and she argues that the way to do this is by cultivating a sense

of responsiveness that is best done through narratives. Schiff's argument is that we make sense of the world through narratives or stories—she builds on the narrative turn in political theory that I introduced in chapter 1. Through narratives we develop a sense of our location in the world, and by doing so we can foster an understanding of how our conduct matters for the experiences of other people. The matter of political responsibility arises when our conduct involves implicating ourselves, because of our actions or choices, in the suffering of other people. Choices such as deciding what products to buy (where were they made, and in what working conditions?), where to buy them (what are the employment practices of that company?), what foods we consume (did they come from sustainable farming?), and so on, reveal that our everyday choices can carry far-reaching consequences that each of us, individually, cannot be held liable for. In politics, the same is the case. Choosing not to vote is such an example, and so too is remaining silent when we see others being hounded and abused.

Political choices are about not keeping silent and recognizing that as members of a diverse society it is incumbent upon us all to listen to each other's narratives and to appreciate how our own actions have consequences that are not direct. Thus, political responsibility requires that we take the first kind of responsibility in regard to our own actions (we are accountable for our decisions and behaviour) but also that our choices implicate us in a wider range of societal and political effects. In this sense, who we align ourselves with requires that we accept the non-linear consequences of doing so. There are clearly important reasons why many supported Trump or Brexit, but doing so also involved supporting the uglier sides of both: misogyny and racism, to name just two.

The question consequently is: does understanding oneself according to a narrative that encourages these views correspond with the sense of who you are, and of who you would want to align yourself with? If the answer is no, but you nevertheless still support actors representing these views, it is the decision that speaks and in a few ways. The first is that the support means that you have not spoken out against the forces of racism and misogyny, but actually enabled such voices. Moreover, supporting a misogynist but then claiming you are not sexist does not work. To accept this is a classic case of self-delusion, so that our sense of who we are fits with our idea of who we think we are, even if our actions tell a different story.

Furthermore, in politics it is the decision that transforms the activity of thinking and makes it public. It is through the decision that, in this case, one enters into the hermeneutic circle, and in a public way. Since politics is about acting with other people and cannot only be in the activity of thinking, it does not matter that we might think of ourselves differently to how our actions suggest. Our entering into intersubjective contact with others has been done by entering into the circle from a position partially characterized by racism and misogyny, as they were key features of the public representation of Trump and Brexit. As such, even though someone who voted for Trump or to leave the EU may not understand themselves as racist or sexist, and they cannot be held liable for what the political leaders do, they are, nevertheless, still responsible.

The strongest counter to this argument is, I would think, to highlight that our political leaders end up doing what they want regardless of what is best for the citizenry, and that politicians do not listen anyway. As such, even if we are politically responsible in a non-liable matter, it is irrelevant because the system is largely broken. Such a response, however, only serves to emphasize the importance of a non-liability model of political responsibility. It is in this example that we see how political responsibility of the indirect type comes into contact with the institutions of our political system, the importance of norms, and with how our political systems reward certain types of behaviour.

Our largely broken political system is a consequence of at least two forces. The first is the distance by which the system exists from the lives of ordinary people. It is very hard to get involved. We have to make it easier for the public to participate in politics, to remove the role of private money and corporate influence. We need to empower the citizenry but also ensure that our citizenry has the resources and the tools to participate.

There is no equality of opportunity without also some equality of condition. We need to strengthen our local governing institutions, but also provide for a robust and universal system of care so that the greatest number of people possible have the opportunity to participate in a meaningful way. This is not just about education—and the need for a liberal arts education that includes training in how knowledge production works, and of methodology—but also about professional opportunities, a functioning infrastructure, and a transparent and accountable system of politics. Another way to think about this is to ask ourselves who ends up participating in politics and whether or not we actually think they are the right people. That we view politicians largely with disdain as liars and cheats should tell us the answer. As such, the question we need to ask ourselves is: why it is that such people end up becoming involved and what can we do to replace them with more suitable people? Our political class is a failure because we have enabled them.

In an interview about Brexit, the former Chancellor George Osborne said that he did not take identity politics seriously and was too concerned about the economy.[100] That Osborne repeatedly failed to meet his economic targets means that we should perhaps not take his interpretation of events at face value. But what is shocking is that he is by no means alone in looking at identity politics as the reason for recent voter decisions. In fact, others, including from the Labour Party, have been making a very similar point, such as Andy Burnham, the former Labour MP, now Labour mayor for Manchester, who made the exact same point, that focusing on the single market (the economy) and not immigration (identity) cost Labour the referendum.[101] What both politicians appear to be buying into is that identity politics have become the driving force of politics. However, identity politics in some form have always been a driving force of politics. It is patently absurd to think that "it's the economy stupid" can somehow displace identity in our political sphere.

What is concerning here is that the identity politics these politicians, and Trump as well, are latching on to provide a very negative understanding of identity politics, one where there is no responsibility. It is negative because what these politicians, and the liberal egalitarians as well, are presuming is that identity functions as a source of division and insecurity. In this view, people feel that immigration harms them and negatively changes their societies and opportunities. What this view undermines is how our narratives inculcate within us the prerogative of responsibility. This is one way in which the intersubjective character of ourselves functions in politics: that identity concerns set up a context in which we then interpret and act in relation to the norms of society that we value or see changing. When they become negative, however, we start to view ourselves as victims, and once this happens we are able to consciously decouple our actions and decisions from ourselves in the first sense of the word responsibility. In this sense, because of the logic of victimhood, one cannot be held responsible for one's actions; it is the (ostensibly stronger) oppressor that is responsible. In the "they made me do it" version of politics, we displace our responsibility in the first sense and thus transform our public political responsibility (non-liable responsibility) from a progressive force into a destructive one, where we lose the idea of responsibility in its future-oriented sense.

When Hans Jonas points out that responsibility is always about the future, he is highlighting a seeming paradox in responsibility, that our responsibility involves referring back to past actions but by looking forward. What we have done will shape the future and because of this we are responsible for both our actions and our inactions. As such, when our identity-based narratives involve a sense of loss or victimhood, when the world appears to be spinning away from us, we start to construct narratives that reaffirm a nostalgic past and thus try to remove ourselves from the future consequences of our actions in a world that we cannot control. The infinite diversity and thus inevitable contingency of the world makes it that way. However, this is only a problem when our narratives resist change. Consequently, to find politics, people have to feel

comfortable in their decisions, but also feel that not getting
your way in the public sphere is not a disaster. The world is
changing, it has always changed, and it will continue to change.
Our political leaders and the people we support into politics
need to help people to feel better about changes, knowing
that they will still have a place in this future.

Conclusion

I have tried to suggest in this chapter and throughout the book
that it is possible to develop an understanding of politics that
is inspired from hermeneutic phenomenology. This argument
brings together the importance of narratives and of identity, of
the contingency of politics and of the failures of liberal thought
to adequately understand what politics *is*. An important part
of this discussion involved exploring the philosophy of Martin
Heidegger, a controversial figure, in order to generate this move
away from the liberal imagination of politics to one where the
people can discover politics. In his treatise on Heidegger's
influence among Jewish scholars, Richard Wolin remarks that
it is decidedly odd how Heidegger "wished ... to be judged
solely on the basis of his work," a position that is a "very
strange stance for a man who coined the term 'thrownness'
(*Geworfenheit*) to describe the fundamental contingent, non
self-generated character of human Being-in-the-world."[102]
Indeed, there are significant intellectual and political difficulties
in taking the philosophy of Heidegger, who was most likely not
a nice man,[103] and using it in the manner that I have done:
to suggest a non-liberal avenue for thinking about politics. I
have done so for a very simple reason.

It is not Heidegger that matters here, it is the idea that as
human beings our existence in the world can only make sense
through our own ability to interpret this world. The methodological starting point for this argument is with Heidegger, and
as such it makes sense to understand what exactly it means to
emphasize the significance of meaning and interpretation for
our being in the world. Once we accord this significance, and
also identify a way to make sense out of it, then it becomes

possible to think politically in a different way than we are used
to; but, I would suggest, we already do this, even if analytic
political theory and most political science suggests otherwise.

Throughout this book I have engaged with newspaper
articles and statements that are in the public domain. I have
quoted Michael Moore at length, along with op-eds in leading
newspapers. The reason for doing so is that through these
sources we can see how people are interpreting the sources of
their political understanding. These public texts are examples
of the contexts that most of us come into contact with in our
thinking about politics. They set out, if you will, a kind of
reference point for how we—the public—understand what
counts as political issues, political debate, and the forms in
which political activities take place. There are many different sources that contribute to this function, and not all of
them are media sources. But the sources I have used are,
I think, helpful in representing many of the central issues
that contextualize our understanding of Brexit and Trump's
election. For example, websites like FiveThirtyEight, with
their extensive polling coverage, provide their own form of
interpretation that contributes to this context. Nate Silver
went to some lengths to point this out when he defended
the polls by arguing that they were not really wrong, but that
there was a small polling error that provided sufficient paths
for a Trump victory.[104] Trevor Noah, of *The Daily Show*, had
some very pointed questions for Silver, challenging him, "I
mean, do we still call them polls if they are wrong."[105] Silver's
reply, which is repeated on his website, is that all he could
provide through his polling conclusions are illustrations of
uncertainty. Here we see a debate about the political role
of polling, from different positions, one that emphasizes its
political consequences and the other focused on an ideal of
defending a set of methods as being apolitical.

Silver's narrative is an interpretation that fulfils the role of
legitimizing the work he does at the expense of how polls are
used, interpreted, and shape public debate. As Mona Chalabi,
a former poll analyst for FiveThirtyEight, wrote, "I've been
concerned by how much faith the public has placed in polling.

Just like you'd check the weather before getting dressed, many people checked presidential polling numbers before heading out to vote."[106] She continued in what is an especially telling couple of paragraphs:

> I spent almost two years working for Nate Silver's website FiveThirtyEight, where I hoped to learn the secrets of political forecasting. I walked away totally disillusioned. It sometimes seemed as though their interpretation of the math wasn't free from subjective bias. There was also a certain arrogance that comes from being part of an elite that "gets the numbers," and an entrenched hierarchy meant that predictions weren't properly scrutinised.
> …
> And so you, the reader, are also complicit in this huge mistake. You probably didn't want to hear "it's complicated". You probably didn't want to have a difficult conversation with your aunt whom you knew was voting for Trump. You probably didn't want to think too much about the fact that the United States is a country deeply divided along racial and economic lines. Instead, you'd rather hit refresh on a little web page that tells you how America will vote. Too bad the numbers were wrong.[107]

Unfortunately, she does not provide evidence of what she saw as subjective bias, but what she highlights is that people do not read polls as though they are merely illustrations of uncertainty. Rather, they read them as facts because that is how polls have to be interpreted in the political sphere if they are to carry any meaning. In this sense, polls provide one character of "thrownness." We produce them but they are not self-generated and they condition our social and political arena.

As a consequence of using polling data as though they can be read like the weather forecast, we forget that what characterizes our political arena are not these facts, but the people who interpret them, which means experts and non-experts alike. In the process of emphasizing data in our analysis we make it too easy to forget that there are people behind these numbers and people interpreting these numbers. We have, in a methodological sense, removed people from our political discussions when we turn to polls—this is why it is possible to insult politicians as having no conviction when we accuse them of governing according to the polls, because they are treated as having no conviction, no ideas of their own of any moral worth. They are empty shells or opportunistic hucksters.

The process of interpretation is a deeply political process. This political character of interpretation is evident in how various forms of power function as a part of the interpreting process. This happens in regard to the use of knowledge to control the terms of public debate. I used the example of Robert's Rules of Order, but Trump does the same thing through his bait and switch Twitter tactics. He knows that by making outrageous statements on Twitter he can divert attention from one story and create another, and thus control the news cycle and the debate (even if the debate ends up being about how outrageous his latest tweet is).[108]

We need to be aware of this aspect of how knowledge and power function, but in our public sphere power functions in another sense as well, the sense meant by Hannah Arendt, in which people come together to act in concert as a group. Groups in politics, however, cannot be monolithic. They can try, but the inevitable plurality of the human condition requires that unless we want to populate our own space station, we will have to come into contact with people who are different from us. The greater the difference, the greater the potential for disagreement, but that does not mitigate the political responsibility to engage with difference knowing that we are all different in some way. This is one of the important lessons from the multicultural literature. One of James Tully's arguments in *Strange Multiplicity* is, in contrast to Brian Barry, especially important in emphasizing that the idea of our political societies as homogeneous nations is itself a political choice, not a representation.[109] Politics, to be meaningful, has to come to terms with this character of our inevitable diversity and take identity seriously. Imagining a political process where culture and identity do not matter is not only the grounds for a fictional dystopia, it is insulting to human beings.

However, in respecting the importance of culture and identity, we also have to be conscious about avoiding the kind of absurd scenarios where identity politics become identified as the cause of our political malaise or insecurities. The way we do this is by turning to the state and demanding that the state works in the interests of the majority of its inhabitants, and enables as many people as possible to find meaning and fulfilment in their lives. This requires that the state provide the means of opportunity for people to make informed choices about their future. There will still be elites, and capitalism, and consumerism, but there also need to be cultural goods to counter these, a robust education system, and the provision of essential goods without prejudice. The market economy works in some areas, but we need to acknowledge that it does not work in all areas (the US health care system is actually one of the least efficient in the world).[110] The more we turn to economics as the main focus of politics, the less we are able to care about what matters to people, which are values as well as goods. Politics has to address both, but in doing so we have to be politically responsible. And identity politics becomes dangerous when, as the contingent grounds on which our politics are based, it becomes the last vestige for our political debates. When all else fails, we turn to identity because that cannot be taken away from us.

Knowledge is always in some fashion political or open to politicization. One way that we have seen this happen is in debate about climate change. There is no doubt within the scientific community that climate change is happening. Yet in political discourse, it is presented as though there is such doubt. Moreover, the media tends to further such doubt by presuming that if climate change is being questioned, the only alternative must be that there is no climate change (as opposed to the more complicated question about how to understand the causes of climate change). As Welch notes, however, there is another perhaps more insidious feature at work in public political denouncement of climate change:

> Politics is already deeply involved in climate science. Like any science that becomes the focus of public attention, climate science struggles to have its "disinterestedness" accepted. Once the scientific community is seen as itself having an interest, as an "industry", that struggle is lost. And when its presentational strategies and rhetorical practices are exposed, as from time to time they are bound to be, the apparent distance of science from ordinary politics is further diminished. The presence of politics in science becomes plain to see, and this must reduce the authority of science *for* democratic decision making.[111]

What we see here are multiple failures of political responsibility. Researchers are irresponsible in assuming that scientific knowledge can somehow function independently of politics. Politicians are irresponsible in how they manipulate data and thus undermine the possibility of using evidence to inform policy, thereby further eroding the integrity of politics. When politicians can ignore evidence or treat evidence as meaningless, it has the perverse effect of damaging the integrity of the process and further alienating people from politics. The reason is because so long as knowledge is treated as a commodity, a good to use when and how we see fit, we remove any accountability for our actions and also any possibility of understanding ourselves as having responsibility in the world and for the world. New evidence can always be produced to justify our decisions, and changes to our knowledge base can be used to justify our reluctance to get involved. One of the most egregious examples of the ability to deflect responsibility in modern times may be the tobacco industry, which knowingly understood the dangers of smoking but decided to cover up this knowledge and produce different narratives instead.

Knowledge is always open to politicization because knowledge cannot be separated from the multiple facets of power. Consequently, what we require is a public sphere where knowledge is used in support of thinking, not as proof in its own right. We have witnessed the removal of thinking and of evidence from politics, turning instead to deploying people's anger,

frustration, and alienation for the short-term professional gain
of politicians. What has been missing in the public sphere is
political responsibility. The responsibility of our leaders to use
evidence fairly, without undermining the process of knowledge
production; of the state to provide the conditions by which
the electorate is able to interpret and engage with politics in
a sustainable way; of the people and our politicians to appreciate
that politics is about compromise not zero-sums; for our own
complicity in how others experience this world. For politics
to work, it will involve disagreement, but it also has to have
respect, and a deep appreciation for the role of our narratives
in how we make sense of a complicated world. Politics will
never be about everybody getting along, and it is not about
the avoidance of conflict. But we do need to appreciate that
politics is meaningless if, in our political decisions, we undermine the conditions for *our* future. To find politics we have
to find political responsibility and appreciate that we live in
an uncertain world of endless diversity and potential for change.

How can we save politics in a post-truth era? I am not going
to provide a list of institutional types of responses or rules (i.e.
this is what government should do, or how the media ought
to behave), as doing so will lead to an infinite regress. Instead,
I am going to summarize three arguments that I suggest can
provide a starting point for a wider conversation for answering
this question, which build on many of the different observations
and critiques I've advanced so far.

First, although narratives are not everything, they are very
important. The greater the argument for un-polluted facts as the
only response to "truthiness," the less our chances of success.
Evidence matters, but narratives are also a form of evidence.
We need to have a space in our public debate for empirical
evidence, but those who produce this evidence need to be
reflexively responsible, understanding the role of what they are
producing in our public debate. This is important because of
our general faith in science and the scientific method. If this
method is to be treated as some kind of gold standard for the
production of knowledge on which all others are judged, its
purveyors and practitioners need to be held accountable for

the consequences of their work. What this means is not that
we should cease polling. Rather, it is to draw attention to the
hubris of those like Sokal who think interpretivism is relativism.
We are at an important moment when politics and methodology are publicly being debated in a way that is exceedingly
rare outside of university methodology seminars. We need to
make greater room for interpretive approaches to knowledge
production and to respect the methodological arguments from
such approaches. One of these is that knowledge claims are
rarely apolitical, and we need to be transparent about the type
of causal assumptions guiding causal claims. How empirical
data is reported is very important here, since a lot of the
time the research findings are more modest than is presented,
or are exaggerated for greater publicity and professional
progression.

Second, the way in which identity is treated and understood
politically is exceptionally important. What this importance
means is that it is crucial to develop ways to allow identity-based
political concerns to inform our public debate. Doing so does
not necessarily open up Pandora's box and unleash it into the
public sphere, as liberal egalitarians and others might want
us to think. However, it does require responsibility. To take
identity seriously requires an acceptance, not just of competing
claims but also of our own fallibilities. Another way to frame
this is to highlight it methodologically, by what could be the
driving principle of all methodological debates: doubt. If there
is anything to philosophy and methodology, it is addressing the
impossible question about how we are able to know anything
at all. Philosophy is largely the history of aporias, of unresolv-
able questions, usually emerging out of inconsistencies. For
both Augustine and Descartes, the solution to doubt was to
emphasize our existence, which brings us back to the centrality
of existence (of being) for how we respond to the impossible
question of how we are able to know anything at all. In this
sense, there is an inescapable relationship between our ability
to know and our having to know who we are. Yet this move
is precisely what Sokal and his positivist allies want to deny,
that we can remove any considerations of who we are from

how we know. Similarly, this move is also denied by those who doubt the significance of identity politics because if who we are shapes our ability to understand the world we find ourselves in, then identity politics necessarily means that there is no single answer, only a multiplicity of positions. The argument against identity politics is actually an argument against difference in pursuit of some kind of certainty that philosophy has never been able to find—hence the significance of the aporia—and which politically is only possible in totalitarianism. What is required, consequently, is confidence in our uncertainty. This is the responsibility of identity: that our identities and thus our knowledge claims are always fragile. What is required is the ability to enable people to accept this fragility. Having this acceptance would go a long way to increasing our ability to work alongside others and to accept the intersubjective character of our being.

Third, political responsibility has to become a defining feature of politics. This will be the great challenge of our age, to identity the institutions necessary for greater responsibility, to develop normative understandings of how to foster greater political responsibility among the populace, and to identify the different kinds of political responsibility that exist and why each of them matters for a healthy democracy. In this chapter I have mentioned three kinds of responsibility: a liability model, an indirect model that emphasizes our complicity, and an ontological model grounded in our long-term survival as human beings. I've now added a fourth: the responsibility of identity. Politics is responsibility in a multiplicity of ways. It is to work out what political responsibility means in conditions of an interpretive and intersubjective existence. That is how we will save politics in a post-truth era. For when we lose responsibility in politics we are lost. It is time to find ourselves.

Notes

1 Heather Stewart and Jessica Elgot, "Labour Plans Jeremy Corbyn Relaunch to Ride Anti-Establishment Wave," *The Guardian,*

December 15 2016. May Bulman, "Labour Plans to Relaunch Jeremy Corbyn as Left-Wing Populist in Bid to Seize on Anti-Establishment Sentiment," *Independent*, December 16 2016.

2 Hochschild, *Strangers in Their Own Land*. Frank, *What's the Matter with Kansas?*

3 BBC, "Young 'to Be Poorer Than Parents at Every Stage of Life' "; Boffey, "Middle-Class Young 'Will Fare Worse Than Their Parents' "; Equality and Human Rights Commission, "Is Britain Fairer?"; Resolution Foundation, "Millennials Facing 'Generational Pay Penalty' "; Cribb, Hood, and Joyce, "The Economic Circumstances of Different Generations."

4 Oxford Dictionaries, https://en.oxforddictionaries.com/definition/post-truth. Accessed February 10 2017.

5 Peter Beinart, "Glenn Beck's Regrets," *The Atlantic*, January/February 2017.

6 Sykes, "Charlie Sykes on Where the Right Went Wrong."

7 Ibid. Emphasis in original.

8 Welch, *Hyperdemocracy*.

9 Ibid., 25.

10 Richard Wolin, *Heidegger's Children: Hannah Arendt, Karl Löwith, Hans Jonas, and Herbert Marcuse* (Princeton: Princeton University Press, 2001), 110.

11 Ibid.

12 Ibid., 102.

13 Robert M. Pirsig, *Zen and the Art of Motorcycle Maintenance: An Inquiry into Values* (New York: Bantam Books, 1974), 109. Emphasis in original.

14 Feyerabend, *Against Method*, 12. Although the entire book is about expanding on this thesis, he elaborates more specifically on this phrase in Appendix I (pages 169–216).

15 Emmanuel Faye, *Heidegger: The Introduction of Nazism into Philosophy*, trans. Michael B. Smith (New Haven: Yale University Press, 2009).

16 Blattner, *Heidegger's Being and Time*, 1.

17 Charles B. Guignon, "Introduction," in *The Cambridge Companion to Heidegger*, ed. Charles B. Guignon (Cambridge: Cambridge University Press, 2006), 1.

18 Dreyfus, *Being-in-the-World*, 9.

19 Heidegger, *Being and Time*, 50. Emphasis in original. See also page 59 (35).

20 Ibid., 59 (35). Emphasis in original.

21 Mark A. Wrathall and Max Murphy, "An Overview of *Being and Time*," in *The Cambridge Companion to Heidegger's* Being and Time, ed. Mark A. Wrathall (Cambridge: Cambridge University Press, 2013), 4.

22 Dreyfus, *Being-in-the-World*, 30.

23 Ibid., 32.

24 Heidegger, *Being and Time*, 59. Emphasis in original.

25 Ibid., 61 (37).

26 Ibid., 62 (37). Emphasis in original.

27 Dreyfus, *Being-in-the-World*, 34.

28 Heidegger, *Being and Time*, 25–26; see also 119 (86).

29 Dreyfus, *Being-in-the-World*, 34.

30 Ibid., 18–19.

31 Blattner, *Heidegger's Being and Time*, 22.

32 Heidegger, *Being and Time*, 195.

33 I would like to thank Elad Lapidot for his invaluable help in working through Heidegger's understanding of the hermeneutic circle.

34 Heidegger, *Being and Time*, 194.

35 Ibid., 195.

36 Ibid., 94–95.

37 Habermas's discussion of Heidegger can be found in Jurgen Habermas, *The Philosophical Discourse of Modernity: Twelve Lectures*, trans. Frederick Lawrence (Cambridge, MA: MIT Press, 1998). Useful summaries of his and other political critiques of Heidegger include: Catherine H. Zuckert, "Martin Heidegger: His Philosophy and His Politics," *Political Theory* 18, no. 1 (1990); Steven B. Smith, "Heidegger and Political Philosophy: The Theory of His Practice," *Nomos* 37, Theory and Practice (1995); Fred Dallmayr, "Rethinking the Political: Some Heideggerian Contributions," *The Review of Politics* 52, no. 4 (1990); Mark Blitz, "Heidegger and the Political," *Political Theory* 28, no. 2 (2000).

38 Smith, "Heidegger and Political Philosophy," 457–58.

39 Hubert L. Dreyfus, "Heidegger on the Connection between Nihilism, Art, Technology, and Politics," in *The Cambridge Companion to Heidegger*, ed. Charles B. Guignon (Cambridge: Cambridge University Press, 2006), 369. Emphasis in original.

40 Ibid., 371.

41 See, for example, and compare, Arendt, *The Origins of Totalitarianism*; Theodor W. Adorno and Max Horkheimer, *Dialectic of*

Enlightenment, 2nd ed. (London: Verso, 1986); Zygmunt Bauman, Modernity and the Holocaust (Ithaca, NY: Cornell University Press, 1991).

42 John Stuart Mill, "A Few Words on Non-Intervention," Fraser's Magazine for Town and Country 60 (1859): 772.

43 Hannah Arendt, Eichmann in Jerusalem: A Report on the Banality of Evil, rev. and enl. ed., Penguin Twentieth-Century Classics (London: Penguin Books, 1994). Iris Marion Young developed an account of political responsibility influenced by Arendt's critique. See, Iris Marion Young, Responsibility for Justice (Oxford: Oxford University Press, 2011).

44 Or rather, with a political philosophy that can be separated from his Nazism. Two works that do, however, find political philosophy within Heidegger are James F. Ward, Heidegger's Political Thinking (Amherst: University of Massachusetts Press, 1995); Frederick A. Olafson, Heidegger and the Ground of Ethics: A Study of Mitsein (Cambridge: Cambridge University Press, 1998).

45 See, Joan Cocks, On Sovereignty and Other Political Delusions (London: Bloomsbury, 2014).

46 Emmanuel Chukwudi Eze, Race and the Enlightenment: A Reader (Cambridge: Blackwell, 1997).

47 Hannah Arendt, Mary McCarthy, and Carol Brightman, Between Friends: The Correspondence of Hannah Arendt and Mary Mccarthy 1949–1975 (London: Secker & Warburg, 1995), 22–29.

48 Dreyfus, "Heidegger on the Connection between Nihilism, Art, Technology, and Politics," 349–50.

49 Ibid., 351.

50 Heidegger, Being and Time, 171.

51 Peter Novick, The Holocaust and Collective Memory (London: Bloomsbury, 1999 (2001)), 13.

52 Michel Foucault, Discipline and Punish: The Birth of the Prison, trans. Alison Sheridan (London: Penguin Books, 1991).

53 Christopher Coker, Ethics and War in the 21st Century (London: Routledge, 2008), 35.

54 Waging War without Warriors? The Changing Culture of Military Conflict (Boulder, CO: Lynne Rienner Publishers, 2002), 106.

55 Mark A. Wrathall, "Heidegger on Human Understanding," in The Cambridge Companion to Heidegger's Being and Time, ed. Wrathall, 182.

56 Ibid.

57 Ibid., 188. Emphasis in original.

58 See, Dreyfus, *Being-in-the-World*.

59 Wrathall, "Heidegger on Human Understanding," 191.

60 Havercroft, *Captives of Sovereignty*, 151.

61 Ibid., 152.

62 Ibid., 154.

63 See, in particular, Jean Bodin and Julian H. Franklin, *On Sovereignty: Four Chapters from the Six Books of the Commonwealth* (Cambridge: Cambridge University Press, 1992); Thomas Hobbes, *Leviathan*, ed. Richard Tuck, Rev. student ed. (Cambridge: Cambridge University Press, 1996); Carl Schmitt, *Political Theology: Four Chapters on the Concept of Sovereignty*, trans. George Schwab (Chicago: Chicago University Press, 2005 (1985)).

64 Gibbons, "Hermeneutics, Political Inquiry, and Practical Reason," 566.

65 Blitz, "Heidegger and the Political," 172.

66 Ibid., 182.

67 Gibbons, "Hermeneutics, Political Inquiry, and Practical Reason," 570.

68 Ibid.

69 Which is not to say that others have not gained success from precisely such an approach. Daniel Goldhagen's book *Hitler's Willing Executioners* is one such example: Daniel Jonah Goldhagen, *Hitler's Willing Executioners: Ordinary Germans and the Holocaust* (New York: Vintage Books, 1997).

70 Henry M. Robert, *Robert's Rules of Order*, 11th rev. ed. (Philadelphia: Da Capo Press, 2011 (1876)).

71 Michel Foucault, *Security, Territory, Population: Lectures at the Collège De France, 1977–78.*, ed. Michel Senellart, trans. Graham Burchell (New York: Palgrave Macmillan, 2007), 87–114.

72 See the discussion in Steven Lukes, *Power: A Radical View*, 2nd ed. (Basingstoke: Palgrave Macmillan, 2005).

73 In addition to ibid., see Havercroft, *Captives of Sovereignty*, 25–27.

74 Arendt, *On Violence*, 44.

75 Note, for example, Hans Morgenthau's classic statement about politics being "a struggle for power." Hans J. Morgenthau, Kenneth W. Thompson, and W. David Clinton, *Politics among Nations*, 7th ed. (New York: McGraw Hill, 2006), 29.

76 Hannah Arendt, *Between Past and Future: Eight Exercises in Political Thought* (London: Penguin, 1968), 163.

77 Havercroft, *Captives of Sovereignty*, 22.

78 Ibid., 23.

79 Ibid.

80 Hannah Arendt, *The Human Condition* (Chicago: Chicago University Press, 1958), 7.

81 Hobbes, *Leviathan*, 89 (Ch 13).

82 For discussions of Arendt and agonistic politics see: Craig Calhoun and John McGowan, eds, *Hannah Arendt and the Meaning of Politics* (Minneapolis: University of Minnesota Press, 1997). For a discussion that brings together both Arendt and Foucault in relation to agonistic politics, see James Tully, "The Agonistic Freedom of Citizens," in *Public Philosophy in a New Key* (Cambridge: Cambridge University Press, 2008).

83 Quoted in Hannah Arendt, *The Jew as Pariah*, ed. Ron H. Feldman (New York: Grove Press, 1978), 241.

84 Ibid., 246; *The Jewish Writings*, ed. Jerome Kohn and Ron H. Feldman (New York: Schocken Books, 2007), 466–67.

85 Nussbaum, *Poetic Justice: The Literary Imagination and Public Life*, 1.

86 Ibid., 380.

87 Ibid., 382.

88 Ibid., 209.

89 Ibid.

90 Walzer, *Politics and Passion*, 110.

91 See, for example, Kern, *A Cultural History of Causality*.

92 Steven Levitsky and Daniel Ziblatt, "Is Donald Trump a Threat to Democracy?," *The New York Times*, December 16 2016.

93 Hedley Bull, *The Anarchical Society: A Study of Order in World Politics*, 2nd ed. (New York: Columbia University Press, 1995).

94 Ludwig Wittgenstein, *Philosophical Investigations*, trans. G.E.M. Anscombe, P.M.S. Hacker, and Joachim Schulte, 4th ed. (Oxford: Wiley-Blackwell, 2009). Wittgenstein summarizes this possibility in passage 219, on page 92 when he writes, "When I follow the rule, I do not choose. I follow the rule *blindly*." Emphasis in original.

95 See also Welch, *Hyperdemocracy*, 6–7.

96 Hans Jonas, *The Imperative of Responsibility: In Search of an Ethics for the Technological Age*, trans. Hans Jonas and David Herr (Chicago: Chicago University Press, 1984).

97   See, Arendt, *Eichmann in Jerusalem*.

98   Young, *Responsibility for Justice*.

99   Schiff, *Burdens of Political Responsibility*.

100 Tom Peck, "'I Was Too Focused on the Economy,' Says Osborne," *Independent*, December 17 2016.

101 Anushka Asthana, "Andy Burnham: Labour Wrong to Put Single Market Ahead of Immigration," *The Guardian*, December 16 2016.

102 Wolin, *Heidegger's Children*, 203.

103 See, for example, ibid. The chapter on Arendt is especially relevant.

104 Nate Silver, "Why Fivethirtyeight Gave Trump a Better Chance Than Almost Anyone Else," http://fivethirtyeight.com/features/why-fivethirtyeight-gave-trump-a-better-chance-than-almost-anyone-else/. Accessed February 10 2017.

105 Alexandra Rosenmann, "Nate Silver Reveals Why We're Not Done with Polls after Trevor Noah Skewers Him for Being So Wrong This Election," www.alternet.org/election-2016/nate-silver-reveals-why-were-not-done-polls-after-trevor-noah-skewers-him-being-so. Accessed February 10 2017. See also Tracy Swartz, "Nate Silver Wears Cubs Hat as he Talks World Series, Election on 'Daily Show'," *Chicago Tribune*, November 15 2016.

106 Mona Chalabi, "Yes, the Election Polls Were Wrong. Here's Why," *The Guardian*, November 9 2016.

107 Ibid.

108 Donald Trump's bait and switch tactics have been increasingly recognized, as evident in reports by CNN, *The New Yorker*, *The Nation*, *The Atlantic*, *Vanity Fair*, *The Washington Post*, and many others. See Raul A. Reyes, "Trump's Cruel Bait-and-Switch on Immigration," CNN, March 1 2017, http://edition.cnn.com/2017/03/01/opinions/trump-bait-and-switch-on-immigration-reyes/index.html. Accessed September 25 2017; John Cassidy, "Donald Trump's Great Bait and Switch," *The New Yorker*, November 14 2016; Robert L. Borosage, "Donald Trump Has Pulled an Epic Bait-and-Switch," *The Nation*, February 14 2017; David A. Graham, "The Bait-and-Switch Presidency," *The Atlantic*, December 14 2016; Tina Nguyen, "Donald Trump Unleashes His Ultimate Bait-and-Switch," *Vanity Fair*, March 8 2017; David Ignatius, "Donald Trump Pulls a Bait and Switch on America," *The Washington Post*,

November 23 2016. His tweets about Obama tapping his phones during the election provide a striking example. While these reports are largely from after the election, it is also the case that during the campaign, when confronted with one issue, he would frequently raise something else, often outrageous, as a distraction. In one example, on September 30, following reports by former Miss Universe Alicia Machado of sexist abuse he had directed at her, and in the context of widespread criticism of his chauvinism and sexism, Trump issued a series of tweets falsely alleging the existence of a sex tape featuring Ms Machado and at the same time attempting to smear Hillary Clinton for alleged assistance in obtaining US citizenship for Ms Machado. See Carolina Moreno, "Alicia Machado Speaks Out After Donald Trump's 'Sex Tape' Accusation," *Huffington Post*, October 4 2016; Ben Mathis-Lilley, "Trump Tweeted at 5:30 A.M. About Alicia Machado's Alleged 'Sex Tape'," *Slate*, September 30 2016. On August 9, a day after tweeting about Megyn Kelly in highly misogynistic language, he tried to deflect attention by claiming that Hillary Clinton's policies and "maybe her emails" had "gotten people killed." Often his bait and switch attacks bore no reflection of empirical evidence, but dwelt on matters that would energize his base. One newspaper compiled a list of Trump's sexist comments: Adam Lusher, "Donald Trump: All the Sexist Things He Said," *Independent*, October 9 2016.

109 Tully, *Strange Multiplicity*.

110 Karen Davis et al., "Mirror, Mirror on the Wall: How the Performance of the U.S. Health Care System Compares Internationally" (The Commonwealth Fund, 2014). David Squires and Chloe Anderson, "U.S. Health Care from a Global Perspective: Spending, Use of Services, Prices, and Health in 13 Countries" (The Commonwealth Fund, 2015).

111 Welch, *Hyperdemocracy*, 126. Emphasis in original.

Bibliography

Adorno, Theodor W. and Max Horkheimer. *Dialectic of Enlightenment*. 2nd ed. London: Verso, 1986.

Agerholm, Harriet. "Donald Trump Wins: French Ambassador to the US Reacts by Posting Tweet Declaring the End of the World." *Independent*, November 10 2016.

Arendt, Hannah. *Between Past and Future: Eight Exercises in Political Thought*. London: Penguin, 1968.

———. *Eichmann in Jerusalem: A Report on the Banality of Evil*. Penguin Twentieth-Century Classics. Rev. and enl. ed. London: Penguin Books, 1994.

———. *The Human Condition*. Chicago: Chicago University Press, 1958.

———. *The Jew as Pariah*. Edited by Ron H. Feldman. New York: Grove Press, 1978.

———. *The Jewish Writings*. Edited by Jerome Kohn and Ron H. Feldman. New York: Schocken Books, 2007.

———. *On Violence*. New York: Harcourt Brace & Company, 1970.

———. *The Origins of Totalitarianism*. London: André Deutsch, 1986.

———. *The Promise of Politics*. Edited by Jerome Kohn. New York: Schocken Books, 2005.

———. *Responsibility and Judgment*. Edited by Jerome Kohn. New York: Schocken Books, 2005.

———. "Thinking and Moral Considerations: A Lecture." *Social Research* 38, no. 3 (1971): 417–46.

Arendt, Hannah, Mary McCarthy, and Carol Brightman. *Between Friends: The Correspondence of Hannah Arendt and Mary Mccarthy 1949–1975*. London: Secker & Warburg, 1995.

Aronowitz, Stanley. "Alan Sokal's 'Transgression'." *Dissent* 44, no. 1 (1997): 107–11.

Asthana, Anushka. "Andy Burnham: Labour Wrong to Put Single Market Ahead of Immigration." *The Guardian*, December 16 2016.

Baron, Ilan Zvi. "The Continuing Failure of International Relations and the Challenges of Disciplinary Boundaries." *Millennium: Journal of International Studies* 43, no. 1 (2014): 224–44.

———. "Jews Were Europeans Even before the EU. That's Why U.K. Jews Should Vote 'Remain'." *HaAretz*, June 20 2016.

———. *Justifying the Obligation to Die: War, Ethics and Political Obligation with Illustrations from Zionism.* Lanham, MD: Lexington, 2009.

———. "The Problem of Dual Loyalty." *Canadian Journal of Political Science* 42, no. 4 (2009): 1025–44.

Barr, Caelainn. "The Areas and Demographics Where the Brexit Vote Was Won." *The Guardian*, June 24 2016.

Barrett, Ted. "Pol: Trump Defended Articles of the Constitution That Don't Exist." http://edition.cnn.com/2016/07/08/politics/sanford-questions-trump-constitution-gaffe/. Accessed February 3 2017.

Barry, Brian. *Culture & Equality.* Cambridge: Polity, 2001.

Barthes, Roland. "Introduction to the Structural Analysis of Narratives." In *Image, Music, Text*, edited by Stephen Heath, 79–124. London: Fontana Press, 1977.

Bauman, Zygmunt. *Modernity and the Holocaust.* Ithaca, NY: Cornell University Press, 1991.

BBC. "Elections 2017 Results: Tories Win Four New Mayors." www.bbc.co.uk/news/election-2017-39817224. Accessed May 6 2017.

———. "Young 'to Be Poorer Than Parents at Every Stage of Life'." BBC News, www.bbc.co.uk/news/business-34858997. Accessed February 5 2017.

Beinart, Peter. "Glenn Beck's Regrets." *The Atlantic*, January/February 2017.

Benhabib, Seyla. *The Rights of Others: Aliens, Residents and Citizens.* Cambridge: Cambridge University Press, 2004.

Bennett, Owen. *The Brexit Club.* London: Biteback Publishing, 2016.

Bialik, Carl. "No, Voter Turnout Wasn't Way Down from 2012." FiveThirtyEight, http://fivethirtyeight.com/features/no-voter-turnout-wasnt-way-down-from-2012/. Accessed February 3 2017.

Blattner, William D. *Heidegger's Being and Time: A Reader's Guide.* London: Bloomsbury, 2006.

Blitz, Mark. "Heidegger and the Political." *Political Theory* 28, no. 2 (2000): 167–96.

Blumenthal, Sidney. "The Clinton Wars." In *The Clinton Wars.* New York: Farrar, Straus and Giroux, 2003.

Bodin, Jean and Julian H. Franklin. *On Sovereignty: Four Chapters from the Six Books of the Commonwealth* [in translation of selections from Six livres de la Re\0301publique.]. Cambridge: Cambridge University Press, 1992.

Boffey, Daniel. "Middle-Class Young 'Will Fare Worse Than Their Parents'." *The Guardian*, October 12 2013.

Bond, Anthony. "French Embassador to the US Says the 'World Is Collapsing' as Donald Trump Looks Set to Become President." *Mirror*, November 9 2016.

Borosage, Robert L. "Donald Trump Has Pulled an Epic Bait-and-Switch." *The Nation*, February 14 2017.

Brait, Ellen. "Princeton Students Demand Removal of Woodrow Wilson's Name from Buildings." *The Guardian*, November 23 2015.

Brown, Wendy. *Undoing the Demos: Neoliberalism's Stealth Revolution.* New York: Zone Books, 2015.

Bull, Hedley. *The Anarchical Society: A Study of Order in World Politics.* 2nd ed. New York: Columbia University Press, 1995.

Bulman, May. "Labour Plans to Relaunch Jeremy Corbyn as Left-Wing Populist in Bid to Seize on Anti-Establishment Sentiment." *Independent*, December 16 2016.

Butler, Judith. *Gender Trouble: Feminism and the Subversion of Identity.* 10th anniversary ed. New York; London: Routledge, 1999.

Calhoun, Craig and John McGowan, eds. *Hannah Arendt and the Meaning of Politics.* Minneapolis: University of Minnesota Press, 1997.

Campbell, David. *Writing Security: United States Foreign Policy and the Politics of Identity.* Rev. ed. Manchester: Manchester University Press, 1998.

Case, Anne and Angus Deaton. "Mortality and Morbidity in the 21st Century." *Brookings Papers on Economic Activity*, BPEA Conference Drafts, March 23–24 2017.

———. "Rising Morbidity and Mortality in Midlife among White Non-Hispanic Americans in the 21st Century." *PNAS* 112, no. 49 (2015): 15078–83.

Cassidy, John. "Donald Trump's Great Bait and Switch." *The New Yorker*, November 14 2016.

Cavell, Stanley. *The Claim of Reason: Wittgenstein, Skepticism, Morality, and Tragedy.* Oxford: Oxford University Press, 1979.

Chalabi, Mona. "Yes, the Election Polls Were Wrong. Here's Why." *The Guardian*, November 9 2016.

Chalmers, A. F. *What is This Thing Called Science?* 3rd ed. Buckingham: Open University Press, 1999.

Chambers, Samuel A. *Bearing Society in Mind: Theories and Politics of the Social Formation.* New York: Rowman & Littlefield, 2014.

Chomsky, Noam. *Profit Over People: Neoliberalism and the Global Order.* New York: Seven Stories Press, 1998.

———. *World Orders Old and New.* New York: Columbia University Press, 1996.

Clifford, James and George E. Marcus. *Writing Culture: The Poetics and Politics of Ethnography.* 25th anniversary ed. with a new foreword by Kim Fortun. Berkeley: University of California Press, 2010.

Cocks, Joan. *On Sovereignty and Other Political Delusions.* London: Bloomsbury, 2014.

Cohen, Robin. "Diasporas and the Nation-State: From Victims to Challengers." *International Affairs* 72, no. 3 (1996): 507–20.

Coker, Christopher. *Ethics and War in the 21st Century.* London: Routledge, 2008.

———. *Waging War without Warriors? The Changing Culture of Military Conflict.* Boulder, CO: Lynne Rienner Publishers, 2002.

Connolly, William. *Identity/Difference: Democratic Negotiations of Political Paradox.* Expanded ed. Minneapolis: University of Minnesota Press, 1991.

Cornwell, Rupert. "Campus Protests: Students Fighting for Free Speech and the Eradication of Racism Should Be Working Together—Not against Each Other." *Independent*, November 14 2015.

Crary, Alice. *Beyond Moral Judgment.* Cambridge, MA: Harvard University Press, 2007.

Cribb, Jonathan, Andrew Hood, and Robert Joyce. "The Economic Circumstances of Different Generations: The Latest Picture." London: The Institute for Fiscal Studies, 2016.

Crotty, Michael. *The Foundations of Social Research: Meaning and Perspective in the Research Process.* London: Sage, 1998.

Dahl, Robert. "The Behavioural Approach in Political Science: Epitaph for a Monument to a Successful Protest." *The American Political Science Review* 55, no. 4 (1961): 763–72.

Dallmayr, Fred. "Rethinking the Political: Some Heideggerian Contributions." *The Review of Politics* 52, no. 4 (1990): 524–52.

Dardot, Pierre and Christian Laval. *The New Way of the World: On Neoliberal Society.* London: Verso, 2014.

Davies, William. *The Limits of Neoliberalism: Authority, Sovereignty and the Logic of Competition*. London: Sage, 2017.

Davis, Karen, Kristof Stremiksi, David Squires, and Cathy Schoen. "Mirror, Mirror on the Wall: How the Performance of the U.S. Health Care System Compares Internationally." The Commonwealth Fund, 2014.

de Tocqueville, Alexis. *Democracy in America*. Translated by Harvey C. Mansfield and Delba Winthrop. Chicago: Chicago University Press, 2000.

Dinstein, Yoram. *War, Aggression and Self-Defence*. 4th ed. Cambridge: Cambridge University Press, 2005.

Doyle, Michael W. "Kant, Liberal Legacies, and Foreign Affairs." *Philosophy and Public Affairs* 12, no. 2 (1983): 205–35.

———. "Kant, Liberal Legacies, and Foreign Affairs, Part 2." *Philosophy & Public Affairs* 12, no. 4 (1983): 323–53.

Dreyfus, Hubert L. *Being-in-the-World: A Commentary on Heidegger's Being and Time*. Cambridge, MA: MIT Press, 1991.

———. "Heidegger on the Connection between Nihilism, Art, Technology, and Politics." In *The Cambridge Companion to Heidegger*, edited by Charles B. Guignon, 345–72. Cambridge: Cambridge University Press, 2006.

Dworkin, Ronald. "The Original Position." In *Reading Rawls: Critical Studies on Rawls'* A Theory of Justice, edited by Norman Daniels, 16–52. Stanford: Stanford University Press, 1975.

Easton, David. "The Decline of Modern Political Theory." *The Journal of Politics* 13, no. 1 (February 1951): 36–58.

———. *The Political System: An Enquiry into the State of Political Science*. New York: Knopf, 1953.

The Economist. "Britain's Immigration Paradox." *The Economist*, July 8 2016.

The Editors of *The Atlantic*. "Against Donald Trump." *The Atlantic*, November 2016.

The Editors of *The Lancet*. "Retraction: Ileal-Lymphoid-Nodular Hyperplasia, Non-Specific Colitis, and Pervasive Developmental Disorder in Children." *The Lancet* 375, no. 9713 (2010): 445.

The Electoral Commission. "EU Referendum Results." The Electoral Commission, www.electoralcommission.org.uk/find-information-by-subject/elections-and-referendums/past-elections-and-referendums/eu-referendum/electorate-and-count-information. Accessed February 7 2017.

Elgot, Jessica. " 'Absurd' Visa Rules on Income Force UK Citizens into Exile, Court Told." *The Guardian*, February 22 2016.

Elshtain, Jean Bethke. *Democracy on Trial*. CBC Massey Lecture Series. Concord, Ontario: Anansi, 1993.

England, Charlotte. "George Orwell's *1984* Sells Out on Amazon as Trump Adviser Kellyanne Conway refers to 'alternative facts'," *Independent*, January 27 2017.

Equality and Human Rights Commission. "Is Britain Fairer? The State of Equality and Human Rights 2015." Manchester, 2015.

European Parliament. "Results of the 2014 European Elections." Europarl, www.europarl.europa.eu/elections2014-results/en/country-results-uk-2014.html#table01. Accessed February 3 2107.

Eze, Emmanuel Chukwudi. *Race and the Enlightenment: A Reader*. Cambridge: Blackwell, 1997.

Fanon, Frantz. *Black Skin, White Masks* [Translated from the French.]. New York: Grove Press, 1967.

Fay, Brian. *Contemporary Philosophy of Social Science*. Oxford: Blackwell, 1996.

Faye, Emmanuel. *Heidegger: The Introduction of Nazism into Philosophy*. Translated by Michael B. Smith. New Haven: Yale University Press, 2009.

Feyerabend, Paul. *Against Method*. 3rd ed. London: Verso, 2010.

Foreman, Jonathan. "Theresa May's Record as Home Secretary is Alarming, Not Reassuring." *The Spectator*, July 15 2016.

Foucault, Michel. *Discipline and Punish: The Birth of the Prison*. Translated by Alison Sheridan. London: Penguin Books, 1991.

———. *Security, Territory, Population: Lectures at the Collège De France, 1977–78*. Translated by Graham Burchell. Edited by Michel Senellart New York: Palgrave Macmillan, 2007.

Frank, Thomas. *What's the Matter with Kansas?* New York: Henry Holt and Company, 2005.

Frankel, Jonathan. *The Damascus Affair: "Ritual Murder," Politics, and the Jews in 1840*. Cambridge: Cambridge University Press, 1997.

Fukuyama, Francis. *The End of History and the Last Man*. London: Hamish Hamilton, 1992.

———. "The End of History?" *The National Interest*, no. 16 (1989): 3–18.

Garfinkel, Harold. *Studies in Ethnomethodology*. Englewood Cliffs, NJ: Prentice-Hall, 1967.

Gaukroger, Stephen. *The Emergence of a Scientific Culture: Science and the Shaping of Modernity 1210–1685*. Oxford: Clarendon Press, 2006.

Gelman, Andrew and Jonathan Auerbach, "Age-aggregation Bias in Mortality Trends." *PNAS* 113, no. 7 (2016): "Letters."

Gibbons, Michael T. "Hermeneutics, Political Inquiry, and Practical Reason: An Evolving Challenge to Political Science." *The American Political Science Review* 100, no. 4 (2006): 563–71.

Giddens, Anthony. *New Rules of Sociological Method: A Positive Critique of Interpretive Sociologies*. New York: Basic Books, 1976.

Gilbert, Margaret. *A Theory of Political Obligation: Membership, Commitment, and the Bonds of Society*. Oxford: Clarendon Press, 2006.

Goldhagen, Daniel Jonah. *Hitler's Willing Executioners: Ordinary Germans and the Holocaust*. New York: Vintage Books, 1997.

Gorski, David. "The General Medical Council to Andrew Wakefield: 'The Panel is Satisfied That Your Conduct Was Irresponsible and Dishonest'." *Science-Based Medicine*, February 1 2010.

Graham, David A. "The Bait-and-Switch Presidency." *The Atlantic*, December 14 2016.

Gray, John. *False Dawn: The Delusions of Global Capitalism*. London: Granta, 2009 (1998).

Grusky, David B., Dough McAdam, Rob Reich, and Debra Satz, eds. *Occupy the Future*. Cambridge, MA: MIT Press, 2013.

Guàrdia, Arnau Busquets. "How Brexit Vote Broke Down." Politico, www.politico.eu/article/graphics-how-the-uk-voted-eu-referendum-brexit-demographics-age-education-party-london-final-results/. Accessed February 3 2017.

Guignon, Charles B. "Introduction." In *The Cambridge Companion to Heidegger*, edited by Charles B. Guignon, 1–41. Cambridge: Cambridge University Press, 2006.

Gunning, Jeroen and Ilan Zvi Baron. *Why Occupy a Square: People, Protests and Movements in the Egyptian Revolution*. London: Hurst & Company, 2013.

Guthman, Julie. *Weighing In: Obesity, Food Justice, and the Limits of Capitalism*. Berkeley and Los Angeles: University of California Press, 2011.

Habermas, Jürgen. *The Philosophical Discourse of Modernity: Twelve Lectures*. Translated by Frederick Lawrence. Cambridge, MA: MIT Press, 1998.

———. *Theory and Practice*. Translated by John Viertel. Cambridge: Polity, 1973.

Hall, Richard. "How the Brexit Campaign Used Refugees to Scare Voters." https://www.pri.org/stories/2016-06-24/how-brexit-campaign-used-refugees-scare-voters. Accessed January 24 2107.

Hartocollis, Anemona and Jess Bidgood. "Racial Discimination Protests Ignite at Colleges Across the U.S." *The New York Times*, November 11 2015.

Havercroft, Jonathan. *Captives of Sovereignty*. Cambridge: Cambridge University Press, 2011.

Heidegger, Martin. *Being and Time*. Translated by John Macquarrie and Edward Robinson. Oxford: Blackwell, 1999 [1962].

———. "The Question Concerning Technology." In *Technology and Values: Essential Readings*, edited by Craig Hanks, 99–111. Oxford: Wiley-Blackwell, 2010.

Heigton, Luke. "Revealed: Tony Blair's Worth a Staggering £60m." *The Telegraph*, June 12 2015.

Hirst, Aggie. *Leo Strauss and the Invasion of Iraq: Encountering the Abyss*. London: Routledge, 2016.

Hobbes, Thomas. *Leviathan*. Edited by Richard Tuck. Rev. student ed. Cambridge: Cambridge University Press, 1996.

Hochschild, Arlie Russell. *Strangers in Their Own Land: Anger and Mourning on the American Right*. New York: The New Press, 2016.

Holbrock, Thomas M. and Aaron C. Weinschenk. "Campaigns, Mobilization, and Turnout in Mayoral Elections." *Political Resarch Quarterly* 67, no. 1 (2014): 42–55.

Holmes, Jack. "A Trump Surrogate Drops the Mic: "There's No Such Thing as Facts"." *Esquire*, December 2 2016.

Horkheimer, Max. *Critical Theory: Selected Essays*. London: Continuum, 1975.

Horton, John. *Political Obligation*. 2nd ed. Basingstoke: Palgrave Macmillan, 2010.

Huang, Jon, Samuel Jacoby, Michael Strickland, and Rebecca K.K. Lai. "Election 2016: Exit Polls." *The New York Times*, November 8 2016.

Ignatius, David. "Donald Trump Pulls a Bait and Switch on America." *The Washington Post*, November 23 2016.

Isaacs, Jeffrey C. "For a More Public Political Science." *Perspectives on Politics* 13, no. 1 (June 2015): 269–83.

———. "Further Thoughts on Da-Rt." www.the-plot.org/2015/11/02/further-thoughts-on-da-rt/. Accessed Janury 27 2017.

Jackson, Patrick Thaddeus. "Causal Claims and Causal Explanation in International Studies." *Journal of International Relations and Development* (2016). doi:10.1057/jird.2016.13.

——. *The Conduct of Inquiry in International Relations: Philosophy of Science and its Implications for the Study of World Politics*. London: Routledge, 2011.

——. "Must International Studies Be a Science?". *Millennium* 43, no. 3 (2015): 942–65.

Johnson, James Turner. *Can Modern War Be Just?* New Haven: Yale University Press, 1984.

——. *Just War Tradition and the Restraint of War: A Moral and Historical Inquiry*. Princeton: Princeton University Press, 1981.

——. *Morality and Contemporary Warfare*. New Haven: Yale University Press, 1999.

Jonas, Hans. *The Imperative of Responsibility: In Search of an Ethics for the Technological Age*. Translated by Hans Jonas and David Herr. Chicago: Chicago University Press, 1984.

Jones, Dan. "Seeing Reason: How to Change Minds in a 'Post-Fact' World." *New Scientist*, November 30 2016.

Kang, Cecilia and Adam Goldman. "In Washington Pizzeria Attack, Fake News Brought Real Guns." *The New York Times*, December 5 2016.

Kenan, Malik. "The Failure of Multiculturalism". *Foreign Affairs* 94, no. 2 (March 2015): 21–32.

Kern, Stephen. *A Cultural History of Causality: Science, Murder Novels, and Systems of Thought*. Princeton: Princeton University Press, 2004.

Khan, Aalia. "Four Ways the Anti-Immigration Vote Won the Referendum for Brexit." *New Statesman*, July 7 2016.

King, Gary, Robert O. Keohane, and Sidney Verba. *Designing Social Inquiry: Scientific Inference in Qualitative Research*. Princeton: Princeton University Press, 1994.

Klein, Naomi. *Fences and Windows: Dispatches from the Front Lines of the Globalization Debate*. London: Flamingo, 2002.

——. *No Logo*. 10th anniversary ed. New York: Picador, 2009.

——. *The Shock Doctrine: The Rise of Disaster Capitalism*. New York: Picador, 2015.

Krauthammer, Charles. "The Unipolar Moment." *Foreign Affairs* 70, no. 1 (1990/1991): 23–33.

Kuhn, Thomas S. *The Structure of Scientific Revolutions*. 3rd ed. Chicago: Chicago University Press, 1996.

Kurki, Milja. *Causation in International Relations: Reclaiming Causal Analysis*. Cambridge: Cambridge University Press, 2008.

Lebow, Richard Ned. *A Cultural Theory of International Relations.* Cambridge: Cambridge University Press, 2008.

Leopold, David and Marc Stears, eds. *Political Theory: Methods and Approaches,* Oxford: Oxford University Press, 2008.

Lévinas, Emmanuel. *God, Death, and Time.* Translated by Bettina Bergo. Stanford: Stanford University Press, 1993.

———. *Is It Righteous to Be?* Translated by Jill Robbins. Stanford: Stanford University Press, 2001.

———, ed. *The Levinas Reader.* Edited by Seán Hand. Oxford: Blackwell, 1989.

———. *Otherwise Than Being: Or Beyond Essence.* Translated by Alphonso Lingis. Pittsburgh: Duquesne University Press, 1993.

———. *Totality and Infinity: An Essay on Exteriority.* Translated by Alphonso Lingis. Pittsburgh: Duquesne University Press, 1969.

Levitsky, Steven and Daniel Ziblatt. "Is Donald Trump a Threat to Democracy?" *The New York Times,* December 16 2016.

Levitt, Steven D. and Stephen J. Dubner. *Freakonomics: A Rogue Economist Explores the Hidden Side of Everything.* Rev. and expanded ed. New York: William Morrow & Co., 2006.

Lilla, Mark. "The End of Identity Liberalism." *The New York Times,* November 18 2016.

Loomba, Ania. *Colonialism/Postcolonialism.* 2nd ed. London: Routledge, 2005.

Lowery, Wesley. "Aren't More White People Than Black People Killed by Police? Yes, but No." *The Washington Post,* July 11 2016.

Lukes, Steven. *Power: A Radical View.* 2nd ed. Basingstoke: Palgrave Macmillan, 2005.

Lusher, Adam. "Donald Trump: All the Sexist Things He Said." *Independent,* October 9 2016.

Magnusson, Warren. *The Search for Political Space.* Toronto: University of Toronto Press, 1996.

Magnusson, Warren and Karena Shaw, eds. *A Political Space: Reading the Global Through Clayoquot Sound.* Minneapolis: University of Minnesota Press, 2001.

Mance, Henry. "Bashing Brussels is Boris Johnson's Brand Not Conviction, Friends Say." *Financial Times,* February 22 2016.

———. "Britain Has Had Enough of Experts, Says Gove." *Financial Times,* June 3 2016.

Mandelson, Peter. "Why is the Brexit Camp so Obsessed with Immigration? Because That's All They Have." *The Guardian,* May 3 2016.

Marx, Karl and Friedrich Engels. "The Communist Manifesto." Chap.
    18. In *Karl Marx: Selected Writings*, edited by David McLellan,
    245–71. Oxford: Oxford University Press, 2000 [1848].

Mathis-Lilley, Ben. "Trump Tweeted at 5:30 A.M. About Alicia
    Machado's Alleged 'Sex Tape'." *Slate*, September 30 2016.

McClintock, Anne, Aamir Mufti, and Ella Shohat. *Dangerous Liaisons:
    Gender, Nations, and Postcolonial Perspectives*. Cultural Politics;
    V.11. Minneapolis: University of Minnesota Press, 1997.

McDonald, Michael P. "United States Election Project."
    www.electproject.org/. Accessed September 25 2017.

McKernan, Bethan. "A Journalist Has Shared a Story About Boris
    Johnson That Completely Undermines His Authority on the EU."
    Independent, https://www.indy100.com/article/a-journalist-has-
    shared-a-story-about-boris-johnson-that-completely-undermines-
    his-authority-on-the-eu-bkoHJPBuVZ. Accessed Janury 24 2017.

McMullin, Evan. "Trump's Threat to the Constitution." *The New
    York Times*, December 5 2016.

Mill, John Stuart. "A Few Words on Non-Intervention." *Fraser's
    Magazine for Town and Country* 60 (December 1859):
    766–76.

Mirowski, Philip. *Never Let a Serious Crisis Go to Waste: How Neolib-
    eralism Survived the Financial Meltdown*. London: Verso, 2014.

Mirowski, Philip and Dieter Plehwe, eds. *The Road from Mont Pèlerin:
    The Making of the Neoliberal Thought Collective*. Cambridge, MA:
    Harvard University Press, 2009.

Moody, Chris. "Trump in '04: 'I Probably Identity More as Demo-
    crat'." CNN.

Moore, Michael. "5 Reasons Why Trump Will Win." http://
    michaelmoore.com/trumpwillwin/. Accessed January 27 2017.

———. "Is Trump Purposely Sabotaging His Campaign?" http://
    michaelmoore.com/TrumpSabotage/. Accessed February 3 2107.

Moreno, Carolina. "Alicia Machado Speaks Out After Donald Trump's
    'Sex Tape' Accusation." *Huffington Post*, October 4 2016.

Morgenthau, Hans J., Kenneth W. Thompson, and W. David Clinton.
    Politics among Nations. 7th ed. New York: McGraw Hill, 2006.

National Assembly of France. "Declaration of the Rights of Man."
    http://avalon.law.yale.edu/18th_century/rightsof.asp. Accessed
    February 28 2017.

Nestle, Marion. *Food Politics: How the Food Industry Influences Nutrition
    and Health*. Berkeley and Los Angeles: University of California
    Press, 2013.

The New York Times. "Presidential Election Results: Donald J. Trump
    Wins." www.nytimes.com/elections/results/president. Accessed
    September 25 2107.

Nguyen, Tina. "Donald Trump Unleashes His Ultimate Bait-and-
    Switch." *Vanity Fair*, March 8 2017.

Nietzsche, Friedrich. *On the Genealogy of Morality*. Translated by
    Carol Diethe. Edited by Keith Ansell-Pearson. Cambridge:
    Cambridge University Press, 1994.

Norris, Andrew. "Political Revisions: Stanley Cavell and Political
    Philosophy." *Political Theory* 30, no. 6 (2002): 828–51.

Novick, Peter. *The Holocaust and Collective Memory*. London: Blooms-
    bury, 2001. The Holocaust in American Life.

Nussbaum, Martha C. *Not for Profit: Why Democracy Needs the Humani-
    ties*. Princeton: Princeton University Press, 2010.

———. *Poetic Justice: The Literary Imagination and Public Life*. Boston,
    MA: Beacon Press, 1995.

Olafson, Frederick A. *Heidegger and the Ground of Ethics: A
    Study of Mitsein*. Cambridge: Cambridge University Press,
    1998.

Oxford Dictionaries. https://en.oxforddictionaries.com/definition/
    post-truth. Accessed February 10 2017.

Pateman, Carole. *The Sexual Contract*. Cambridge: Cambridge
    University Press, 1988.

Peck, Tom. "'I Was Too Focused on the Economy,' Says Osborne."
    Independent, December 17 2016.

Petrini, Carlo. *Slow Food Nation: Why Our Food Should Be Good,
    Clean, and Fair*. Translated by Clara Furlan and Jonathan Hunt.
    New York: Rizzoli Ex Libris, 2007.

Pew Research Centre. "America's Shrinking Middle Class: A Close
    Look at Changes within Metropolitan Areas." Washington DC:
    Pew Research Centre, 2016.

———. "The American Middle Class is Losing Ground: No Longer
    the Majority and Falling Behind Financially." Washington DC:
    Pew Research Centre, 2015.

Pinker, Steven. *The Better Angels of Our Nature: A History of Violence
    and Humanity*. New York: Penguin, 2012.

Pirsig, Robert M. *Zen and the Art of Motorcycle Maintenance: An
    Inquiry into Values*. New York: Bantam Books, 1974.

Plato. *The Last Days of Socrates: Euthyphro, Apology, Crito, Phaedo*.
    Translated by Hugh Tredennick and Harold Tarrant. London:
    Penguin Books, 2003.

————. *The Republic of Plato.* Translated by Allan Bloom. New York: Basic Books, 1986.

Pluckrose, Helen. "How French 'Intellectuals' Ruined the West: Postmodernism and its Impact Explained." *Areo*, March 27 2017.

Pollin, Robert. *Contours of Descent: US Economic Fractures and the Landscape of Global Austerity.* London: Verso, 2005.

Pomerantsev, Peter. "Why We're Post-Fact." *Granta*, July 20 2016.

Popper, Karl. *The Logic of Scientific Discovery.* London: Routledge, 2002 [1959].

Putnman, Robert D. *Bowling Alone: The Collapse and Revival of American Community.* New York: Simon & Schuster, 2000.

Rallings, Colin and Michael Thrasher. "Local and Police and Crime Commissioner Elections." Plymouth: Elections Centre, Plymouth University, 2016.

Rehm, Diane. *How Journalists Are Rethinking Their Role Under a Trump Presidency.* The Diane Rehm Show, November 30 2016, 49:072016. http://thedianerehmshow.org/audio/-/shows/2016-11-30/how-journalists-are-rethinking-their-role-under-a-trump-presidency/114095.

Remnick, David. "An American Tragedy." *The New Yorker*, November 9 2016.

Resolution Foundation. "Millennials Facing 'Generational Pay Penalty' as Their Earnings Fall £8,000 Behind During Their 20s." News release, July 18 2016, www.resolutionfoundation.org/media/press-releases/millennials-facing-generational-pay-penalty-as-their-earnings-fall-8000-behind-during-their-20s. Accessed September 25 2017.

Reyes, Raul A. "Trump's Cruel Bait-and-Switch on Immigration." CNN, March 1 2017, http://edition.cnn.com/2017/03/01/opinions/trump-bait-and-switch-on-immigration-reyes/index.html. Accessed September 25 2017.

Ricci, David. *Politics Without Stories: The Liberal Predicament.* Cambridge: Cambridge University Press, 2016.

Rich, Nathaniel. "Inside the Sacrifice Zone." *The New York Review of Books*, November 10 2016.

Riesman, Abraham. "Stephen Colbert is Pissed at the Oxford Dictionary, Says 'Post-Truth' Is Just a Rip-Off of 'Truthiness'." *Vulture*, November 18 2016.

Robert, Henry M. *Robert's Rules of Order.* 11th Revised ed. Philadelphia: Da Capo Press, 2011 [1876].

Romm, Cari. "Where Are All the Female Test Subjects?" *The Atlantic*, September 4 2014.

Rorty, Richard. *Contingency, Irony, and Solidarity*. Cambridge: Cambridge University Press, 1989.

Rosenmann, Alexandra. "Nate Silver Reveals Why We're Not Done with Polls after Trevor Noah Skewers Him for Being So Wrong This Election." www.alternet.org/election-2016/nate-silver-reveals-why-were-not-done-polls-after-trevor-noah-skewers-him-being-so. Accessed February 10 2017.

Said, Edward W. *Orientalism*. Penguin Classics. London: Penguin, 2003.

Sanghani, Radhika. "Inside Britain's 'Worst' Immigration Removal Centre at Christmas." *The Telegraph*, December 24 2014.

Saul, John Ralston. *The Unconscious Civilization*. CBC Massey Lecture Series. Concord, Ontario: Anansi, 1995.

Schiff, Jade Larissa. *Burdens of Political Responsibility: Narratives and the Cultivation of Responsiveness*. Cambridge: Cambridge University Press, 2014.

Schmitt, Carl. *Political Theology: Four Chapters on the Concept of Sovereignty*. Translated by George Schwab. Chicago: Chicago University Press, 2005 [1985].

Schwartz, Barry. *The Battle for Human Nature: Science, Morality and Modern Life*. New York: Norton, 1986.

Scott, James C. *Seeing Like a State*. New Haven: Yale University Press, 1998.

Silver, Nate. "Why Fivethirtyeight Gave Trump a Better Chance Than Almost Anyone Else." http://fivethirtyeight.com/features/why-fivethirtyeight-gave-trump-a-better-chance-than-almost-anyone-else/. Accessed February 10 2017.

Smith, Steven B. "Heidegger and Political Philosophy: The Theory of His Practice." *Nomos* 37, Theory and Practice (1995): 440–63.

Sokal, Alan D. *Beyond the Hoax: Science, Philosophy and Culture*. Oxford: Oxford University Press, 2008.

———. "A Physicist Experiments with Cultural Studies." *Lingua Franca* (1996).

Solomon, John and Matthew Mosk. "In Private Sector, Giuliani Parlayed Fame into Wealth." *The Washington Post*, May 13 2007.

Spence, Peter. "Government Faces Worldwide Hunt for Trade Negotiators, Experts Warn." *The Telegraph*, July 3 2016.

Spivak, Gayatri Chakravorty. "Can the Subaltern Speak?" In *Marxism and the Interpretation of Culture*, edited by Cary Nelson and Lawrence Grossberg, 271–313. Urbana and Chicago: University of Illinois Press, 1988.

Squires, David and Chloe Anderson. "U.S. Health Care from a Global Perspective: Spending, Use of Services, Prices, and Health in 13 Countries." The Commonwealth Fund, 2015.

Steele, Brent J. *Defacing Power: The Aesthetics of Insecurity in Global Politics*. Ann Arbor: University of Michigan Press, 2010.

Stewart, Heather and Jessica Elgot. "Labour Plans Jeremy Corbyn Relaunch to Ride Anti-Establishment Wave." *The Guardian*, December 15 2016.

Stiglitz, Joseph. *Globalization and Its Discontents*. London: Penguin, 2002.

———. *Making Globalizaiton Work: The Next Steps to Global Justice*. London: Penguin, 2006.

Strange, Susan. *The Retreat of the State: The Diffusion of Power in the World Economy*. Cambridge: Cambridge University Press, 1996.

Suganami, Hidemi. "Agents, Structures, Narratives." *European Journal of International Relations* 5, no. 3 (1999): 365–86.

———. "Bringing Order to the Causes of War Debates." *Millennium: Journal of International Studies* 19, no. 1 (1990): 19–35.

———. *On the Causes of War*. New York: Oxford University Press, 1996.

———. "Stories of War Origins: A Narrativist Theory of the Causes of War." *Review of International Studies* 23, no. 4 (1997): 401–18.

Swartz, Tracy. "Nate Silver Wears Cubs Hat as he Talks World Series, Election on 'Daily Show'," *Chicago Tribune*, November 15 2016.

Sykes, Charles J. "Charlie Sykes on Where the Right Went Wrong." *The New York Times*, December 15 2015.

Taylor, Charles. "Interpretation and the Sciences of Man." *The Review of Metaphysics* 25, no. 1 (September 1971): 3–51.

———. "Neutrality in Political Science." In *Philosophical Papers: Philosophy and the Human Sciences*, edited by Charles Taylor, 58–90. Cambridge: Cambridge University Press, 1985.

———. "The Politics of Recognition." In *Multiculturalism*, edited by Amy Gutmann, 25–74. Princeton: Princeton University Press, 1994.

Tickner, J. Anne. "You Just Don't Understand: Troubled Engagements Between Feminists and IR Theorists." *International Studies Quarterly* 41, no. 4 (December 1997): 611–32.

Tobin, Ben. "One in Three Middle-Class Brits Would Struggle to Pay a £500 Bill." YouGov, https://yougov.co.uk/news/2016/06/08/third-middle-classes-would-struggle-pay-sudden-500/. Accessed January 24 2017.

Travis, Alan. "What Does Theresa May's Record as Home Secretary Tell Us?" *The Guardian*, July 18 2016.

Truman, David B. "The Implications of Political Behaviour Research." *Items (Social Science Research Council)* 5, no. 4 (December 1951): 37–39.

Tully, James. "The Agonistic Freedom of Citizens." Chap. 4 In *Public Philosophy in a New Key*, 135–59. Cambridge: Cambridge University Press, 2008.

———. *Strange Multiplicity: Constitutionalism in an Age of Diversity*. Cambridge: Cambridge University Press, 1995.

Wakefield, A.J., S.H. Murch, A. Anthony, J. Linnell, D M. Casson, M. Malik, M. Berelowitz, *et al.* "Retracted: Ileal-Lymphoid-Nodular Hyperplasia, Non-Specific Colitis, and Pervasive Developmental Disorder in Children." *The Lancet* 351, no. 9103 (1998): 637–41.

Wallace, Gregory. "Voter Turnout at 20-Year Low in 2016." CNN.

Waltz, Kenneth N. *Man, the State, and War: A Theoretical Analysis*. Revised ed. New York: Columbia University Press, 2001.

Walzer, Michael. *Arguing About War*. New Haven: Yale University Press, 2004.

———. *Interpretation and Social Criticism*. Cambridge, MA: Harvard University Press, 1987.

———. *Just and Unjust Wars: A Moral Argument with Historical Illustrations*. 3rd ed. New York: Basic Books, 2000.

———. *Politics and Passion: Toward a More Egalitarian Liberalism*. New Haven: Yale University Press, 2004.

———. *Spheres of Justice: A Defense of Pluralism and Equality*. Oxford: Basil Blackwell, 1983.

———. *Thick and Thin: Moral Argument at Home and Abroad*. Notre Dame: University of Notre Dame Press, 1994.

Ward, James F. *Heidegger's Political Thinking*. Amherst: University of Massachusetts Press, 1995.

Warren, James. "The Press Blames Itself for Trump Win." *Vanity Fair*, November 10 2016.

The Washington Post. "2016 Election Exit Polls." November 29 2016.

Watt, Nicholas. "EU Referendum: Vote Leave Focuses on Immigration." www.bbc.co.uk/news/uk-politics-eu-referendum-36375492. Accessed September 25 2017.

Weber, Max. *The Methodology of the Social Sciences*. Translated by Henry A. Finch and Edward Albert Shils. London: Transaction Publishers, 2011 [1949].

Welch, Stephen. *Hyperdemocracy*. London: Palgrave Macmillan, 2013.

———. *The Theory of Political Culture*. Oxford: Oxford University Press, 2013.

Wells, Tom and Jonathan Reilly. "Blueprint for Britain: It's Time to Bring Back the Famous Dark Blue UK Passport as a 'Symbol of Our Independence' after Brexit." *The Sun*, August 1 2016.

Westervelt, Amy. "The Medical Research Gender Gap: How Excluding Women from Clinical Trials is Hurting Our Health." *The Guardian*, April 30 2015.

Wintour, Patrick. "UK Lacks Expertise for Trade Talks with Europe, Says Top Civil Servant." *The Guardian*, June 28 2016.

Wittgenstein, Ludwig. *Philosophical Investigations*. Translated by G.E.M. Anscombe, P.M.S. Hacker and Joachim Schulte. 4th ed. Oxford: Wiley-Blackwell, 2009.

Wolin, Richard. *Heidegger's Children: Hannah Arendt, Karl Löwith, Hans Jonas, and Herbert Marcuse*. Princeton: Princeton University Press, 2001.

Wolin, Sheldon S. "Political Theory as Vocation." *The American Political Science Review* 63, no. 4 (December 1969): 1062–82.

Wong, Alia and Adrienne Green. "Campus Politics: A Cheat Sheet." *The Atlantic*, April 4 2016.

Wrathall, Mark A. "Heidegger on Human Understanding." In *The Cambridge Companion to Heidegger's* Being and Time, edited by Mark A. Wrathall, 177–200. Cambridge: Cambridge University Press, 2013.

Wrathall, Mark A. and Max Murphy. "An Overview of *Being and Time*." In *The Cambridge Companion to Heidegger's* Being and Time, edited by Mark A. Wrathall, 1–53. Cambridge: Cambridge University Press, 2013.

Yoon, Dustin Y., Neel A. Mansukhani, Vanessa C. Stubbs, Irene B. Helenowski, Teresa K. Woodruff, and Melina R. Kibbe. "Sex Bias Exists in Basic Science and Translational Surgical Research." *Surgery* 156, no. 3 (2014): 508–16.

Young, Iris Marion. "Feminist Reactions to the Contemporary Security Regime." *Hypatia* 18, no. 1 (2003): 223–31.

———. *Responsibility for Justice*. Oxford: Oxford University Press, 2011.

Zakaria, Fareed. "The Rise of Illiberal Democracy." *Foreign Affairs* 76, no. 6 (November/December 1997): 22–43.

Zimmer, Ben. "Truthiness." *The New York Times Magazine*, October 13 2010.

Zuckert, Catherine H. "Martin Heidegger: His Philosophy and His Politics." *Political Theory* 18, no. 1 (1990): 51–79.

Index